# Things Fall Apart?

# Things Fall Apart?

The Mission of God and the Third Decade

MICHAEL PAGET-WILKES

*Foreword by Justin Welby*

WIPF & STOCK · Eugene, Oregon

Wipf & Stock
An Imprint of Wipf and Stock Publishers
199 W. 8th Ave., Suite 3
Eugene, OR 97401

www.wipfandstock.com

PAPERBACK ISBN: 978-1-5326-9728-9
HARDCOVER ISBN: 978-1-5326-9729-6
EBOOK ISBN: 978-1-5326-9730-2

Manufactured in the U.S.A.   05/28/20

To Richard F., who walked the walk as well as talking the talk;
To Richard and John who are always there in the background;
and to all our grandchildren, who will face the Mission of God
in the third and ensuing decades.

# Contents

# List of Illustrations

# Foreword

*By the Most Reverend Justin Welby,
Archbishop of Canterbury*

I have known Michael since he was Archdeacon of Warwick, and I was Rector of Southam in the 1990s. Even in those days he engaged widely with life outside the church, observing changes in society and philosophy, and encouraging the church to think more carefully about how these changes would affect its mission.

His book is written from an Anglican perspective but makes use of a range of examples from the wider church. In fact, throughout the book Michael provides engaging evidence to illustrate how the church might respond to the leadership challenge that the third decade of the millennium presents.

In part one he begins with an overview of the state of the world, technology, markets, and related issues. He has insights into current technology and theories about the ethical questions surrounding development. His conclusion is that the age of information innovation may be for many an age of uncertainty, something we have observed around us in recent years. As a result, he encourages those who believe the church still has much to offer to engage with these uncertainties, to find out what he calls "the edge of chaos," to refresh our understanding of what ministry looks like. He poses the profound question about what ordination means and involves: whether it is principally about doing or being and how this differs from the early understanding of the Ministry of the Baptized.

In part two he uses a management SWOT analysis of the Church of England, advocating significant change in the structure in favor of an emergent bottom-up pattern. He returns to this rationale throughout part three.

Part three is the most challenging section as it is about the ministry of Christ and how it intersects with society. In polemical and provocative style, he presents truths that he believes the church must face, always based on a sense of opportunity and hope. His high view of both culture and Gospel enables him successfully to engage the two in a constructive and critical conversation with each other.

One of the areas that is both most provocative and most timely is his challenge to the church as to whether it is human centered or has as its primary purpose the protection of its structures, its authority, and its hierarchy. He argues that the tensions that are sometimes visible between bishops, clergy, and laity arise from a mismatch of expectations of the nature of the church.

While I might not agree with everything he says, as is always the case with Michael, his book will leave his readers stirred and interested.

# Preface

W. B. Yeats wrote "The Second Coming" in Dublin in 1920 within the mael-strom of the emerging Irish Free State, with a bitter civil war looming ahead. Knowing how history continues to repeat itself, this poem can easily be seen to be pertinent to both British society and the Christian faith/church—they all face radical change—on entering the twenty-first century.

We are moving from the Industrial Age to the Information/Data Age, from hierarchical order to networking innovation, from absolute to relative values, from planet pollution to eco-friendliness, from outright material-ism to growing spiritual enquiry, from Western neo-liberal capitalism to an uncertain future, from a national mindset towards overwhelming globaliza-tion and then back to reemergent localism.

How then does both society and the faith/church face these chang-ing circumstances? Which elements of the past will crumble into insignifi-cance, and which are worth holding onto? What are the already emerging new signs of life, and the fresh questions that accompany them? In what direction is society traveling, and what inspirational guidance has the faith/church to offer?

In seeking to reflect on these questions, I will undoubtedly draw on my previous life experience: from being an agricultural development worker in Tanzania; to inner-city youth and community ministry in Canning Town, Wandsworth, and New Cross; to Midland urban and rural ministry in Rugby and Warwickshire; to aid/church consultancy in Khartoum, Juba, and the surrounding countrysides; to engaging with extreme Muslim and secular governments who faced defiant Christian communities seeking to be fully participating citizens of Sudan and South Sudan.

I have approached this task as a practical theologian: one who reflects theologically and biblically on all experience, both within society, and within the church. My work has taken me to a rich variety of communities, places, and responsibilities. It has involved working through the rapid social change environment of Arusha Declaration "ujamaa" villages of Tanzania in the 1960s—which has a counterpoint in Chimamanda Ngozi Adichie's book *Americanah*; juxtaposing Latin American liberation theology with the racially torn, inner-city London melting pot of the 1980s;[11] engaging with the urban/urban shadow of the West Midlands, as the church has sought to come to terms with decaying structures and the challenge of postmodern, postindustrial society; and participating side by side with a living church, in the traumas of war, peace, persecution, and the corruption of the divided multicultural Sudanese countries.

It was only when I left all of these spheres of work and experience that I had time and clarity of mind to objectively analyze and reflect on the issues in which I had been deeply immersed. Networking with other practitioners and following these discussions with further research/reading led me to discern and articulate an overall response to my search, which is the book that follows.

Throughout all of this it is clear that both society and the church, be they British or African, have found it difficult to survive intact as secularization, postmodernism, and technological change have engulfed global society and opened up an uncertain future.

Hopefully the conclusion to this journey—with Yeats's poem in mind—will include both a deeper understanding of the church's predicament, and a facing up to the distinct possibility of its center falling apart, and yet at the same time, a belief that there is a constructive way forward. By looking both seriously and critically at the context, and by rediscovering the purpose and relevance of the mission of God, it is argued, the church could be reimagined so as to become the wild beast that "slouches toward Bethlehem to be born,"[22] participating afresh in the inauguration of God's mission amidst the excitement of the third decade. The hope and expectation behind all of this is that once again the falcon might alter its course, following the guidance and cry of the falconer.

1  See Paget-Wilkes, *Poverty, Revolution and the Church*.
2  Yeats, quoted in Childs, *Modernism*, 39.

# Acknowledgements

This book has been a team effort from the very beginning, with so many people contributing to the final outcome. Central to this has been the group who met in Burford: Richard Cooke, John Benington, and Andrew Kirk, together with the advice from afar from Ann Morisy, Jenny Bickmore-Brand, Jean Hartley, Paul Wignall, and Tony Bradley. In particular, Richard Cooke, Director of Ministry at Coventry Diocese, made up for my deficiencies theologically, and John Benington, Professor Emeritus at Warwick Business School, gave advice and shape to the chapters in part one. I am deeply indebted to Karen Czapiewski for manuscript preparation, together with Angie and Yvette who so patiently typed earlier manuscripts. My whole being still benefits from working alongside Ezekiel in Khartoum, and Harriet, Enoch, and Pauline in Juba. I am grateful to Jessica, Claire, and Rory, who kept me in touch with contemporary thinking, and to Gillian for her patience and support during the gestation of this work. Finally, it is the thought of our grandchildren, entering future decades of life, that has encouraged me to articulate a lifetime of thoughts onto paper.

# Introduction

For the past sixty years the world has been engulfed in rapid social change. Since the millennium, the speed and scope of this change have been increasing and expanding exponentially. Being immersed within that experience makes it difficult to identify what is happening objectively, or to offer thoughts on the direction and endpoint of travel. So to step to the side and consider what is happening is both an exciting and daunting task. It requires looking back, standing still, and imagining the future, all at the same time. The challenge this book hopes to kick-start is a process that others of future generations will continue to explore and expand upon.

The three parts of this book will juxtapose three aspects together: the changing societal context in which we live; the development of the Christian faith from New Testament times up until the millennium; and a reimagining of the mission of God within the Western church as it approaches the third decade following the millennium.

Stimulation to write this book has come from the single Chinese character that denotes both crisis and opportunity. As the paradigm shift in Western culture becomes clear, and new horizons open up, the Christian faith/church is becoming increasingly aware of a crisis looming. Both the church's structures and the traditional articulation of its faith are being threatened by the oncoming age, with the distinct possibility of disintegration for the church as we have known it.

At the same time, the paradigm shift in culture is offering the church an opportunity, in the eye of the storm, to reassess its core message and represent it, not only recontextualized but also counter-culturally, to western society. This paradigm shift is unnerving to the whole of society, leaving it open to alternative views as to what is happening and alternative suggestions concerning the way forward. It is bemused by the fresh issues/questions being thrown up that have no easy answer or response. This therefore is an opportunity for the church to understand and acknowledge its own failings and then to represent its message with a confident countercultural stance to an ever-evolving society that is hesitantly treading, step by step, into an uncertain future.

## THE CONTENT

The content of this book is divided into three parts.

Part one looks at twenty-first century Western society in flux. It refers to analysis/interpretations that have been made, and notes examples that illustrate those changes/developments. These relate not only to institutional and political structures but also to the marketplace of ideas, ethics, and morals, together with reference to the apparent winners and losers in this maelstrom of change. Chapter one covers structural and technological development right up to the possibilities of genetic engineering, molecular manufacturing, sentient computers, and superhumans. Chapter two covers the outworkings of these in social, political, economic, and global structures. Chapter three looks at the philosophies underlying society, and the ethical questions raised in this melting pot of development.

Part two takes us on a journey through the development of the Christian faith/church, from Pentecost right up to the present day. Dividing the time into four eras, chapter four considers the time between Pentecost and the edict of Emperor Constantine in AD 313, the legitimizing of the Christian faith, and the initiating of a long association between the church and state rulers. Chapter five continues that story up until the Renaissance/Enlightenment, including the Protestant Reformation. Chapter six takes the story on from the rise of modern life sciences through to the millennium, from when the rise of individualistic humanism and the centrality of fact over value and belief broke the liaison between church and state, relegating faith to the private lives of its followers. Postmodernism continued that trend, undermining absolute truth with its relativist claims, and pointing onward to the fourth postmillennial era.

Chapter seven takes us into more detail on the various crises facing the church around the millennium, leading up to the point when the church is faced with the arrival of this fourth era. It highlights both the threats and the opportunities present as structural difficulties threaten its very existence.

Arising out of this journey, four key issues/disjunctions are identified that appear regularly throughout these eras of historical development. These same disjunctions remain with us today as the faith/church face yet another paradigm shift. They are:

1. The attraction of the church towards prerogative power in society as compared to Jesus' dependence on the power of vulnerability.

2. The centrality of hierarchy, control, and coercion for the church as compared to the networking, digital, innovative, and emergent dynamic within today's society.

3. The pivotal, functional, dominant role of "ministerial order" as compared to the "ministry of the baptized."

4. The church's efforts to contextualize and assimilate being "in the world" as compared to its responsibility to be countercultural, prophetic, and challenging to society—being "not of the world."

It is these four disjunctions that continue on into this fourth era.

Part three immerses itself in this fourth era within which we live. It seeks to reposition both faith and church as the mission of God for the third decade. It is concerned that the medium should reflect the message, that contextualization does not obliterate its prophetic countercultural role. It takes the four key questions raised in chapter six, and offers ways forward. Chapter eight looks at power and vulnerability: the disjunction between the medium of the church, and the message of Christ's identification with the marginalized. Chapter nine begins by delineating three choices facing the church as it enters this postmillennial period.

The first option is to reemphasize a conservative, orthodox, *laager mentality*. The second is to continue along the lines of a *mixed economy*. The third is to take a step towards becoming an *emergent organism*.

These choices center around how the hierarchy responds to the networking society around it: whether an ordered structure could be transformed into an emergent Holy Spirit empowered experience arising from the periphery. Chapter ten looks at the dualism encompassing "representative" orders and the "ministry of the baptized." It seeks a holistic synthesis, spearheaded by lay vocation and supported by an iconic servant ministry. Chapter eleven returns to the question of balance between contextual relevance and countercultural activity in ethics, reality, relationships, reconciliation, and spiritual warfare. Chapter twelve raises a number of these issues/questions as an agenda that the whole body of the church should address.

The overall thesis of the book stresses the cruciality of these deep-rooted, longstanding issues as the Christian faith engages with this post-humanist, algorithmic, technological, brave new world, a world which raises as many questions as it does innovations/achievements. The book will highlight that, despite the incredible transformation of the Western world, through the exponential rise of computer power, the Christian faith remains totally relevant to the unresolved questions concerning the nature of society, humanity, and reality. So far many of them lie unresolved, beyond humanity's hope, expectation, and belief that power, possessions, and problem-solving potential can solve them.

Alternatively, the thesis will firstly stress that the faith/church's identification with the "least in society" could provide a firmer and more sustainable base from which to serve the whole of humanity. Secondly, it will show that the vulnerability of relational love can oil the wheels of structures more effectively than coercion, dominion, control, and prerogative power. Thirdly, it will stress that the very nature of God can emerge from the bottom up through transformed, individual life empowerment by the Holy Spirit, as seen in New Testament times. Fourthly, it will point toward a more balanced contribution between the necessary contextualization required and appropriate countercultural contributions—the mission of God in the third decade.

Returning to the stanzas of Yeats's poem, the conclusion/postscript suggests that this third decade will bring the issues facing the church/faith, to a head. Having laid out these key issues, and offered three possible responses in part three, the postscript will stress that this third decade will be a pivot upon which the future of the present church will hinge—a point of no return. Choices and actions will need to be taken by the church, otherwise they will be forced upon the church. The key dynamic pointed out will be whether the church identifies the mission of God as a giant leap of faith, like a free-fall base jumper launching off from the top of the Shard; whether it goes for the hybrid option, choosing to take the express lift instead; or whether, enveloped by its pre-Enlightenment past, it attempts to "laager" and "lock down," slowly descending the central staircase, settling simply for survival.

The book radically believes that the center, in its present form, should not hold, but that the falcon should refresh its connection with the falconer. In doing so it believes that "the rough beast," with its hour fast approaching, will "slouch toward Bethlehem to be born."

## POSTSCRIPT

With regard to terminology I have sought to use the generic term "church" as much as possible. Although it has often referred to the Roman Catholic/ Anglican denominations down the centuries, I believe it still has relevance to other denominations/community churches. Uses of the terms "threefold order" and "ministry of the baptized," again often relate more to Roman Catholics/Anglicans, but I believe they can be easily equated to the concepts of "ministry leadership" and "church membership." And just as the influence of the Enlightenment and postmodernism has assimilated itself into church life comparatively undetected, so too I believe elements of Anglican dynamics have been absorbed into nonconformist structures far more than is recognized.

# PART 1

## Western Society in Flux

Turning and turning in the widening gyre
The falcon cannot hear the falconer;
Things fall apart; the centre cannot hold;
Mere anarchy is loosed upon the world[1]

---

1. Yeats, "The Second Coming," in Childs, *Modernism*, 39.

## INTRODUCTION

### WHAT DOES THE FUTURE HOLD?

There are Jim, Jean, Kevin, and Stuart on a council estate in a Midlands town, trying to make ends meet, supporting their children, mentoring their growing number of grandchildren. There are Sally and Harry; Sally, a health operative spending so much of her free time with youngsters excluded from school, and open to the attractions of "county lines." There are retired businessmen in a coastal village of Northumberland, praying for their village to come alive with faith. Within the Birmingham urban shadow there is a car manufacturing executive living in one hamlet, and a University professor in another, both seeking to contribute to society in their day jobs, whilst at the same time doing their best to uphold their historic village churches as a witness of faith.

There are Sanjay, Jenny, and Bill, all living under the shadow of Canary Wharf, and ministering to those who are buffeted by the stresses and strains of inner-city life. There is Maxine, living on the Welsh border, fresh into secondary school, seeking to find her way and her faith in a teen world of friends, social media, and, often, anxiety. Then there are commuter couples in Cotswold villages, where one leaves on the 6:27 and returns on the 8:09; whilst the other looks after the children, and finds a job share as a jobbing architect or an estate agent's assistant, with short day working hours.

Each one of them is being blown along by the strong winds of change both in society and in the Christian faith, which never seem to die down. Yet far too often the sailing boat—the church within which their faith is nurtured—has a hull that is riddled with holes below the water-line. They have to spend so much time baling out the water just in order to stay afloat. Just what does the future hold for people like them—and us? How are we to participate in the mission of God today, and to find hope and purpose in this epoch of volatility and uncertainty?

We live in fast-changing times, in a world of increasing uncontainable complexity. The last five centuries have led the West through global exploration, from agricultural societies through the Industrial Revolution, the information and communications revolution, into our present digital age. Ahead of us lies an algorithmic and undreamed-of future, a point of posthuman "singularity" as the physicists say, where machines can think faster than humans, and where artificial intelligence—AI—can either liberate, enslave, enhance, or supersede humans as the dominant species on this planet.

## SHENZHEN—THE MEGA-CITY OF THE WORLD

Nothing illustrates the speed of change better than the city of Shenzhen, just north of Hong Kong. Forty years ago it was a fishing village surrounded by rice paddy fields in the Pearl River Delta. Today it is populated by up to fourteen million people, and surrounded by an urban area of more than 120 million people. It has more skyscrapers over 200 meters than any other city—eighty-two in 2019, with a further sixty under construction. Initiated by Deng Xiaoping as a Special Economic Zone, described as market capitalism guided by ideals of socialism with Chinese characteristics, it now claims to be a global center for scientific and technological innovation. Development may well be initiated in Silicon Valley, but Shenzhen is becoming the ultimate capital of innovation, production, and sale—including its famous Huaqiangbei Shopping District; a cashless tech market with all purchases being made by QR code.

Increasingly, through open source/open innovation on hyper-speed—the New Shanzhai—it is at the forefront of creative development, with 2019 offering, for instance, flying bikes, drones that deliver your fast-food meals, three-dimensional interactive imaging that can model traffic flow through a whole city, and facial recognition security cameras that can feed into Government data banks. It's no wonder the youth of Hong Kong are prepared to fight for their own independence at the barricades.

Such an unimaginable future is made possible not just by the assistance of technology, but by its speed and accelerated expansion. This is best illustrated by Moore's Law, that computer power will double every eighteen to twenty-four months, that microprocessing boards double their capacity by 50 percent every year, that the acceleration of technology will fuel the transformation of life, leaving us in the death throes of the Anthropocene era, where humans have irreversibly altered the ecological balance of nature, putting at risk soils, rivers, forests, the climate, and other species.

Such change will bring complexity that both excites and frightens, that heralds both opportunity and crisis, that will offer societal choices over reduction in menial labor for all, and further rises in inequality. Not only does it increase our abilities to create and wield power, but it also raises timeless questions of meaning, of value, and of human relationships. Despite the extended horizons of human potential, we all search for an answer to creation, evolution, chance, and purpose. Scientists, following Stephen Hawking and others, still strive for a grand unified theory of everything. Others expect to achieve John von Neumann and Ray Kurzweil's point of singularity, which will usher in a posthuman age. The human brain stands out as the most complex computer of all, but we are still discovering and debating the meaning of the mind and its relationship to the body and soul.

The framework of Western society has been shaped by Christendom, renaissance, reformation, enlightenment, humanism and Western capitalism, but the twenty-first century has revealed deep-seated cracks in this configuration, suggesting that they may struggle to survive the consequences of political economic globalization, the shift of power and empire away from USA and the West towards China and the East, the continuing discoveries of the life sciences and neurosciences, and the outworking of the latest wave of digital, technological innovation, automation, and machine-generated algorithms.

No wonder W. B. Yeats's poem, following the Easter uprising and the dawn of Irish independence in Dublin, still resonates so strongly in western and global society today. "Things fall apart; the centre cannot hold"[2] are the unuttered thoughts floating deep within the hearts and minds of so many today. The amazing potential for good is acknowledged, but the depravity of self-obsessed individuals, globalized capitalist markets/mammon, and populist, dictatorial governments can so easily destroy all that has been gained through the long struggles for liberal democracy. There are many therefore who fear in their blood that "Our Iceberg is Melting."[3]

So as the Christian faith seeks to be a serious signpost for those living in the twenty-first century, and attempts to understand and engage with today's changing context, what are the issues that both excite and confront it? Innovation and technology mushroom with benefits, and yet also hint that automation will bring significant unemployment with it. Finite resources might well be replaced by technological development. But will the ensuing automation bring with it massive unemployment, shrinking consumer demand, and dwindling growth? Globalization has swept the board through industrial conglomerates and internet giants, but now nationalism has reemerged, and national governments have begun to recognize and respond to the power of the Silicon Valley elite. The need to confront climate change has been accepted in principle, but national positions frequently rebel against carbon reductions. Increased automation will, in turn, foster growing inequality between the developed West, and poor continents such as Africa. Worldwide population growth, water and food shortages, together with the demography of an aging population in developed countries, will exacerbate already-existing social instability.

---

2. Yeats, "The Second Coming," in Childs, *Modernism*, 39.

3. Kotter, *Our Iceberg is Melting*.

As a part of all of this, ensuing turbulence will continue to feed the world migration and refugee movements.

So how do we evaluate the issues of change confronting us? How do we identify a shaft of positive hope to guide us through the narrow channel between the shifting sandbanks that could so easily ground us?

Part 1 looks at Western society in flux. Chapter 1 introduces us to some of the key changes that are impacting and transforming twenty-first-century lives. It begins with the evolving nature of institutions and organizations that make up the heart of our ordered society, including the shift from hierarchies and markets to networks. It analyzes growth through information, innovation, and reformation, leading on to the dynamics of coercion and collaboration, chaos and order. These are followed by the issues of complexity, emergence, algorithms, and data-flow. It concludes with the debates on what it means to be human, whether machines will ever usurp the role of human beings—the singularity—and whether and how an enhanced superhuman might come into being.

Chapter 2 then discusses globalization and nationalism, markets and the crisis facing capitalism, and issues arising from automation, unemployment, and reduced growth.

Chapter 3 unpacks some of the intransigent issues surrounding the tension between power and meaning: substance and relationship; coercion and collaboration; individuality and community; the question of worldviews; the challenge to secularization/humanism as the only show in town. It goes on to touch on the point raised by the film *Blade Runner 2049*, "What is real? What does it mean to be human?," the decoupling of intelligence and consciousness, and, finally, our morally inept approach to these issues, from individual self-centeredness to new ways of conducting war.

# Chapter 1

## Western Society in Flux and Transition

### *Political, Economic, Social, Technological, and Ecological Change*

Western culture has undergone successive waves of ecological, political, economic, social, technological and organizational change. The ruptures with the past and the new opportunities kickstarted by the Industrial Revolution in the nineteenth century are mirrored in some ways by the Digital Information Revolution in the twentieth century. Both have also led to new divisions in society, within class, race, wealth, and age, with a growing division between the information-rich and the information-poor, between those who have access to and an affinity for the web, internet, social media, fast broadband, and global interconnectedness, and those who don't.

Three factors interact, amplify, and multiply these influences. First, the speed of change, for example, in computing power, has an exponential impact on everything. To use a borrowed example. a car traveling at 5mph, takes one minute to cover 440 feet. If you double its speed every minute, in the fifth minute it will cover a mile, reaching a speed of 80mph. In twenty-seven minutes its speed will be 671 million mph and it will have traveled 11 million miles. Five minutes more would take it to the moon.

Second, the complexity of change. Natural scientists—particularly in physics, chemistry, and biology—are increasingly recognizing the limitations of traditional reductionist explanations, which explain things by reducing them to separate component parts and analyzing linear patterns of predictable cause and effect. Reductionist thinking is relevant and fit for purpose when the problems being addressed are relatively "tame" or technical, when there is little dispute about either the causes or the solutions to the problems. Reductionist thinking was effective in resolving many of the technical engineering challenges which drove the industrial revolution.

However, many of the problems now facing society—climate change, drug and alcohol abuse, caring for an ageing population—are wicked rather than tame, and complex rather than technical. Neither the causes nor the solutions to the phenomena are understood or agreed upon; the effects of interventions cannot be predicted accurately because new phenomena emerge unexpectedly. In these conditions scientists find that they need to move beyond reductionist thinking and methods, and instead explore new holistic forms of explanation and engagement with these continuously fluid inter-connected complex adaptive systems.[1]

Complex adaptive energy systems include the formation of atoms at the Big Bang right through to the CERN atomic particle collider in Switzerland, where some of those self-same atoms are split, giving off immense heat and energy. Or consider the complexity of the human brain: What we know is that it is made up of neurons, 86 billion of them, that relate to each other through synapses, operating on a whole range of levels—deep neural networks—with each grouping of these nerve ends responsible for the actions and activities of different parts of the body.

Third, artificial or machine intelligence. Our world has been significantly influenced by the use of machine-generated algorithms defined in the House of Lords Report[2] as "a series of instructions for performing a calculation or solving a problem," or as Yuval Harari has put it, "a methodical set of steps that can be used to make calculations, resolve problems, and reach decisions (not a) particular calculation, but the method followed when making the calculation."[3] Harari goes on to describe them as "arguably the single most important concept in our world."[4] By having algorithms built into its software, a computer can develop further algorithms that enable it to solve problems and find solutions to increasingly complicated questions within infinitesimally small amounts of time. This ability to process data so much faster than the human brain and to use algorithms give computers

---

1. Benington and Moore, *Public Value*, ch. 1.
2. House of Lords Report, *AI in the UK.*
3. Harari, Homo Deus, 97.
4. Harari, Homo Deus, 97.

immense potentiality—posing great challenges for the changing relation-ships between human beings and artificial intelligence. Some argue that we are entering a posthuman era.

As individuals, however, we are influenced not just by ideas and systems but also by organizations and cultures. Changing centuries have brought on immense changes in those organizations themselves and how people participate and operate within them. Perhaps two of the most influ-ential starting points for understanding organizational change at the turn of the millennium are to be found in *Markets, Hierarchies and Networks* by Grahame Thompson, Jennifer Francis, Rosalind Levacic, and Jeremy Mitchell,[5] and in *The Network Society* by Manuel Castells.[6]

## 1.1 MARKETS, HIERARCHIES, AND NETWORKS

Thompson et al.'s work proposes three models of coordination of social life: markets, hierarchies, and networks; it then considers how they interact to-gether as a framework of understanding as to how human society is ordered. Such "models of coordination" they suggest, can provide "an analytical framework for understanding the way social life in general is organized."[7]

---

**SOCIAL EVOLUTION**

These authors suggest that, as the twenty-first century unfolds, we are moving from a society that was organized and coordinated primarily through the model of *hierarchy*, with its vertical dynamics, towards a society of *networks*, with a growing variety of horizontal communications. *Markets coordinate* the arena of private or commercial production, and distribution of goods and services. Each of the three spheres overlap, interact, and depend upon the other. It is as though there are three torches, each with a beam of light: sometimes there are three separate pools of light; sometimes two or even three of them overlap, making cooperation, understanding, and a unified view possible. But the predominant trend is that so-ciety is proliferating cross-cutting networks (as a result of globalization and new digital information technologies) whereas hierarchical structures are waning.

---

A more recent reflection on this area comes from Niall Ferguson,[8] who ar-gues that both hierarchies and networks have been in tension with each

---

5. Thompson et al., *Markets, Hierarchies, and Networks*.
6. Castells, Network Society, Preface.
7. Thompson, *Markets, Hierarchies, and Networks*, 1.
8. Ferguson, *Square and the Tower*.

other all throughout history. He identifies, as an example, the printing press in the late fifteenth century, which initiated the rise of the network through the widespread increase in access to books and reading, until the eighteenth century. He suggests that from then until the 1960s hierarchies dominated, with the networking revolution of the Information Age only reasserting itself from the seventies onwards. As well as identifying these eras as being dominated by one dynamic or the other, he also proposes that these two can work integrally with each other. He cites the example of Siena in Italy. There, the Tower, representing hierarchical power, overlooks the Market Square, representing the economic and social networks which are central to the functioning of the city. Both need the other for the city to operate. Rather than accepting that networks will totally replace hierarchies, he suggests that our present century will be a time of increased tension between the two: witness the engagement between the networking power of social media's Facebook, compared to traditional party politics in the 2016 election of the hierarchical President Trump. Ferguson goes on to argue that a world run by networks alone would be a recipe for anarchy—illustrated by the spread of such groups as ISIS—and that therefore, the presence of both hierarchies and networks provide a healthy balance.

## 1.2 SUSTAINING INNOVATION IN AN INFORMATION AGE

In the decade preceding the turn of the millennium, an underlying change in institutions was therefore being identified: hierarchical organization was giving way to networking forms of engagement. Manuel Castells,[9] Pekka Himanen,[10] and Dee Hock[11] all argue that we are living in a transition period between our past Industrial Age and a new Information Age. Whereas we have been used to infrastructural, command/control organizations, we are now surrounded by infostructural networks of sharing and information: central organizational control is giving way to dispersed leadership, to the significance of the periphery; central initiatives give way to innovative problem solving, imagining, and planning for the future; the production line workforce gives way to the growth of innovation, with a significant convergence between information technology and globalization.[12]

9. Castells, Network Society.

10. Himanen, Challenges of the Global Information Society.

11. Hock, *Birth of the Chaordic Age,* 262.

12. Baldwin, *Great Convergence.*

Himanen points out that this Information Age is not necessarily simply based on new technologies, but on a new way of doing things. Information society is a "network form of organization and growth that is based on innovations."[13]

The work of Alberts and Hayes interlinks with this analysis.[14] In an information age, both society and organizations within it grow and change through the sharing of information. Such activity and resultant transformation depend on innovation—both sustaining innovation and disruptive innovation. Alberts and Hayes draw out the significance of each of these two if an organization is to grow and maintain growth.

---

### INNOVATION

Alberts and Hayes see "sustaining innovation" as the way an established organization fine-tunes its purpose/product throughout the life cycle of the organization: "individuals and organizations get better at doing what they have been doing,"[15] whereas they see "disruptive innovation" as referring to disruptive, discontinuous change, occurring at particular critical points in the organization's lifecycle. For instance, in manufacturing it may result in a new product being developed; from being a fringe line, then, as the market changes, it becomes a dominant, mainstream product. They see this disruptive innovation as crucial to organizational transformation. Indeed they conclude "in a nutshell, disruptive innovation changes the very nature of the endeavor, or the enterprise."[16]

---

The concepts of sustaining and disruptive innovation have a relevance to many twenty-first-century organizations. Not only is it clearly applicable to the US military, and to manufacturing industries and commercial businesses, but it could have considerable relevance to church structures. Whereas up until now the church has continued primarily through sustaining innovation, today's information age is challenging it to be conscious of the need for more disruptive innovation.

Similarities can be drawn between Alberts and Hayes's terminology and the terminology of Castells.[17] Castells identifies three different types of identity that go to make up the social/cultural nature and evolution of every society or organization. He terms them "legitimizing identity," "resistance identity," and "project identity." Between these three influences the whole

---

13. Himanen, "Challenges of the Global Information Society," 337.

14. Alberts and Hayes, *Campaigns of Experimentation*.

15. Alberts and Hayes, *Campaigns of Experimentation*, 42.

16. Alberts and Hayes, *Campaigns of Experimentation*, 43.

17. Castells, *Power of Identity*.

ethos of an organization, society/culture is formed and developed. And whereas the first two are primarily resistant to change, linking them with Alberts and Hayes's sustaining innovation, the third one, projective identity, is specifically looking to the future and to change, linking it with Alberts and Hayes's disruptive innovation.

Up until the present the church—the Anglican Church particularly—has existed by sustaining itself and legitimizing itself through adherence to hierarchical tradition/biblical text and has resisted radical organizational change to a considerable degree—with the obvious exception of the Reformation. It has discouraged disruptive innovation/projective identity for fear of its traditional stability and unity being threatened. It has not been prepared to trust or respond to the evidence of those who raise genuine issues, such as those who raised, in the past, the issue of sexual abuse in church life.

---

### CASTELLS

The first, "legitimizing identity generates, reproduces and rationalizes the status quo of civil society,"[18] it cements and holds together an established institutionalized power structure, it controls and irons out any disruptive ideas that might surface, and incorporates them into the existing framework.

The second, resistance identity, is when an organization or society is being threatened. In its attempt to reject the oncoming threats, it allows resistance groups to rise up against its primary body. It then deals with them by marginalizing them into sidelines or ghettoes, and in the process it defuses them.

The third, projective identity is "when social actors, on the basis of whatever cultural materials are available to them, build a new identity that redefines their position in society, and by doing so, seek the transformation of overall social structure."[19] They are not prepared to be sidelined or ghettoized, nor are they satisfied with building defensive barricades to protect their ideas. Their identity is expressed by "expanding towards the transformation of society."[20] Again, this projective identity links in with Alberts and Hayes's disruptive innovation.

---

## The Sigmoid Curve

Running parallel with the above concepts of sustaining and legitimizing tradition and disruptive innovation for change and transformation, lies the

18. Castells, *Power of Identity*, 8.
19. Castells, *Power of Identity*, 10.
20. Castells, *Power of Identity*, 10.

work of Charles Handy,[21] W. R. Scott, and others on organizational trajectories. One common trajectory is that of the Sigmoid Curve—innovation, expansion, plateauing, and contraction/decline.

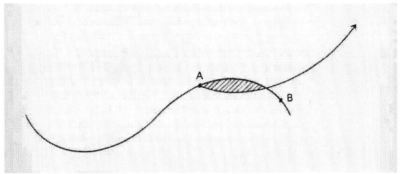

**Figure 1. The Sigmoid Curve**

An institution may start with innovation, with the seed of a product, idea, and purpose, and expands in a rising curve. At some point it may plateau and then, later, follow an inexorable decline into stagnation. But, Handy says, there is a way to avoid this decline, by acting at a certain point on the rising curve, before it plateaus. He calls that Point A and suggests that at that point, a new curve needs to be inaugurated with fresh purpose, products, and infrastructure. The initial upward curve he puts down to sustaining innovation—linking with the research of Alberts and Hayes. But before the plateau is reached, whilst there is still enthusiasm, momentum, and success in the initial venture, a different kind of innovation is required—disruptive innovation. Although the initial venture still believes it is following a path to success, Handy suggests that disruptive innovation needs to be given space by the so-far-successful existing leadership so as to enable fresh growing, flowering, and blossoming, which then becomes a second curve of innovation.

If that opportunity is not taken before reaching the plateau—whilst the operation is still seen to be in success mode—the organization will struggle to resist eventual stagnation and decline. There is, however, a point on the decline curve, Point B, when decline can at last be acknowledged and where a belated attempt to reinvigorate the organization can be made, often called a sharp-bend turnaround.

21. Handy, *Empty Raincoat*.

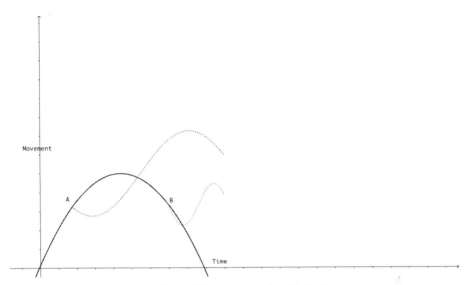

Figure 2. Sigmoid Curve arising from Point B

But such attempts are often beleaguered by a culture of bitterness, division, recrimination, and pessimism which hinder and hold back much chance of a second upward curve of organizational innovation taking off.

## 1.3 COERCION, COLLABORATION, CHAORDIC

Returning to the comparison between hierarchies and networks, a significant question has been raised concerning the intrinsic dynamic operating in each mode. Dee Hock[22] points out that the primary dynamic of a hierarchy is one of coercion, compelled behavior, and control from the top of the pyramid—the senior leadership establish rules and regulations, which are to be followed by all those lower down the pyramid. Walter Wink similarly describes dominating hierarchies based on "the right of some to lord it over others by means of power, wealth sharing, or titles."[23]

On the other hand, a networking organization/culture can be seen to work more on collaboration, integration, trust, and purposefulness. Walter Wink suggests that there have been alternatives to the domination model. He talks of partnership societies that may have existed in earlier times, which were characterized by actualization hierarchies—where communities are served by the leader. Indeed there is evidence to suggest

22. Hock, *Birth of the Chaordic Age*, 10.

23. Wink, *Engaging the Powers*, 112.

that this kind of leadership—based on the importance/significance of the land and its creator—was used by Australian aboriginal society for many thousands of years, long before Europeans came and brought their own domination model.

Dee Hock has illustrated this more collaborative approach in more recent times, in the creation of Visa International.[24] Whereas the parent bank, Bank of America, had a typical hierarchical, top-down, dominating structure, with the Board making the key decisions, Hock describes Visa's inauguration, with all participating banks having an equal say. He claims that decisions were taken by all equally, on a basis of the purpose and principles of the organization, through collaboration and negotiated trust between all partners. He argues that such an approach can be seen to be more appropriate "in the face of exploding diversity and complexity of society worldwide."[25] In this kind of organization, it is argued that power resides at the edge as well as in the center, and that networking, collaboration, and trust are the driving forces of creativity, innovation, and expansion. Such an approach suits a society where work is less and less a matter of repeating standardized actions on a production line, mass producing the same item through routinization of processes and a division of labor. This contrasts with a network society that is growing through innovation, digital information, artificial intelligence, and machine technologies, where top-down rules and instructions are being replaced by emergent discovery and creativity at the edge.

## DEE HOCK

Dee Hock, founder and CEO Emeritus of Visa International, puts forward the proposal that we are moving into a "chaordic" age, where chaos and order can be constructively combined together. He finds "organizations increasingly unable to achieve the purpose for which they were created, yet continuing to expand as they devour resources, decimate the earth, and demean humanity. . . . We are experiencing a global epidemic of institutional failure that knows no bounds."[26]

The primary reason he cites for this failure lies in the concept of organization intrinsically based on domination, compelled behavior, and monetary measured "substance." Such an approach, he suggests, is not able to handle "the exploding diversity and complexity of society, and the systemic nature of seemingly intractable social and environmental problems."[27]

24. Hock, *Birth of the Chaordic Age*, 10.
25. Hock, *Birth of the Chaordic Age*, 5.
26. Hock, *Birth of the Chaordic Age*, 5.
27. Hock, *Birth of the Chaordic Age*, 10.

His response is to suggest that, rather than organizations being based on domination, "organizations of the future will be the embodiment of community, based on shared purpose calling to the higher aspirations of people."[28] He calls for the emergence of a Chaordic Age, where both chaos and order are simultaneously combined and held together by individuals and organizations, "releasing what people desire in the depths of their being, the passion they have for it—the integrity they bring to the attempt,"[29] with organizations, rather than being centered around compelled behavior, being about relationships and community.

He goes on to describe (in terms not dissimilar to the approaches of viral change, cooperative enquiry, and Rohr's reflections on substance and relationship,[30] referred to later) how such a newly emerging organization can come about through a process: a mutual journey of discerning the primary *purpose* of community, the *principles* that should undergird it, and the *people* who are to be involved. From there the *concept* of the organization can be determined, and only then is the *structure* to be identified and the *practice* established.

A chaordic organization is not a destination, a linear process, a static entity. Rather, it is a journey, a community engagement, evolving out of very "different dynamics of judgment, behavior, capacity, and ingenuity."[31] It takes seriously the complexity of society, and the imaginative, innovative nature of each individual within the community. It is a reconception for our twenty-first century, of what organization could be about—all illustrated by Hock's own personal experience of creating and developing Visa International.

Hock found that forgoing control through order didn't necessarily lead to chaos if control could be replaced by mutual engagement and trust. He realized that coercion could be replaced by cohesion. He sought to build up horizontally networked relationships as an alternative to the compelled behavior of top-down, vertical command and control. Primarily he discovered that the success of a twenty-first-century organization should not start with the structure of the organization but rather with the mutually agreed purpose and principles central to that organization. Hock's experience in creating Visa International out of the traditional concept of organization—exhibited by Bank of America—indicates that our contemporary environment asks fresh questions, offers different alternatives, and requires a variety of new skills and working practices, as compared to past practices, requiring more time, trust, and effort in developing horizontal relationships. In

28. Hock, *Birth of the Chaordic Age*, 6.
29. Hock, *Birth of the Chaordic Age*, 2.
30. Rohr, *Divine Dance*.
31. Hock, *Birth of the Chaordic Age*, 6.

the end it can lead to a more flexible, fluid, fluent community, encouraging creative innovation, responding speedily to ever-changing circumstances, coping with the ever-increasing complexity of our time. This example of turning away from hierarchical control towards networking relationships of trust offers both a practical illustration and hope to the church if it were to consider a similar leap of faith.

## 1.4 COMPLEXITY

Returning again to this primary trend, from hierarchies toward networks, brings us to the subjects of complexity and emergence. Complexity has been a part of creation and humanity from the very beginning, but has come into a clearer focus since the end of the last century. Complexity began when the primordial soup of amino acids coalesced to become living cells, individual cells came together to form organisms such as the amoeba, and neurons and synapses came to make up the most complex of all systems: the human brain.

---

**THE BRAIN**

Alan Turing once remarked "How wondrous a thing the brain is. A one-litre, liquid cooled, three-dimensional computer. Unbelievable processing power, unbelievably compressed, unbelievable energy and efficiency, no overheating. The whole thing running on 25 watts—one dim light bulb."[32]

---

Now whereas complexity was first identified in the life sciences, it has more recently been applied to organizational networking systems. The basis of complexity is that systems themselves can self-organize in such a way as to create a system of even greater complexity. They do this through spontaneous interaction between agents, by novelty and innovation, sometimes including human intervention. What results are more intricate systems that have adapted out of a simpler format but which are living, dynamic, and vibrant, occurring in any part of a society or organization.

The crucial point comes when a novelty or innovative idea comes up against, or emerges out of, an existing static-ordered structure. Mushrooming explosions of innovation, amplified by the networking nature of digital information, challenge the existing order as illustrated by Castells, Alberts and Hayes, and Charles Handy. That area of confrontation, or border, has been described as the edge of chaos, where the simpler, traditional, often hierarchical order of the past is confronted with the often-chaotic

---

32. Kemp, "Machines Like Me by Ian McEwan Review," 27.

complexity of creative, interactive, networked innovation. So the direction of movement is from, as Pickard notes, "order that emphasized fixity and stability, to a dynamic of order that involves change, adaption, and capacity for novelty."[33] This complexity is fed by the ever-expanding information network age, where our structures and activities are organized around electronically processed information networks.

This border at the edge of chaos, described by Hock as chaordic, is where creativity, spontaneity, and adaptive dynamics can be harnessed for the benefit of the established order, where coercion from structured power can be replaced by collaborative horizontal networking.

Now whereas this chaordic border—at the edge of chaos—is often feared by existing structures, advice comes from a surprising, 2,500-year-old source. In the Denma translation of Sun Tzu's collection of Chinese writings—*The Art of War*—the Sage Commander, the general of the military organization, is expected to live with and harness this chaos. Chaos and order, it is said, are part of the same whole. "It is part of the totality of our experience, the good, the bad, the confusion and clarity—all interconnected and constantly shifting."[34] For example, a low-pressure weather system bringing a hurricane, storms, high winds, and lashing rain may come suddenly with great power, resulting in much fear, but it is actually only part of a much larger weather system or pattern. Those on England's west coast have every reason to fear the hurricane, but overall it is part of the same system that brings rain and sunshine for our agricultural ecosystem throughout the year. The Sage Commander calls us to feel at home in chaos and conflict, and to learn how to harness them for our positive purposes. Chaos and opportunity come from the same holistic approach: we are to use this border on the edge of chaos for the benefit of all; we are to welcome these complex adaptive systems that can help us to handle the explosion of knowledge, intelligence, and interactivity which accelerating technology brings.

## 1.5 EMERGENCE

Complexity is closely allied to the concept of emergence. Networking capability expanded the printing press revolution 500 years ago,[35] but a basic form of emergence is rooted in the whole concept of networking. Emergence ideas can also be traced back to John Stuart Mill in the nineteenth

33. Pickard, *Theological Foundations*, 132.

34. Tzu, *Art of War*, 91.

35. Ferguson, *Square and the Tower*.

century. After lying fallow, emergent evolution reemerged in one of Alan Turing's last papers in 1954, which in turn was developed much more extensively in the 1970s by psychologists and philosophers of the mind—C. D. Broad—and then on into this century. The principle at the heart of emergence is that simple systems with simple parts can generate very complex behaviors: what appears to be a simple organism or system can have within it the potential to develop into a complex adaptive system or organism.

---

### SLIMEMOULD

One of the best-known illustrations of the concept of emergence can be found in the "organizational structures of slimemould,"[36] an algae that creeps from dead branch to dead branch in the woods, eating up the rotten leaves decaying in its path. Without a pacemaker/leader, these cells successfully aggregate together, cross obstacles to find and devour food, and then disappear again. To do this they use acrasin (cyclical AMP) and pheromones that they give off and receive as a kind of communication network. Their behavior, "a movement from lower levels to higher level sophistication," is called "*emergence*": whereby "disparate agents can unwittingly create a higher-level order"[37] where the whole becomes more than the sum of the parts; where both parts and whole contribute to the creation and functioning of a new entity.

Although slimemould aggregation is now seen as a classic case study of bottom-up behavior, two other biological case studies live all around us. Both ants and bees have very complex societies. Yet neither is centered around a leader who calls the shots. Their structures are based on a communication network using pheromones[38] that guide the activities of all ants and bees. Such an ant colony might survive for fifteen years, despite the fact that an average ant life is miniscule in comparison. Although there are queen ants they don't fulfill hierarchical roles. Ant nests emerge out of "swarm logic" whereby ants "think and act locally, but their collective action produces global behaviour."[39] In humans, research is focusing on the possibility of babies receiving pheromones from their mother, directing them towards her nipple for milk in the same way as piglets are thought to do with the sow's teats.

---

From American history the Apache tribe illustrated how an apparently uncivilized culture, could cause chaos to a highly organized and experienced army with a centralized command. When the Spanish Army, having

36. Johnson, *Emergence*, 90.
37. Johnson, *Emergence*, 100.
38. Johnson, *Emergence*, 92.
39. Johnson, *Emergence*, 64.

subdued both the Incas and the Aztecs, moved north through Mexico to the United States, the Apaches had no central leader or headquarters. They worked as bands of raiders with a spiritual leader. If he was killed, another warrior immediately took his place. To the Spanish it looked a chaotic organization, but in reality it was "an advanced and sophisticated society—it's just that a decentralized organization is a completely different creature."[40] Interestingly, that very same approach, originally used by General Sir Walter Walker in the Borneo and Malaya campaigns, is now adopted by the Active Service Units of the SAS and other military groups. Whilst in action there is no leader, all members are leaders; if one is killed, the rest continue. Undoubtedly the al-Qaeda and ISIS movements work on exactly the same principle. In a completely different context, Alcoholics Anonymous groups work on a similar basis. The organization has no central command. Each group runs itself. It is held together by its members, its purpose, and its limited rules. Similarly, emergent and decentralized organizations feed off the internet/social media. During the Tottenham riots of 2015, the rioting spread like wildfire via mobile texting and through social networking. There was no central organization. It happened by finger on the keypad.

So emergent, decentralized, often relational organizations/structures are everywhere around us, from slimemould to Airbnb. So many institutions and organizations with static hierarchical structures, who began life as a centralized organization, are being challenged by emergent characteristics, and by the changing innovative nature of our network society.

## 1.6 ALGORITHMS AND DATA-FLOW

Now whereas emergence was initially detected in biological contexts, that then appeared to be transferable to systemic, organizational structures, algorithms were developed more in the mechanistic world and are now being related to human and biological contexts.

The story began in the industrial factory setting, with certain tasks in the assembly process and machine tool industry being done by Computer Numerical Controlled (CNC) machines taking the place of human shop floor operatives. These machines were soon followed by increasingly more complex robots, as seen in car assembly line production. A more domestic example can be seen in a food hall stand. If you want a bowl of Japanese soup for lunch, you can buy a carton with all the fresh ingredients, vegetables, chicken, chili and noodles prepared mechanically beforehand. All that

---

40. Brafman and Beckstrom, *Starfish and the Spider*, 21.

needs to be done is to add boiling water. Dependence on a chef to produce a meal is minimized by machines.

CNCs and robots have now all become part of industrial history. Such automation began to filter through from unskilled into semi-skilled and then skilled jobs, like the machine tool industry. Now it has also penetrated skilled, professional worlds such as medicine and law.

---

### WARFARIN MEDICATION

When having warfarin—medication for heart disease—levels checked there is no need to see a doctor every time. It is all done by taking blood readings and then feeding them into a computer that has one's previous readings. The computer assesses the present INR reading and prescribes appropriate warfarin dosages for the coming weeks—possibly with greater accuracy than a doctor's recommendation.

---

This leads us into the world of algorithms, "a methodical set of steps that can be used to make calculations, resolve problems, reach solutions."[41] The above warfarin/INR software program was an automated task, but it was done by algorithms. Algorithms lie behind the work of supercomputers, such as IBM's Big Blue and Watson, and Google's Go, Deep Mind, and its recent sibling, AlphaZero. In the case of popular games such as Chess and Chinese Go, and in the TV show *Jeopardy!*, when the computer took on human opposition, the software was fed astronomical amounts of data and possible options, which were all processed to find the appropriate algorithms with which to play against the human opposition. At the start, very few believed that the computer could outsmart the human contestants. But the computers did, in each competition, through the use of algorithms.[42] On the more negative side, in the financial markets, algorithms created a number of "flash crashes"—May 6, 2010, and April 23, 2013—and then produced new algorithms to correct themselves in between three and six minutes. However, during the space of those few minutes some investors made huge losses, whilst others made corresponding profits.

These algorithms have now become the bedrock undergirding computer capability. Any human task that has a predictable outcome, however large or complex, is in danger of being made redundant by algorithmic software. And whereas the process began with mechanical and memory centered tasks, it now even stretches to cancer research; composing classical music; and even writing Japanese haiku poetry. It all depends on crunching

---

41. Harari, *Homo Deus*, 97.
42. Harari, *Homo Deus*, 373.

vast amounts of information, described as big data. Personal phones and laptops may still talk about megabytes and gigabytes of storage, but today's supercomputers deal with thousands of exabytes—a billion gigabytes. They even have a name for the number of bytes that has thirty-three noughts— domegemegrottebyte. Moore's Law applies to the exponential increase in big data memory as well as the ability to compute it. In the beginning, this fact-crunching capacity only applied to what is called "structured" informa- tion: information that lies directly behind the task in hand, with an out- come that is, in principle, predictable. Now, however, algorithms can search through vast amounts of unstructured information and draw out informa- tion pertinent to a highly specific target—which points towards the concept of thinking computers.

The next step from programming algorithms into computer software is for computers to program themselves, by developing self-learning algo- rithms. This has evolved from computers with deep learning networks that have drawn information from huge, wide-ranging sources and then direct- ing them toward specific targets. Apple used this process to develop SIRI, its speech pattern and analysis recognition system, as did Google with its translation software. Behind this software that enables instantaneous trans- lation for most languages, was the mining of big data over each and every language included, and the processing of that data into specific targeted requirements, so that accurate translation could be simultaneous. This is a machine-learning process that writes its own programs. Such a process was used by Google to develop a highly complex computer designed for one single task alone. Once they had built the computer they then put it on four wheels and called it a driverless car. Others are in the advanced stages of doing this for transport distribution lorries.

Imagine three people decide they want to create a new product that would fit perfectly into future market demands. They might rent two offices, employ three extra members of staff, and persuade serious venture capitalists to invest in their idea. They could use 3D printers to develop the item, market it online, distribute it by a fleet of automated driverless vehicles to central hubs, from which local delivery would be organized.

Such a scenario has initiated a rethinking of Charles Handy's Sigmoid Curve of the 1990s. As the third decade of the twenty-first century approaches, it is the S-curve that becomes significant, not centered around people's relation- ships within an organization, but rather centered on algorithms and on the deep learning capacities of a machine learning system. Whereas Sigmoid was homocentric, S-curves will be data-centric, dependent on data flow and its exponential explosion.

---

### S-CURVES

Martin Ford[43] defines S-curves as "an S shaped path in which accelerating—or exponential—advance ultimately matures into a plateau." Although similar to Handy's Sigmoid Curve, Ford's concept is of a whole staircase of ascending S-curves resting on each other. He illustrates this through aircraft development. The first S-curve is illustrated by propeller-driven aircraft from 1903 and culminating in the Spitfire of the 1940s. The second curve began during the Second World War with Frank Whittle's jet engine, which built on, and then overtook, the technology that had climaxed in the Spitfire. Now a third curve has already started through forms of rocket propulsion spearheaded by the likes of Richard Branson and Elon Musk.

---

Competition to be the first with any form of innovation—the winner takes all—raises a wide range of questions. To develop innovation often requires considerable investment. The incentive to be first motivates the venture capitalists. The stakes are high. At present our economy is dominated by Silicon Valley giants such as Google, Apple, Facebook, Microsoft, Amazon, and Netflix, who all form a growing stranglehold on marketing consumption and media. How those tech companies relate to governments and legislation and to ordinary individuals will be addressed later. But automation, algorithms, and data-flow are certainly in areas where Silicon Valley giants are heavily investing, particularly in the possibility of AGI—Artificial General Intelligence—or the singularity.

## 1.7 ARTIFICIAL GENERAL INTELLIGENCE— THE SINGULARITY, NANOTECHNOLOGY— MOLECULAR MANUFACTURE

With the exponential rise of computer power, an unanswered question lies in wait. It can take different forms but it is the same issue. Could computers ever develop to the point where they exceed human intellectual capability? Could they exceed the power and complexity of the human brain? If so, what will happen to humanity? Is there a next stage of human development—superhuman intelligence—a combining of digital computer power with the complexity of the brain itself?

---

43. Ford, *Rise of the Robots*, 68–70.

Stephen Hawking warned against dismissing lightly "the notion of highly intelligent machines as mere fiction," going on to say "this would be a mistake, and potentially our worst mistake ever."[44] Hawking was reflecting on issues that first appeared in the 1950s, with Alan Turing and Irving Good, who talked of an intelligence explosion, and with John von Neumann, who first coined the term singularity, for the creation of a sentient computer. This was then developed in the 1960s by Ray Kurzweil, the futurist inventor and Google's Director of Engineering, who warned that it could rupture the fabric of history, and usher in a new age. Similarly, in the 2000s, Eliezer Yudkowsky raised the same concerns referred to by Hawking. He posted a series of blogs entitled the "sequences," out of which the Rationalists Movement was developed. Most recently James Lovelock and has added further reflections in his book *Novacene.*

Artificial Intelligence, as a subject, has taken two different roads. Technological research and development into robots and algorithms has followed the path of specialized or narrow artificial intelligence directed at specific areas/specific tasks, such as IBM's Watson. However, there is a second area of research and imagining—Artificial General Intelligence—described by Alan Turing as a "genuinely intelligent system,"[45] that would in itself "exceed human intellectual capability."[46]

AGI has also been referred to by the term "singularity—attributed to John von Neumann in the 1950s, Vernor Vinge in 1993,[47] and Ray Kurzweil. The word is taken from physics, describing the point within a black hole where gravitation breaks down and light appears unable to escape. They then use it in the technological sphere to describe "a discontinuity in human progress, that would be fundamentally opaque until it occurred,"[48] before calling it "a point where development of technology becomes so fast that humanity will no longer be able to keep up with it" and "a machine that can conceive new ideas, demonstrate an awareness of its own existence, and carry on coherent conversations."[49] Such a machine would be the holy grail of artificial intelligence. It is researched by eminent academics, such as Nick Bostom of Oxford University and Max Tegmark at MIT. It is that to which so much investment from Silicon Valley giants—such as Elon Musk's Open Philanthropy Project—is directed. For many it is like the discovery of the

---

44. Hawking, "Will Robots Outsmart Us?," 33.
45. Ford, *Rise of the Robots,* 226.
46. Ford, *Rise of the Robots,* 228.
47. Vinge, quoted in *Rise of the Robots,* 229.
48. Kurzweil, quoted in *Rise of the Robots,* 229.
49. Kurzweil, quoted in Baddiel, Sunday Times, 22/10/2017.

Higgs Boson particle of CERN's hadron collider. It is talked about for many years before ultimately being discovered. But whereas identification of the Higgs Boson caused a scientific celebration, the advent of the singularity would inaugurate a new era of human history, where the human species was no longer the dominant or center point.

The main fear is that, having been asked by humans to fulfill a task, a computer will achieve that and then go on to reprogram itself in ways that cannot be stopped by its human operator. In Yudkowsky's oft-quoted reflection, "The AI does not hate you, nor does it love you, but you are made up of atoms which it can use for something else." A second fear centers around uncertainty concerning the speed at which it develops—from being quite smart, to becoming vastly cleverer than the human mind. In this epoch of novelty and hybridization, the speed of such exponential growth is hard to perceive; from the time when a scientist programs a computer, to the time when the computer resists any attempt by the scientist to switch it off—for instance, in the controlling of nuclear weapons. Many believe we are in that timeframe now, with no way of knowing if or when it will end.

Another such radical conception, initiated by K. Eric Drexler in the late 1970s and articulated in book form in 1986,[50] and which is still in gestation today, is that of nanotechnology: nano-scale molecular machines that could in effect take atoms from one molecule and rearrange them so that they become a very different molecule, and hence a different substance. For instance, Drexler imagined a factory that could take certain basic materials, work on them through various nano-stages from molecular level upwards, until they ultimately became a car in a matter of minutes. "The essence of nanotechnology is the ability to work at the molecular level, atom by atom, to create large structures with fundamentally new molecular organization."[51]

Initially the US Congress funded research into nanotechnology. However, later on, two interpretations of the word "nanotechnology" began to circulate. What received US funding was not Drexler's original concept of molecular manufacturing, but rather anything that was being manufactured at tiny molecular levels. But, even so, as with the singularity, the concept of molecular manufacturing didn't go away. Both Manchester University and research funded by Silicon Valley investors continue the search.

50. Ford, *Rise of the Robots*, 226.

51. Drexler, quoted in *Rise of the Robots*, 239.

## 1.8 INTELLIGENCE AND CONSCIOUSNESS

This kind of debate has been put in a different format by Yuval Harari,[52] where he talks about the decoupling of intelligence and consciousness. He sees computers outstripping humans in intelligence and technological ability, but he differentiates that from human consciousness. He speculates that, not only could computers take the place of humans in driving vehicles, but the supercomputer could actually manage the whole traffic system of a city, and hence eliminate all accidents arising from human failure or miscalculation. However, although this artificial intelligence could easily surpass human intelligence, it may never attain a consciousness exhibited in humans. This makes us consider in depth what human consciousness offers, that is not mechanically quantifiable.

> Consciousness has been defined as a quality of awareness: a human ability to be aware of, to examine, to analyze one's own thoughts, one's own feelings; to experience objects around one; an ability to respond to one's surroundings and to one's own inner feelings; an understanding and sense of being oneself, a personal self, different from others.

At the core of humanism is the importance and centrality of human consciousness. Our human relationships with others, and our personal expressions of them, are central to Western culture. Other expressions of consciousness include the significance of self, and even the possibility of a human soul: both of which can have built-in senses of values such as right and wrong, of feelings and emotions, and in the case of the Christian faith— of that preparedness to lay down one's life for someone else, or something we value.

> The action of Vasili Archipov, a Soviet submarine commander in the 1962 Cuban missile crisis, has been said to be the single most valuable contribution to humanity in human history, when he refused to obey instructions from Moscow, to launch nuclear missiles at US warships close by. If "the red button" had been controlled by a computer algorithm, rather than a conscious human being, then no one knows what our world would be like today.[53]

Having feelings, empathy, and solidarity with others over beliefs, values, and rights are all central to human consciousness. Some of those feelings would

---

52. Harari, *Homo Deus*, 356–408.
53. Davis, "Soviet Submarine Officer," para. 6.

come from memory, personal history, and actualities that have not been recorded or included in big data's memory for algorithmic development. One illustration of such feelings is that of love. How could awareness of other people, through feelings of love, be absorbed into an algorithmic world? Such an encounter was visualized in *Blade Runner 2049*, between agent K and Joi—a 3D visual robot prostitute, created and made available to him by the replicant producer organization. An element of human feeling from K toward Joi was shown, only to be destroyed forever by K's pursuer from the organization, who destroyed his mobile phone. In an instant, Joi who had been such a companion to him, disappeared for ever. Agent K, expressing devastation about the loss of Joi, was illustrating some degree of consciousness programmed in by the organization, whereas Joi, who participated in the relationship, was purely an algorithm. Surely this poignant relationship highlighted the intrinsic chasm between consciousness and intelligence.

As well as this ability to be objectively aware of people, activities, and values from the past, David Baddiel[54] raises the point of "doubt." AI, he suggests, is inherently arrogant. It cannot conceive that it might be wrong, that it might have come to the wrong conclusion. It cannot doubt the validity of its own calculations. Doubt is surely a significant attribute that makes us human, encourages us to reconsider, exhorts us to think more deeply or widely or search for other material that might help us to improve our conclusion. It was doubt in the mind of the Soviet submarine captain that led him to question the values and decision of Moscow, which in turn resulted in him not precipitating a third world war.

Maybe one way of recoupling intelligence with consciousness, and bringing about a move toward singularity, might be by interfacing and connecting up the complexity, creativity, and innovation of the brain with the extraordinary computing capacity of machine-learning algorithms. The brain itself functions through very complex deep learning neural networks. Increasingly computers are developing similar neural networks, with different levels of connection and interaction, into their algorithms. On the one hand, this brain/computer interface could evolve into upgraded superhumans. On the other hand, it could result in a more conscious, algorithmic, sentient computer. Certainly, the complexity and size of the brain's neural network computer should not be underestimated. But advances in neuroscience have led to massive steps being taken by tech organizations—such as Facebook, Elon Musk's Neuralink, and OpenWater—side by side with the Pentagon and the Chinese Government's AI research programs. Many

---

54. Baddiel, Sunday Times, 22/10/2017.

accept that through the brain/computer interface—human symbiosis with AI—humans are swiftly moving toward communicating telepathically.

Some, such as Neuralink, are making invasive connections, implanting chips through polymer threads right into the brain. Others, such as OpenWater, are working on noninvasive devices, such as a ski hat or bandage. The University of California has used noninvasive electrodes to record the brain activity of epilepsy patients, and algorithms to deduce the words being formulated, with considerable accuracy. Harari quotes other examples of neuroprosthetics. Hadassah Hospital Jerusalem has been treating depression through implanting computer chips into people's brains. Whilst the American military are experimenting with "trans-cranial stimulator" helmets that could assist soldiers on the battlefront.[55]

One of the issues arising from all of this concerns how this research should be regulated. On the one hand, mind-reading, if used malevolently, would violate the privacy of the human mind. On the other hand, the potential of manipulating/programming people to act involuntarily, as in *The Minority Report* and the Jason Bourne films, could be abused by governments and commercial interests alike.

There is also intense debate between the technologists and the biologists over reverse engineering the brain. The complexity of the brain means it would be extraordinarily difficult to recreate it in a computer. This is stressed by biologists. However, the technologists are already learning more and more about how particular parts of the brain work, especially in the area of deep learning neural networks. It is they who are more optimistic about linking the two together, and about reverse engineering the brain's capacity into advanced computer capability. Watch this space.

## 1.9 SUPERHUMAN

One of the most far-reaching sides of digital technological development has been that of genetic engineering. Since the discovery of DNA and the identification of the human genome, research has gone on in the area of genetic manipulation: the editing, insertion, and deletion of genes.

In medicine—with the identification of illness-causing genes—this research has been dramatic, leading toward the ability to adapt/delete parts of human DNA, often referred to as self-designed evolution. Identifying single genes that cause a particular illness, such as leukemia, muscular dystrophy and cystic fibrosis, has led to faulty genes being repaired. DNA-editing systems—such as in the way CRISPR, a bacterial DNA oddity, is used—are

55. Harari, *Homo Deus*, 334–36.

continually developing, with the possibility of moving from single-gene fault to far more complex, multi-gene combinations that lie behind many sources of illness, such as cancer or schizophrenia.

However, as both Stephen Hawking and Sir Martin Rees[56] have pointed out, a distinction is emerging between medical interventions that remove something harmful and deploying techniques to offer enhancement. The first is already happening, but the second is clearly possible. Hawking points out that we will soon be in a position to modify more complex areas, such as intelligence, instinct, and human characteristics like memory, resistance to disease, and length of life. Both these eminent scientists foresee such a development leading to the possibility of enhancement, toward the appearance of superhumans. The self-designing of beings—creating children with particular advanced characteristics, resistance to disease, increased longevity—will be targeted, despite government legislation expected to curb such innovation. Choosing the sex of one's baby is only one stepping stone ahead of He Jiankui's boundary-breaking research. His team cut out a gene carrying HIV from an embryo at the single-cell stage and allowed that embryo to develop and give birth to twins Lulu and Nana in Shenzhen, South China in 2018, against all international protocol.

Both scientists go even further to hint at a concept of life beyond DNA/macromolecular development. Hawking dreams of humans transforming themselves into posthuman inorganic beings, creating digital surrogates—machines that would become a new life form based on mechanical and electronic components rather than on macromolecules, with the potential to replace DNA-based life. Rees agrees with Hawking, in that "a bio-hacked super-race is inevitable, that we will transcend our human bodies and go electronic."[57] Neither sees this in the near future but as a possible future scenario. Hawking expects this because the comparatively slow biological evolution of humanity will not be able to compete with exponential digital technology.

## ENDNOTE

So, algorithms, singularity, data flows, molecular manufacturing, human and machine intelligence, and consciousness and genetic engineering are all inputs into a complex, ongoing debate. Some steps have been achieved and others are simply sci-fi. Some quote the fact that the expected flying cars haven't materialized. Others quote the increasing capability of a new breed

56. McConnachie, "What's in Store for Us?," 36.
57. McConnachie, "What's in Store for Us?," 37.

of supercomputers, and the expected tie-up between quantum computing and artificial intelligence. So, with Moore's Law undoubtedly being sur-passed—with Silicon valley giants such as IBM and Google investing heav-ily—the future appears at present to be both exciting and, at the same time, unimaginable. How that leaves the ordinary individual, what impact it has on human society, what values it creates and destroys, and who wins or loses as a result, are all matters that need wide-ranging discussion. From a gov-ernment perspective, the House of Lords Report on artificial intelligence[58] has a number of reflections on these issues, which we shall consider later. Similarly, such an exponential explosion of intelligence and knowledge, as it ushers humanity into a new and uncertain world, will surely be an area for Christian reflection and perceptive contribution.

58. House of Lords Report, *AI in the UK.*

# Chapter 2

## Marketization, Globalization, Climate Change

### INTRODUCTION

Today's society has underlying traits which have developed over the last 300 years. One of the basic assumptions in Western society has been a belief in progress and increasing prosperity: forward movement that brings greater achievement and fulfillment for humanity. That prosperity is expected to be built around the growth of production, increasing the size of the pie rather than redistributing the segments of the pie. Prosperity is seen primarily in material terms: as a substance to be consumed, with individual freedom, rights and choice privileged over communal identity, roles, and responsibilities. Such material prosperity, Yuval Harari suggests, has emerged out of the optimistic liberal humanist alliance between scientific progress and economic growth, achieved through the capitalist system of investment, credit, loans, and innovation.[1]

By the end of the twentieth century many had become convinced that such prosperity and progress could be best achieved through a capitalist rather than a socialist or communist society. However, during the first two decades of the present century it is becoming increasingly uncertain as to whether capitalist values, systems, growth, and prosperity can or will be sustainable into the third decade—but more of that later.

---

1. Harari, *Homo Deus*, 237.

Within that western liberal ethos of prosperity, progress, and uncertainty, the Western Christian faith/church will need to understand, engage with, and contribute to the exciting but disruptive sociological changes taking place. Not only is this society a multicultural melting pot, many would argue that it is at a critical open-ended moment in its development.

One of the most significant previous paradigm shifts has been from the Industrial Revolution to the Information/Digital Age. However, we are now facing yet another profound paradigm shift, from an anthropocentric mindset to a machine or data-centric era. The driving force for these changes is not so much national governments but rather global, supranational financial markets and technological forces, that operate beyond the control of many democratic governments and that are the engine room and power house of what is understood to be progress. What drives the future? The answer used to be "The economy, stupid!" However, seismic societal changes are now taking place which are increasingly being driven by rapid innovations in artificial intelligence, big data, and algorithms, and by global corporations, financial systems, social media giants, and supranational speculators behind this latest phase of capitalist evolution.

If the church is to survive and contribute to societal development, it has to understand and participate in the evolving political, economic, and sociological processes. In the past, capitalists used to talk about the invisible hand of the market. But for a just, righteous, and balanced society to develop, those invisible forces need to be brought out into the open, so that a wide-ranging democratic debate, and the voice and rights of the majority, and of many diverse minorities, have a chance to be heard and to flourish. In the past century, the alternative to democracy was dictatorship of one particular form or another. However, today's influential dictatorships are often based on economic and technological power rather than on merely military dominance. They are increasingly led by the new behemoths like Facebook, Google, Amazon, Baidu, Alibaba and WeChat, who innovate by exploiting the potential of digital devices to gather and analyze data on the whole global population, through their appropriation of data from phone usage, texts, e-mails, and social media. This has been identified by some as "surveillance capitalism."[2] Again, more of that later.

So how do Christian beliefs and values stand up beside these emerging trends? How do they view marketization, globalization, and climate change, all of which are becoming key factors after the turn of the millennium? Let us, in this chapter, look at some developing trends, before looking at, in

---

2. Zuboff, *Age of Surveillance Capitalism*.

chapter 3, some of the issues arising. Then, in part 2 we will consider past and present Christian participation in societal development.

## 2.1 MARKETIZATION

In chapter 1 we noted that sociological analysis highlighted three key factors in our move toward an age of information hierarchies, networks, and markets. We now need to look in greater depth at markets.

Markets, in theory, are places of public exchange and debate: places of buying and selling; of supply and demand; of addressing competition; places where the aim is to find an equilibrium between those who bring goods, and those who wish to buy goods. The market is also assumed to be a place where information is equally available to all consumers, and where those transactions can be exchanged peaceably and without conflict; where the diverse needs of those attending are all reasonably satisfied. Such reasonable satisfaction however, is not necessarily accepted by all parties in the marketplace. With hindsight it can be seen that, globally, capitalism has developed in one of three ways: through laissez-faire (free trade), welfare capitalism (today's socialism), or state capitalism (today's communism). Within those three approaches lie different conceptions of the interaction between state, civil society, and free competitive markets that supposedly find their own equilibrium as state intervention molds and enhances them through social policy, control, and investment.

In Britain there have been a number of political economic permutations since the second world war. As the country emerged out of that conflict, John Maynard Keynes's theories dominated economic policy development in the UK. He argued that free competitive markets could not respond adequately to the crisis of depression and high unemployment which prevailed after the war, and argued persuasively that state-led investment in infrastructure, (e.g., building roads, rail, and other public works) was needed to kickstart demand in the economy and to give people wages to spend in the marketplace. In the seventies, Keynesian thinking was challenged by Milton Friedman and the Chicago school of neoliberal economists, who influenced the monetarist policies of Thatcher and Reagan with a belief in shrinking the state and leaving laissez-faire, "blind," free markets to shape priorities.

However, this approach has led toward an increasingly self-regulating role for the private sector, with privatization of state operations and public services, and deregulation of trade restrictions. This has involved a doctrine of austerity, cuts in public expenditure, and constraint in public services, such as health and education, policing, law and order.

This neoliberal ideology held sway until the global financial crash of 2008, which most economists and governments (apart from UK chancellor and then-prime minister Gordon Brown) failed to predict: like a balloon suddenly being pricked with a pin. Most neoliberals had assumed that its synthetic statistical economic model, based on scientific criteria, mechanical logic, and human rationality, had no limits to growth, that it was ensured against risk and uncertainty. In the end this led to a ceiling being reached, followed by a crash, for which the banks were blamed for overreaching themselves and for failing to maintain adequate levels of growth—the lifeblood of progressive capitalism. Public and private debt had been allowed to build up, which fueled consumer spending, in order to maintain those growth rates. In the march of progress, inequality of both wealth and income had become accepted between those who invested to accumulate and those who struggled to survive, whilst wages failed to rise in line with the cost of living and productivity.[3] Or as Harari has put it "when disaster strikes, the poor almost always suffer far more than the rich, even if the rich caused the tragedy in the first place."[4] Despite the crash, government policies continued and those who caused the crash were not adequately penalized.

Around this time French political scientist Chantal Mouffe had been calling for a "populism of the left." Reflecting on the triumph of Margaret Thatcher she argued that "neoliberalism became so dominant that politics was reduced to technical experts, foreclosing meaningful popular debate,"[5] a condition she describes as "post democracy." This was further articulated and developed within the British context by a group of economic students who formed a postcrash economics society, later to become Rethinking Economics. They criticized the "science" of economics taught at universities as being uncritical of itself, as being a "distinct system that can be managed by using and being dependent on a very narrow set of logical scientific criteria,"[6] that didn't take any account of social, historical factors or irrational behavior. Secondly, they saw economists as a group of self-proclaimed experts who, because of the complexity of today's world, could claim to be the only ones who could really understand the economy, the only ones competent to advise on the way forward. They were mirroring the earlier thinking of David Bakan, who wrote about a leadership approach of "mystery/mastery" whereby those with presumed superior knowledge, ability, and control made decisions on a one-way basis on behalf of followers who

---

3. Streeck, *How Will Capitalism End?*, 35.

4. Harari, *Homo Deus*, 251.

5. Longo, "Book Review," para. 2.

6. Chakrobortty, "*Econocracy* Review," para. 11.

did not have, or could not obtain, equivalent knowledge, understanding, or ability. By claiming such expert mastery/status everyone else was de-skilled, and democratic debate on the subject was stifled. Thirdly, they criticized the lack of questioning of existing government policy, and the unprepared-ness to consider any other alternatives. They pressed this by asking why the architects of the 2008 crash were still in power—a point raised similarly by protest movements such as Occupy Wall Street—but they received very little response.

---

### CRASHED

This point has been endorsed in a recent book by Adam Tooze.[7] The 2008 crash, when the global economy teetered on the brink of irretrievable disaster, initi-ated by a collapse in the US sub-prime housing mortgage market, led to an un-precedented bailout from UK, US, and European government funds, to shore up overextended, undercapitalized, free-market financial institutions. Because of the intensity of the crash, funding was made available from public funds—help Wall Street in order to save Main Street—with alacrity. But no one has ever been identified as being responsible or brought to account for the original failures. The global free market capitalist system should have been held accountable by shareholders and governments. But the need to act speedily to avoid disaster, and the absence of institutions of global governance, meant that no fundamental enquiry into what went wrong to begin with took place—a view endorsed by Gordon Brown.[8]

---

The Rethinking Economics students suggested that little account was taken of what might be called heterodox economics, which did take account of so-cial conditions, sustainability, pollution, and historical factors—all of which demonstrate the unpredictability of human choice as it reacts to contem-porary circumstances. Fourthly, the group discerned that economics had infiltrated every aspect of political life, with politics being the servant of economic theory, rather than the other way around. As Roger Scruton has put it, "the most deplorable intellectual failing on the conservative side . . . lies in reducing every question of law, constitution, culture and society to a question of economics."[9]

Over the past decade this neoliberal ideology has led to economic contradictions and crises—a reducing growth rate, a significant increase in both national and personal debt—and a distinct rise in inequality. Although

---

7. Tooze, *Crashed.*
8. Brown, *Beyond the Crash; My Life, Our Times.*
9. Scruton, "Tories will Stay Lost," 20.

the wealthy have been able to take advantage of the circumstances of the twenty-first century to increase their wealth and bonuses, the less fortunate have seen little wage or income increase, and have faced the brunt of the stringent austerity measures, and restrained public service investment. So our present western political/economic approach is being seriously questioned with growth stagnating; public service investment constrained, and innovation/productivity struggling to replace reducing natural resources.

Market econocracy, therefore, following the present economic model, has enabled the wealthy to increase their wealth and, at the same time, has reduced the ability of the voting public to influence the democratic debate on economic policy. Mouffe's populism of the left challenges that oligarchical trend on the basis of social justice, by addressing exploitation, domination, and discrimination. Failure to address such present capitalist tendencies leads to an increased inequality and a reduction of democratic debate, highlighting in the process the weaknesses of the present manifestation of capitalism.

With academic, business, and political leaders failing to articulate an effective critique and alternative policies, the church—as in Margaret Thatcher's time—has taken on the role of prophetic challenge to government policy. Archbishop Justin Welby has criticized this present form of capitalism, calling alternatively for a more inclusive capitalism "offering the opportunity for people's potential to be realised . . . for responsibility from the rich and powerful, not merely through redistribution, and certainly not only through philanthropy and charity, but through openness that overcomes barriers human beings so easily set up."[10] He also suggests that capitalism needs to have a deep sense of gratuity and a "generosity of spirit that doesn't always seek the greatest return; and above all being alongside those who are suffering."[11]

Over the same decade and developing out of this neoliberal approach to the market economy, Western society has become increasingly transformed by growing monopoly control by five or six giant global conglomerates. These Silicon Valley companies have so disrupted both the culture and the economy that they are in the process of changing how we communicate, shop, and watch and search for information. They include the "Fangs" group of Facebook, Amazon, Netflix, and Google, together with Microsoft and Apple. Between them they have created what is coming to be seen as unacceptable monopoly power. Some of these companies, such as Apple and Microsoft, make goods. Others dominate the internet through advertising

10. Welby, "Inclusive Capitalism," para 6.
11. Welby, "Capitalism Must 'Draw Alongside Suffering,'" para 4.

and distribution, such as Google, Amazon, Alibaba and Instagram. Still others, such as Facebook and Netflix, dominate the social media and our social lives.

This increasing domination of the Western economy by giant conglomerates has been highlighted particularly by Mouffe, Tooze, Zuboff, and Streeck. Running alongside Wolfgang Streeck's book *How Will Capitalism End?* has come Shoshana Zuboff's book suggesting that we are fast entering into a period of "surveillance capitalism." Referring to Hal Varian, Google's Chief Strategist, she suggests that key global players such as Google and Facebook—who make profit solely on information gathering, which is later sold on to advertisers—and to a lesser degree Apple, Microsoft and Amazon—who have other substantial sources of profit—are using their vast powers of digital surveillance to turn themselves into what has been termed as The Big Other, "a distributed and largely uncontested new expression of power which constitutes hidden mechanisms of extraction, commodification, and control that threatens core values such as freedom, democracy and privacy."[12] Put in plain language, they are researching us digitally, through our own computer usage, and then analyzing this data, termed "rendering data exhaust". It involves researching the whole background of the internet surfer, the who, the what, and the why, the past and the future, the likes and dislikes, tastes and preferences of each person. This information habituation is then rendered and sold to advertisers, who can then use it to target their advertising directly and appropriately. In other words, as we use our computers, phones, credit cards—all GPS tracked—and participate in social media, we are giving away information about ourselves which the mega-corporations extract and use for their own benefit, making us, in effect, part of their digital colonies.

This development of data extraction /analysis, together with the potential, exponential benefits arising from quantum computing power, gives a huge advantage to large organizations such as the big six—together with China's Baidu, WeChat, Tencent, and Alibaba. As we shall see, they are acquiring an elite status by using automated algorithms in their digital platforms to discern our needs and then provide what we want—in very large quantities. In using their surveillance mechanisms in this way, they are, in effect, removing humanity from the marketplace. Our needs, feelings, consumption, impulses, and dreams are all harvested by algorithms, taking the human choice and judgment out of the exchange. In the process our future is being hijacked. Silicon Valley giants, and their Chinese equivalents, now own and shape the future without society yet fully realizing what is actually

---

12. Zuboff, "'Big Other': Surveillance Capitalism," 75.

happening. Venture capitalists and investors in turn, realizing that substantial profits lie in these fields, are attracted to these Silicon Valley conglomerates, and are making capital available to develop further technological research and innovation, and increasing further that controlling position.

Such research and innovation often lead to increased profits on a winner-takes-all basis. The first company that develops a new product is most likely to monopolize the production and marketing of that product in the future. Instead of governments being feared for holding information about us—Big Brother is watching you—the twenty-first century has discovered that it is the Data Barons, who have become the Big Other, which, Zuboff warns "is a form of tyranny that feeds on people but is not of the people."[13] Those who master information, stocks, and flows, are fast developing a form of gilded age capitalism, giving them a huge advantage in the marketplace, and making them resistant to government legislation or control. Data protection is now being upgraded by legislation, but many would say that it is too little, too late.

Not only is there disquiet about the present state of capitalism on the left, but dissenting voices are also to be heard from ardent capitalists themselves. On receiving an award from *First Magazine* in May 2019 for Responsible Capitalism, Guy Singh-Watson declared contemporary capitalism to be "an imminent threat to our planet and civilization . . . my understanding of the words 'responsible' and 'capitalism' would seem to suggest that they are incompatible."[14] He illustrated his disquiet by selling his company to his employees—an Employee Ownership Trust—at 25 percent of its value. Similarly, Julian Richer sold 60 percent of Richer Sounds to his employees in the same way.

But perhaps the most critical voice comes from Ray Dalio, founder and co-Chief Investment Officer of one of Wall Street's largest hedge funds, who, in a Linkedin essay, concluded that capitalism was not working. He noted the lack of real income growth for years, that both the income and wealth gap between rich and poor was increasing, that lack of investment into health and education for the poorest in society led to a deterioration of benevolent stability and considerable ongoing societal costs, that the income, education, and wealth gap had a built in self-reinforcing feedback link, and that one of the key factors in the overall productivity of society can be directly correlated to the quality of personal development made available to every sector of that society.[15]

13. Appleyard, Review of The Age of Surveillance Capitalism, 31.

14. Wheatcroft, "Capitalism that Makes Everyone Richer," 9.

15. Dalio, "Why and How Capitalism Needs to Be Reformed," 7.

His overall analysis of Western society was that "most capitalists don't know how to divide the pie well, and most socialists don't know how to grow it well,"[16] that we have to work together or we will face conflict and some form of revolution,[17] that there needs to be a bi-partisan approach to "re-engineer the system to simultaneously divide and increase the economic pie better,"[18] and that there should be a "redistribution of resources that will improve both the well-beings and the productivities of the vast majority of the peoples."[19]

So, with similar analyses of Western economic strategy from both left and right, Dalio's call for a bi-partisan response to the ever-increasing wealth/poverty gap is surely one that needs to be heard, not just in one country or another, but globally. With so much of the developing world mimicking or chasing after a western model, there is a considerable danger of collapse or disintegration.

Monopolies of wealth, power, and control are not just limited to global technological conglomerates; they can also be identified in the financial and accountancy sector. This is dominated by four huge conglomerates (KPMG, Deloitte & Touche, Ernst & Young, and PricewaterhouseCoopers). Between them they audit all of Britain's top public companies, 90 percent of top American companies, and 80 percent of top Japanese public companies.[20] These four have developed an effective "cartel status," but at the same time have attracted public criticism for being complicit in a number of high-profile financial crashes, such as Carillion, Lehman Brothers, and HBOS.[21] Because they are dependent on holding onto huge consultancy contracts, they have been somewhat lenient in their criticisms within their audit brief, for fear of losing the lucrative fees or consultancy contracts, which they also have with the firm in question. So far this incongruence remains largely unaddressed by government regulators.

The changing varieties of capitalism, from Keynesianism through to monetarism, from neoliberalism towards new forms of elitist dominance, are now being turbo-charged by the new digital revolution which is allowing the automation of mental processes as well as manual labor; the services sector as well as manufacturing; white-collar as well as blue-collar work. The speed and scale with which business can now be done has greatly expanded

16. Dalio, "Why and How Capitalism Needs to Be Reformed," 1, 14.

17. Dalio, "Why and How Capitalism Needs to Be Reformed."

18. Dalio, "Why and How Capitalism Needs to Be Reformed," 12.

19. Dalio, "Why and How Capitalism Needs to Be Reformed," 13.

20. Arlidge, "Held to Account," 34.

21. Arlidge, "Held to Account," 34

and intensified the opportunities for global trade, and for the displacement of human intellect by digital systems. Indeed it could be argued that such digital technology and artificial intelligence is now driving our whole economy, and hence society itself. As has been said by many, society is its economy."

## 2.2 PROSPERITY AND GROWTH

Martin Ford[22] makes a classic case for technological/digital development molding our twenty-first-century society and economy. He suggests that, at the heart of our system is the desire for prosperity and progress, empowered by economic growth. Yuval Harari similarly states that contemporary society "is based on the firm belief that economic growth is not only possible, but absolutely essential . . . if you have a problem, you probably need more stuff, and in order to have more stuff, you must produce more of it."[23] He goes on to quote Deng Xiaoping as endorsing his view, "development is the only hard truth . . . it doesn't matter if a cat is black or white, so long as it catches mice."[24]

However, growth in an economy isn't as simple as it used to be. Increasingly a number of factors are constraining and reducing the speed of growth; and by implication the nature of the whole capitalist storyline. The primary constraint is being recognized as the curtailment of a "virtuous loop," or positive feedback, in self-regulating markets.

---

**VIRTUOUS LOOP**

The loop starts with a car being made. An assembly line workforce makes the car and is paid for it. They have money to spend and can do that by buying a new car, and in doing so create a demand for more cars to be made. This keeps them in work and provides them with more wages with which to keep up demand for more products, and so on, *ad infinitum*.

---

This loop will gradually be eroded and undermined by technology replacing the workforce: first through CNC machines, then through robots, then algorithms, then into the future through 3D printers, sentient computers, and even possibly through molecular manufacturing. In the long term, reduction in employment and productivity is threatening growth, because it leads

---

22. Ford, *Rise of the Robots*.
23. Harari, *Homo Deus*, 240.
24. Xiaoping, quoted in Harari, *Homo Deus*, 242.

to unemployed people having no spending power/demand to stimulate that growth. So humans will become less involved in the production of cars, while simultaneously being less essential when it comes to driving them.

Over the past fifty years there has been a fundamental shift in the balance between the workforce of a company, and the machines the company uses to produce its product. In more and more cases the machines are actually the workers, rather than being aids to production, not only on the shop floor, but at every level of an organization—even to the point of having a computer algorithm with a seat on the company board! Although, at present, innovation is creating new jobs that, in effect, fill the gaps, that scenario will not be easy to sustain across the whole spectrum.

Governmental influence and societal prosperity are also affected by reductions in capitalism's positive feedback in the shape of tax revenue; with fewer people employed, less tax revenue is collected, leading to less investment in essential services such as health and education. As well as that, large global conglomerates go to extraordinary lengths to avoid paying national governments their tax, again circumscribing what that government can provide in the way of essential public services.

## 2.3 DISRUPTION

One other significant area in the field of growth concerns the role of innovation and disruption, when existing provision is challenged by future possibilities. These occur in all areas of organizational life, be it in the public and voluntary sector, as well as the more obvious economic and commercial worlds. Most organizations from government, finance, health, police, social and voluntary services, together with the church, all work towards an equilibrium between innovation and stability in order to establish and then maintain a sustainable model. Technological innovation has not sat easily with equilibrium because, in essence, it is primarily disruptive. Silicon Valley particularly prides itself in its disruptive skills. This can be illustrated by the designing of driverless cars, by the way Uber and automated taxis will revolutionize the whole world of taxis, by driverless lorries and drones delivering goods, by software that can actually manage traffic flow in cities and in smart motorways. Now these conglomerates not only think in terms of innovating products, but also see themselves at the cutting edge of sociological policy development. They are happy to stand alongside governments and offer alternative concepts of transport for example, that would reduce traffic congestion. As disruption becomes a major instrument of change in its own right, it could severely threaten the structure of society as a whole.

If innovative disruption led to unemployment, combined with growing inequality, and climate change ecological meltdown, then combinations of these disruptions could have a very serious effect.

Before looking at the connection between the breakdown of the virtuous loop, and the emerging concept of the universal basic wage, we need to make brief reference to three other significant disruptions in the production cycle—algorithms, data flows, and 3D printing. Mention has already been made of algorithms, but the speed, complexity, and accumulating effect of these together, with the amount of data they can access, compute, and analyze, has the potential to disrupt the workplace and production dramatically. With such algorithms creating their own software and being capable of digesting huge amounts of unstructured data, the thinking and analyzing role of the human is—more and more—going to be overtaken by the machine, which will in the end be able to overshadow human capability. Similarly, the concept of 3D printing can be expected to grow and expand in capability, significance, and size: taking over more and more areas of production. And were the potential of molecular construction and manufacture to be realized, then the place of humans within production would be unimaginable.

## 2.4 UNIVERSAL BASIC INCOME/WAGE

It is for all these reasons and many more that serious discussion has taken place concerning the concept of a universal basic income/wage (UBI/UBW), Basic Income Guarantee (BIG), or Citizen's Dividend (CD)—the concept of every individual having the right to a basic income whether they work or not. This debate crystallizes the position in which humanity might find itself. Surprisingly it attracts both the left and right of the political spectrum, but for different reasons. On the right, Friedrich Hayek, Milton Friedman, and Charles Murray saw it as an insurance against adversity, a kind of basic safety net: a way to rekindle growth in the market economy: the providing of an alternative income available to increase consumer demand; a reasonable redistribution of purchasing power, to energize growth and expansion. On the left, it would be welcomed as a basic safety net to alleviate poverty, and a fresh constructive approach to wealth redistribution within society.

A wider critique of this whole situation is now surfacing. The present capitalist approach has seen a growth in inequality—highlighted by Thomas Piketty on the left[25] in his earlier book, and Ray Dalio on the right[26] in his challenging essay published in Linkedin—as technology produces a smaller

25. Piketty, *Capital in the Twenty-First Century*.
26. Dalio, "Why and How Capitalism Needs to Be Reformed."

and an ever-reducing elite who dominate and control innovation, investment, disruption, and production dividends. Increasingly the Silicon Valley giants, together with their accountancy counterparts, and others such as Uber, Airbnb, and some supermarket chains, are mutating into new forms of monopoly. As has been said, whoever innovates and enters the market first tends to dominate and monopolize it.

With smaller numbers of people involved in innovation and production through algorithmic computer centrality, and with investment for this expensive research provided by a small group of wealthy venture capitalists, this central group of wealthy owners are increasingly threatening democracy and government legislation. At the other end of the scale there is a growing underclass of modern-day serfs who are in danger of being marginalized by society. Technological innovation has birthed a technofeudalist society which, in its present development, risks becoming dystopic.

Steve Hilton, adviser to David Cameron when Prime Minister, is intensely critical of this societal trend. He advocates that technology should foster a "world where people, not Silicon Valley, come first."[27] Arguing against UBW, he stresses that work is a primary element in the nature of humanity. "Doing meaningful work and being rewarded for it is a basic human need. Depriving people of that is morally evil."[28] He goes on to state, "It's revoltingly patronizing for the great geniuses of Silicon Valley to say 'we can continue our fascinating work and earn vast incomes, so we can live in our gated communities, guarded by robots and drones. But sadly you won't. Don't worry though, we will pay you not to work.'"[29] Hilton has put his finger on a deep-seated dissonance. Technological innovation may well increase prosperity in material ways, but at the same time it appears to encourage an inequality that threatens our understanding of human meaning, purpose, and achievement. At present there appears no way out—except a dystopic future. Surely this needs to be addressed. Otherwise technofeudalism, by seeking to alleviate poverty through an UBW algorithm, will at the same time reduce the fullness of humanity for the majority: denying them opportunities to create, work, and find fulfillment, not only for their own satisfaction, but also for the benefit of wider society.

Yet another serious critique of elite dominance over technological innovation and profit margins comes from Martin Ford. He points out that, "today's enormous technological account balance results from the efforts of

---

27. Hilton, in Arlidge, "Humans Aren't Working," 17.

28. Hilton, in Arlidge, "Humans Aren't Working," 17.

29. Hilton, in Arlidge, "Humans Aren't Working," 17

countless individuals and organizations over the course of decades."[30] This stretches back to the nineteenth century with Charles Babbage's mechanical difference engine, and to the seminal work of Alan Turing and John von Neumann. Today's entrepreneurs are now leveraging their own efforts on the back of this historical accumulation of knowledge and expertise. Ford questions the right, therefore, of this present-day elite to use these historical benefits for their own personal estate. He notes also that much of this earlier research and development was done at the taxpayers' expense. So, should not a levy or tax be imposed on entrepreneurs benefiting from this historic accumulation of technological innovation and expertise? Surely "the population at large have some sort of claim on that accumulated technological account balance,"[31] an idea similar to the concept of a citizen's dividend. Others, such as Thomas Picketty,[32] have suggested a global wealth tax; Martin Ford writes about sovereign wealth funds[33]; Dalio calls for a redistribution of resources, and a coordination of monetary and fiscal policies,[34] all of which could tie into raising levels of basic income.

## 2.5 TECH AND DEMOCRACY

Reflecting on the way contemporary capitalism is adapting to technological/digital advance, there is a growing concern over the balance between the tech giants/data barons who have established market domination, the national governments whose powers are gradually being eroded, with the Silicon Valley giants, with their significant grasp of data, innovation, and investment funds, often being well ahead of government legislation, societal norms, democratic processes, and national/global taxation systems.

The issue is seen most clearly in two particular areas: monopoly/competition and platforming/publishing. On the first area, government regulators have been faced with the dilemma of how much to legislate to restrict monopolies developing, whilst at the same time avoid policies that would stifle incentives to innovate. It comes down to the point of not throwing out the baby with the bathwater. Already it has been noted that the lighter regulatory touch of the US has allowed these tech giants to develop, whereas tighter controls in Europe have constrained their development. It is the more liberal approach of the US that has allowed/encouraged Google to

---

30. Ford, *Rise of the Robots*, 82.

31. Ford, *Rise of the Robots*, 82.

32. Picketty, *Capital in the Twenty-First Century*.

33. Ford, *Rise of the Robots*, 274.

34. Dalio, "Why and How Capitalism Needs to Be Reformed," 13.

become one of the largest monopolies of the world, and Amazon to overwhelm twenty-first-century commerce.

In the US, there are now political calls for these giants to be broken up. In the EU (following US regulators' case against Microsoft) regulators are handing out increasing fines for breaches of anti-trust rules—fair competition—particularly to Google. Both sides of the Atlantic are struggling to drain the bathwater whilst not losing the benefits of the baby. An illustration of the way innovation can so easily keep ahead of regulation is highlighted in the field of automated transport. Technology development companies have for some time been working on new theories on methods of transport and traffic-control approaches, long before national governments have planned or developed policy documents. As we have already noted, this is seen in the whole area of Uber taxis, car sharing, automated driverless vehicles, flying cars, automated transport systems, city traffic-flow systems, and including the use of drones for delivery services. Such innovative, disruptive research and development can so easily outstrip the time it takes for government to research the issues and develop policy/action.

Over the matter of tax, giant corporations have developed effective global tax avoidance strategies, outsmarting many national governments, with investors benefiting hugely from low taxes on their profits. For example, Apple valued the development at Apple Park at about $50 million, whereas US tax authorities valued it at $7 billion; Apple thought tax due might be in the region of $5 million, whereas the US tax department thought it would be closer to $50 million.[35]

On the second area, of platforming/publishing, widespread publicity highlights the difficulties faced in policing the internet, particularly with regard to subjects such as terrorism, pedophilia, and self-abuse. The issue centers around whether social media sites such as Facebook are acting as a platform or as a publisher. Early legislation by President Clinton allowed platform sites such as Facebook to avoid publishing regulations. In light of the myriad anti-social posts, self-regulation by the social media conglomerates is seen to be totally inadequate. Policing these social media posts effectively appears to be unachievable and extremely oppressive to those having to do it. Calls are being made to bring such sites under new government regulations. Anxiety has also been expressed concerning the market power of a totally integrated Facebook/Instagram/WhatsApp world-dominating SuperApp—in global competition with China's WeChat. For government to meekly allow such a monopoly to develop will surely severely limit consumer choice.

35. Bartlett, "Secrets of Silicon Valley."

With such anti-competitive, monopolistic, and lightly regulated practices, exerted through these giant tech conglomerates—together with advertising revenues—societal, democratic, and governmental rights are surely being seriously undermined. This is further compounded by the turbo-charging effect of gathering, collating, and cross-checking data surveillance on a global scale—again bypassing democratic national governments. Having harvested such mega-data, they are in a position to influence both production/consumption and the needs of society on a global scale. They then consolidate their elite positions by selling that data to advertisers. Being the masters of the code enables them to secretly manipulate the algorithms that shape and reshape every aspect of society to their own advantage. Jamie Bartlett sums up this domination by these giant corporations as, "in exchange for the undeniable benefit of technology . . . we have . . . allowed other components of a functioning political system to be undermined: control, parliamentary sovereignty, economic equality, civil society, and an informed citizenry."[36]

All in all, the concept of a comparatively stable market equilibrium, established for the benefit of all and ordered by democratic processes, is more threatened than we realized: changes in contemporary capitalism appear to be undermining established norms by creeping in under the radar. This, kind of surveillance capitalism, dominated by elite, data-manipulating, innovative mega-organizations, and backed by extremely wealthy investors, is coming to dominate and change national/global economics and democratic societies. This leads us neatly on to the whole area of globalization and nationalism.

## 2.6 GLOBALIZATION, NATIONALISM, AND GLOBALISM

Donald Trump's campaign to "Make America First" and Britain's choice of Brexit are classic illustrations of a resurgence of nationalism, the rising tide of identity politics, and the divisive effects of globalization.

Initially, "globalization" was a term associated with the rise of multinational companies—mergers that turned national companies into world players without one central base or national identity. Such globalization, combining technological innovation with investment, is illustrated in the emergence of the Silicon Valley conglomerates. These organizations develop a monopoly of control over competitors, and advance a step ahead of national legislation/taxation. The investment in and use of technological advance is now appearing to overtake the traditional global divisions between the West, the far East, India, and South America. Instead of cheap labor

36. Cavendish, Review of *People vs. Tech*, 36.

influencing manufacturing and import/export flow, global technological advance is becoming more significant.

However, today the term has taken on an additional meaning, which raises more contemporary issues for debate. Globalization also includes global issues, as well as multinational conglomerates. These include the threat of weapons of mass destruction, both nuclear and chemical, as well as autonomous AI-controlled weapons, as highlighted by Stuart Russell in his recent book, *Human Condition*, together with the effects of climate change, global pandemics such as Covid 19, African migration into Europe, Central American migration into the USA, disruption caused by technological innovation, and the taxation of global brands. Each are global issues which have an impact on many national states and which would benefit from a global response.

The challenge facing nations today is how to address these global issues. The attempts of the last century have had some success, but these are inadequate for tomorrow. Many contemporary issues are not amenable for single nations to address, they need a global approach. But the means and mechanisms required are not present. Other than the United Nations and the World Health Organization there are few effective forums for debate and decision. National interests and identities continually thwart global resolution. Donald Trump's withdrawal from the Iran deal over nuclear development is an obvious example. At present there is little sign of global policy or decision-making.

However, as well as the rise of this global consciousness, there has been a corresponding rise in the articulation of local and community issues: identity politics, authentic tribal language, trading, religious, and racial issues have all given rise to demands for individual and political recognition. Movement identities, such as those seen in ISIS, al-Qaeda, the Basque country, America First, Brexit, Scotland, South Sudan, give preference to special interests over national ones. At a community level, people are coming together over particular issues—Black Lives Matter/#MeToo. There are those, therefore, who argue that local and ethnic special interest groups are rising whilst the national level is beginning to fade. Others such as Francis Fukuyama suggest that the rise in these special identities and movements is breaking down the position of traditional left/right politics, hence the instability of traditional party politics.[37]

An illustration of the difference between the local—part national—and global approaches to life has been described by David Goodhart as Somewheres and Anywheres.[38] He offers fresh analysis of British attitudes that move on from class, race, and politics.

37. Fukuyama, *Contemporary Identity Politics*.
38. Goodhart, *Road to Somewhere*.

## SOMEWHERES/ANYWHERES

Goodhart breaks down British society into two general attitudes/tribes, Anywheres and Somewheres—with an in-between position between the two—an overlay to our already-existing class, political, and economic divisions. Before the seventies, the Somewheres held sway, with their commitment to community of place, class, and solidarity based on collective institutions like trades unions, working men's clubs, local authorities, and parish churches.

Somewheres have more of an ascribed identity—Welsh farmer, Yorkshire housewife, working-class Geordie. They are often older, less educated, less affluent, less comfortable with cultural, economic, and technological aspects of change, more deeply socially conservative, reasonably nationalistic, journey less than others, center themselves around local communities, are less at home with traveling abroad/engagement with globalization, have not made the most of educational developments, the internet, the achievement society, and struggle with graduate employment and the move towards a postindustrial agenda.

From the seventies onward the Anywheres gained increasing influence, power, and control. The Anywheres are described as having an achievement identity and being committed to life and individual self-realization. They are part of a meritocracy that have made the most of educational opportunities, and have taken advantage of technological/digital innovation. They engage with European and global horizons, handling change, new issues—such as immigration and human sexuality—with ease. They exude openness, confidence, and excitement towards the future.

The third group, in-betweeners, identify with both sides, and change sides on different issues. They engage to some degree with the digital/international horizons, and yet at the same time value the strengths and traditions of the local community.

The three groups are not completely separate: most people have an affinity to what is expressed in each view, but at the same time, rest in one camp more firmly than the other. Goodhart considers that roughly 50 percent of our population are "Somewheres," 20–25 percent are "Anywheres," with the rest being inbetweeners.[39]

Around the populous uprising of Brexit, the Somewheres democratically renewed their feelings with considerable force.

Roger Scruton offers another illustration of divided sociological attitudes. Using the Greek word for house, he divides society between those who are

---

39. Goodheart, *Road to Somewhere*, 4.

rooted to a physical place—*oikophiles*—and those for whom place or nationhood means very little—*oikophobes*.[40] These ingrained approaches to life suggest that many global issues will never be easily resolved.

Yet another illustration of this divide will be given later through the research of James Fowler. Looking primarily into American society, Fowler detects two groupings that transcend both political and religious divisions. He calls them "orthodox" and "progressive."[41] These two groups have strong similarities with Goodhart's and Scruton's analyses, and interestingly can be clearly seen today in the opposing pro-/anti-Trump camps.

## 2.7 DEMOGRAPHY

Global issues already mentioned include demography in a number of guises. Population growth in the Far East is well known, and African countries, such as Nigeria, are following a similar path. Feeding populations, maintaining peaceful boundaries, sharing scarce resources, particularly water, will fully occupy the minds of governments/legislators.

One of the side effects of increased populations, scarce resources, and changing climates has been the manifestation of growing migration, from areas of poverty to pockets of wealth. Not only has this been identified between Western and Eastern Europe, between America, Central America, and Mexico, but now the African/Europe axis of movement is here to stay. These wealth migrations will never be easy to address. These frictions also have a past; with many old colonial regimes having built their success on the backs of immigrants and cheap imports from underdeveloped countries. As one character in the film *Blade Runner 2049* put it, "Every great civilization is built on the back of a disposable workforce."

## 2.8 CLIMATE CHANGE

As has already been mentioned many times, climate change is undoubtedly one of the most crucial issues facing global society today. This has been well documented elsewhere—particularly by Bringhurst and Zwicky, Berry, and the Intergovernmental Panel on Climate Change, who "provide policy-makers with regular scientific assessments of climate change, its implications and potential future risks, as well as put forward adaption and

---

40. Scruton, *State of Britain*.

41. Fowler, *Faithful Change*, 171–72.

mitigation options."[42] Recognizing the significance of these findings leads many to the conclusion that delaying tactics for reducing $CO_2$ gases is taking us closer and closer to tipping our fragile ecological equilibrium toward ecological meltdown. The Paris Accord—despite US withdrawal—was a step in the right direction, but many would still argue that it was shutting the stable door after the horse has bolted.

---

### DESERTIFICATION

The desertification of the Sahel—that border between the desert of the Sahara and the rich fertile soil of equatorial Africa in the south and the highly populated coastal regions of North Africa—is a trend that creeps inexorably year upon year. The flooding of low-lying islands, and the overpopulated delta region of Bangladesh, continually flash up red alert signs of uncontrollable suffering. Both of these illustrate the way that, so often in cases like global warming, disenfranchised societies suffer the most despite the fact that developed countries predominantly cause the problem.

---

Once again, the inadequacies of global mechanisms to grasp and contain this threat means that the problem is just passed on to future generations. At that point it will be far more difficult for them then to resolve than it is for us now.

## 2.9 ENDNOTE

All in all, the factors raised in chapters 1 and 2 are the significant issues with which the third decade is faced. They form the context within which the faith/church needs to survive, operate, and indeed contribute. Historically there is reason to believe that the faith can, once again, transpose itself into a new era. But these contemporary issues will need to be recognized and grasped. Chapter 3 will seek to identify the salient issues rising out of this paradigm shift in culture. As the critical issues become clear, questions as to how the faith/church should express itself counterculturally, as well as contextually, will emerge. So, let us now identify in chapter 3 some of the issues arising from this technologically driven paradigm shift described in the first two chapters.

---

42. Intergovernmental Panel on Climate Change, para. 1.

# Chapter 3

## Matters Arising from the Melting Pot

### INTRODUCTION

Over the last three decades we have journeyed from the Industrial Age to the Information/Digital Age. Scientists seek to discern a grand unified theory of everything. A new common story is emerging from the Big Bang onwards, where simple organisms emerge, evolve, and lead on to incredible complexity. We now engage with a world of algorithms and data flows. In front of us lies the possibility of a singularity—where machines could surpass humans in every way—where molecular manufacturing could enable something to be created out of something else, where genetic engineering could enhance human life, and where haptic connectivity could enable us to physically participate as we watch 3D programs. Yet all around lies the perversity of human nature, that can react negatively as equally as positively; where the capability to innovate often overwhelms consideration of the appropriateness of any given innovation; where utopia is a dream and dystopia the recurring nightmare; where achievement highlights the pinnacle of humanity, with underachievers taking the position of also-rans.

Along this journey a multitude of fresh questions arise: What is real? What is human? Does inequality have to increase? Are humans simply biological algorithms or do they have a soul? Will computers program our future, or are truth, beauty, and peace beyond their perception? What is the ultimate purpose, meaning, or value of everything? What happened before the Big Bang?

Up until now Western thought has been dominated by two contrasting approaches: the Christian tradition and rational humanism. After the development of Greek philosophical thinking, the advent of Christ brought about the dominance of Christian thinking. This remained until the Renaissance/Enlightenment when rational humanism took center stage. As we face the questions above, the tension between the two is palpable. One has only to look at a humanist historian, such as Yuval Harari, who on the one hand is happy to deride the Bible as fake news on YouTube, yet at the same time he admits in his book, *Homo Deus*, that the humanist, anthropocentric world view is being superceded by the rise of a technocentric and datacentric environment—surely making humanism itself fake news.[43]

So the third decade of this century will become an exciting forum where these complex issues will be addressed, where the Christian faith has an opportunity to contribute and reposition itself within society. This chapter will explore two different approaches to the variety of issues raised, before we move on to part 2, where we look in greater depth at the Christian faith/church, and its previous responses to the challenges of change and development in the Western world. But before that, we need to acknowledge the issues and questions that technological development has raised or highlighted, and the contrasting approaches which seek to make sense of this brave but complex new world.

## 3.1 CONTRASTING WORLDVIEWS

It all goes back to the way people have experienced and interpreted human history from the beginning. Lesslie Newbigin[44] quotes Dr. Harold Turner as suggesting three views as to how to understand human existence: atomic—a billiard ball; oceanic—an ocean; and relational—a net. The atomic, influencing Western thought and derived from Greek philosophy, sees reality in terms of individual units, such as the atom, with the human being seen as the autonomous center of knowledge and the ultimate constituent of society. The oceanic sees all things merged into one identity, both soul and material existence, typified in eastern religions such as Hinduism and Buddhism. The relational draws existence from relationships in both material society and human encounter, within which the biblical triune God engages with created order.

Without difficulty, one can begin to discern the arteries that bring blood to our contemporary debate. The roots of humanism are found in

43. Harari, *Homo Deus*, 232.
44. Newbigin, *Gospel in a Pluralist Society*, 171.

classical Greek, Stoic, Roman, and even Western Christian thought, where human reason is seen as the organ for discovering truth and discerning substance. On the other hand, an alternative, holistic, relational approach considers that the human spirit, through mystical experience, is able to discern the ultimate source of being and truth,[45] typified in a biblical approach. In Eastern thought, the oceanic approach was owned, but sadly this didn't have serious impact on Western thought until the last century.

Throughout the centuries these two main arteries, and the presuppositions of their bloodlines, contended with each other continuously. And although the Christian faith dominated from the time of the Roman Emperor Constantine, that changed decisively with the Renaissance/Enlightenment and the advent of modern science. On the one hand, Enlightenment humanism offered the self-sufficiency and moral autonomy of the individual to *reason* and evaluate experience as the instrument of knowledge and emancipation. It turned to *nature* and the discoveries of modern science as a source of true insight. It had confidence in *progress*, illustrated through invention and materialism, on through the development of civilized society and through the containment of disease by way of understanding and remedies. On the other hand, the Christian faith contended that truth emerged from a more subjective, mystical-natured and value-oriented belief arising out of the given nature of a personal and loving Creator, enshrined in history. This debate between the two approaches could be epitomized by the famous claim made by the humanist Lessing—"accidental truths of history can never become the proof of necessary truths of reason."[46]

As the Enlightenment spread into every public sphere of Western culture, fed by the growing discoveries and expansion of modern science, the dominant authority/tradition of the church—with the Bible as its source text—waned; it was forced to retreat into the private sphere of personal belief, that no longer held credence in the norm of the day. Locke, Hume, and Voltaire concluded that "what was reasonable" was that "God is a product of human imagination."[47]

However, as digital technological development has overwhelmed the twenty-first century—with its exponential expansion, speed of change, and computer capability—cracks have begun to emerge in the liberal humanist/capitalist position. Whilst on the other side the Christian faith—playing off the bench as a substitute—is beginning to realize that it can play the

---

45. Newbigin, *Gospel in a Pluralist Society*, 2.

46. Lessing, *On the Proof of the Spirit*, 53.

47. Voltaire, quoted in Harari, *Homo Deus*, 454.

super-sub role, which could make a significant contribution to the crucible of societal debate and development in this oncoming decade.

This view is vividly endorsed by Tom Holland in "Dominion: The Making of the Western Mind." He stresses the revolutionary and transformative nature of the faith, arising from two deeply subversive views at heart: that all people are equal and that the weak are heroic, that there is an inherent dignity to every human, with a premium to be placed on the weakest of the weak. Far from being overwhelmed by humanism, secularism, and atheism, it can be argued that the Christian faith has not only contributed to the emergence of these philosophies, but is now looking to offer more pertinent and engaged contributions at this critical time.

The cracks in the humanist position are made clear by the inability of capitalism to address inequality, by optimistic liberal humanism—humanity can resolve every eventuality—succumbing to a pessimistic dystopic viewpoint where communal conflict and social inadequacy is passed down from generation to generation, by anthropocentricity being overtaken by technocentricity and—as is becoming increasingly clear—by datacentricity. Much of this is articulately acknowledged by the reasonable logic of one of humanism's recent historians—Yuval Harari. Following *Sapiens*, his volume on human history, his next book, *Homo Deus*, sees humans as gods who can rule the world. However, he concludes that the centrality of the human person will become irrelevant as it is superseded by the centrality of the machine and data flows. Harari lists the varieties of humanism, such as liberal, socialist, and evolutionary, all of which are struggling to accommodate the fact that machines are becoming more intelligent than humans, and are replacing them in many areas. He sees humanism threatened as humans lose their significance and value to machines: that humanity will lose authority as the center of existence; that a small elite group of superhumans will emerge, thus creating intrinsic inequality.[48] Others have described this outcome as neofeudalism, made up of data barons and subservient serfs. Harari goes on to describe a technohumanism, where certain humans can manipulate algorithmic capability and harness the growing resource of data flow, which in turn would lead to dataism, worship of the decision-making prowess of data flow as the ultimate supreme source of intelligence.

A further chink in the armor becomes evident when Harari asks "Is there something in the universe that can't be reduced to data?"[49] Underlying that question is the whole matter of presuppositions. Following somewhat narrow basic humanist principles, it seems that everything can be reduced

---

48. Harari, *Homo Deus*, 403–4.

49. Harari, *Homo Deus*, 459.

down to mathematical, problem-solving, atomic, reasonable logic. Starting from that point one can easily see the data flow threat to individuality and human authority. However, if one is to consider wider presuppositions: that humanity is much more than intelligent, problem-solving, materialist human progress and prosperity, that humanity consists of body, mind, spirit, personality, and emotion in all their networked complexities, then the answer might be that human life consists of far more than data flows and profit margins. Harari hints at this in his decoupling of knowledge from consciousness, but doesn't pursue it into the internal world of feelings, emotions, and dreams.

When these wider presuppositions concerning where truth lies are considered, the answer could be very different. Instead of insisting on an analytical world centered around the rights, expectations, and abilities of individual humans, one could alternatively consider the world in terms of relationships: between peoples, between people and their environment, between substance and emotions, between what is known and what is inexplicable, between body and soul, between constructiveness and destructiveness, between a bootstrapping evolution of chance/power, and the possibility of a given "Other" as the source of all purpose and meaning. Such a worldview—taken by the Christian faith, but also by Sun Tzu, the Chinese writer of *The Art of War*—takes greater account of the fullness, width, and potential of the whole human person within the context of a beautiful world and an ever-expanding, unexplained universe. If that background is taken into account, then contemporary issues as they arise will be so much more interesting to grapple with, and far beyond the limits of data flows. So, let us now turn to some of these issues thrown up by the speed and complexity of technological development, as it impacts, challenges, and transforms Western and indeed global society.

## 3.2 POWER AND MEANING

Facing issues that have popped up over the last thirty years, it is clear that technological development has both accelerated and amplified change, giving added intensity to each issue. Many of these questions have been around for some time, but have come into sharper focus since the millennium. The interaction between power and meaning, between the how and why of humanity, is reflected in the Enlightenment alliance between scientific progress and economic growth. For a thousand years or more before the Enlightenment, both power and meaning were orchestrated by a coalition of church and state. The rule of kings/statesmen provided the power which was legitimized and authenticated by the Christian church—the divine right of kings. At the same time, the church offered value-added meaning to civilization and to all existing social structures. However, that alliance was shattered, particularly by the advent of Renaissance culture and modern science. So began the process of secularization within which we debate today. Modern science increasingly took the place of the church in upholding states and governments, particularly through its ability to instigate economic growth. So, whereas the Christian church had provided meaning behind the development of Western society, scientific discovery/explanation brought prosperity, growth, and progress to whole populations. Popular understanding began to rely less on the meaning and purpose of life, centered around a supreme creator being, and more and more upon the human ability to discover, create, and grow its own destiny for its own enjoyment and fulfillment. Gradually the power to become took the place of the meaning behind living the life.

Now although this tension between power and meaning has been part of Western culture over the past 300 years, it has come into much sharper definition as Moore's Law of digital computer capability has accelerated technological growth. Power in the hands of computer algorithms has exploded exponentially and will continue to do so. The energy source of that power is growth through technological innovation which results in prosperity. The fuel for that growth has become innovation linked to investment within a capitalist market economy. This accentuated power, which increasingly lies in the hands of a diminishing number of people, has resurrected the deeper subject of meaning. What does a society think about this exercise of power? Where is the meaning behind it all? Continuous growth in itself has raised questions for ecology—global warming and climate change; limits to the use of nonrenewable resources, and a whole range of ethical questions. The tension is increased by growing concern that the investors, owners, and controllers of this technological innovation are making up the rules of the game as they go along, before democratic debate and legislation have been put in place at either the national or global level.[50] The purpose, place, and meaning of life are now coming back into focus, but many would say that it is already too late.

Technological development centers around the concepts of research, innovation, mechanistic and materialistic development, and prosperity. Increasingly, computer algorithms surpass human decision-making and control. Little account is taken of ethics, values, safeguards, codes of practice, or life qualities—all of which are the lifeblood of a healthy society. For

50. Baddiel, Sunday Times, 22/10/2017.

instance, it may be accepted in Enlightenment society that individuals can claim their free will and their human rights so they can develop their lives as they see fit, but the flipside of that assumption is "what happens when two people's expectations clash?" Surely societal norms, ethics, and values need to be in place from within the community to resolve differences of interest and opinion between individuals.

Take another example of power and meaning arising from narrow Artificial Intelligence—AI. We are all consciously aware of the positive effects of AI on our lives, especially in the field of health research and education. A Parliamentary Report from the House of Lords reviewed and affirmed a great deal, but raised some significant questions, particularly concerning data protection: the monopolization of control and unfettered use of large amounts of data by big tech corporations.[51] The report doubts whether AI is actually increasing productivity at the same time as reducing jobs:[52] it asks whether sufficient ethical standards are in place to evaluate possible "systems malfunctions" or the use of "malicious purposes,"[53] and raises the possibility of data manipulation.[54] It referred to the lack of any ethical criteria,[55] and the need for a right balance in the educational curriculum between computer science and the arts/humanities, which have links to "creative thinking, communication, and the understanding of context."[56] It concludes with offering a five-point proposal for a shared ethical framework.[57]

But maybe the most important point that came out of the report was AI's impact on social and political cohesion,[58] with particular reference to inequality and redistribution. The Charities Aid Foundation commented that AI "could exacerbate the situation by concentrating wealth and power in the hands of an even smaller minority of people who own and control the technology and its applications."[59] The reality of neofeudalism and surveillance capitalism is increasingly being recognized and queried.

This point was put effectively by a contribution from *Financial Times* journalist Sarah O'Connor:

51. House of Lords Report, *AI in the UK*, 5.

52. House of Lords Report, *AI in the UK*, 6.

53. House of Lords Report, *AI in the UK*, 6–7.

54. House of Lords Report, *AI in the UK*, sec. 265, Summary, and 251.

55. House of Lords Report, *AI in the UK*, sec. 247.

56. House of Lords Report. *AI in the UK*, sec. 242.

57. House of Lords Report, *AI in the UK*, 7.

58. House of Lords Report, *AI in the UK*, secs. 260–71.

59. House of Lords Report, *AI in the UK*, sec. 268.

The big question that people in the economics and labour market world are thinking about is: how will those gains be distributed? If indeed AI leads to vast increases in efficiency, using far fewer workers, does that mean that all the wealth that is created from that will go to the people who own the AI—the intellectual property—and the data that feeds into it? If so, what does that mean for the people who might be displaced out of jobs? Will there be new jobs to replace the old ones? If there are, will they be of the same quality?[60]

The report then went on to stress the government's role in retraining[61] and possible redistribution options, including the universal basic wage (UBW),[62] Bill Gates's idea of a robot tax,[63] and the recognition of regional as well as social inequality.[64] The report left no doubt that although the economic potential of AI was unlimited, the societal and regional impact of it was a matter that the government needed to address most urgently.[65]

Of course, it doesn't take a parliamentary report to highlight these issues. As far back as 2000 the tech world itself, in the form of Bill Joy, Chief Scientist at Sun Microsystems, expressed deep concern surrounding adequate ethical debate as tech development mushroomed. In an article in *Wired*, he referred to the fact that we were, "being propelled into the future with no plan, no control, no brakes"; calling for a kind of "Hippocratic oath requiring scientists and engineers [to] adopt a strong ethical conduct,"[66] and the encouragement of whistleblowing where necessary. More recently, Satya Nadella, head of Microsoft, repeated the same need in the whole area of AI: "What I think needs to be done in 2018 is more dialogue around the ethics, the principles we can use for engineers and companies that are building AI."[67] What those ethics should consist of and how they are to be agreed upon on a global scale are difficult questions that few have dared to address, leading to very little being done. That in itself should spur the government to implement its own report.

Clearly, with such unprecedented tech development and growing inequality within society, the debate is highlighted between the unfettered

---

60. House of Lords Report, *AI in the UK*, sec. 268.

61. House of Lords Report, *AI in the UK*, sec. 270.

62. House of Lords Report, *AI in the UK*, sec. 271.

63. House of Lords Report, *AI in the UK*, sec. 272.

64. House of Lords Report, *AI in the UK*, sec. 273.

65. House of Lords Report, *AI in the UK* AI, secs. 269, 273, 276.

66. Joy, "Why the Future Doesn't Need Us," 14.

67. Nadella, "I Believe Right Now," 5.

power/potential of human innovation as compared to the meaningful development of a benevolent society.

## 3.3 WHAT IS REAL? WHAT IS BEING HUMAN?

Whereas the twentieth-century, Enlightenment-influenced mindset focused on Jean Valjean's song "Who am I?" in the musical *Les Miserables*, the postmillennial period is epitomized by the questions uttered by Deckard and Officer K in the *Blade Runner* films, "What is real?" and its relative "What does it mean to be human?" These two questions arise out of a whole series of trends in our postmillennial world, that are influencing how we see reality.

The latest *Blade Runner* film and its predecessor identify the difference between replicants—robot-type people with AI—and humans. Only humans have the ability to form connections, empathize with others, love, and have values—all of which can lead to acting, resisting, and fighting for those values. As one rebel leader in the film states, "Dying for the right cause is the most human thing you can do."[68] In the latest film there is a controlling authority—Replicant Manufacturing Corporation—and then there is the last remaining small group of rebels—Replicant Freedom Movement—standing against them. These two groups see what is real in very different terms. The rebels are not taken in by the control of the predominant authority and its subservient replicants. Both groupings see what is real somewhat differently.

The film poses the question as to whether what we think we see is reality, or is simply a view of reality seen through a whole series of lenses superimposed over reality. "Now we see but a poor reflection as in a mirror.[69] It puts into our mind the following questions: What is the basis upon which we form our understanding of reality? What are the trustworthy sources upon which we can depend, and what are simply lenses, just in front of us, that complicate our understanding of reality? In the past we might have trusted some newspapers, the BBC, a University education, our Trades Union, our profession, our friends and family upbringing. Today, however, we are encompassed by fake news, filter bubbles, Wikipedia, competing views on the internet, posts and tweets and blogs on social media, and the power of advertising. More than ever we are having to question every element of the ground upon which we stand as we seek to define and understand reality.

68. *Blade Runner 2049*, a rebel leader.

69. 1 Cor 13:12.

A second illustration of this divide between what is real/human and what is virtual comes from *Snow Crash*, a crypto sci-fi novel.[70] In it there are two worlds: reality and the Metaverse. Reality is a broken-down version of America, where the central government has seceded power to states, corporations, foreign powers, and mafia crime syndicates. The wealthy live in "burbclaves," and the poor live in containers. Reality is a broken-down dystopic society, epitomized by the Harley-Davidson owner who keeps a nuclear torpedo in his sidecar. On the other hand, there is the Metaverse, a virtual reality game accessible through goggles and dominated by avatars, a kind of next-level internet. Everybody's data is stored by Government Security. AI software, having been programmed by humans, is able to think for itself. The plot of the novel centers around a government that has lost control of tech development, and a nerd who intends to crash the whole system by infecting the minds of all those on the network, through the mental equivalent of a hard-drive failure. Although written before the millennium, so much of the book is already happening, with undoubtedly more to come. It predicts a dystopic reality, and an escape route through tech alternatives that circumvent the need to take reality seriously.

A third illustration/reflection on the same question as to what reality is can be discerned through Harari's evaluation of AI. In it he differentiates between intelligence and consciousness. Intelligence is knowledge, known by humans, but also by computer software. Using this knowledge, allied to complex algorithms, will easily enable computers to supersede human ability in specific areas, such as cancer research, gene recognition, and surgical operations, with incredible detail and accuracy. On the other hand, he sees consciousness as a significant and central human attribute—although shared to some degree with a limited number from the animal kingdom. Instead of being restricted to more empirical facts and their implications, it emanates from the mind as "a flow of subjective experiences, such as pain, pleasure, anger and love. These mental experiences are made up of interlinking sensations, emotions and thoughts."[71] Others have described human consciousness as being the ability to make connections and associate ideas: to conceive creatively, to have powers of reasoning and judgment, to have doubts, to possess a variety of senses, values, and intuition. So, for many, consciousness delineates the line between humans and machines. Consciousness is also identified as the line computers have to cross if they are to achieve the holy grail of singularity: Artificial General Intelligence (AGI). But in the end maybe *Blade Runner 2049* has the best definition—already

70. Stephenson, Snow Crash.

71. Harari, *Homo Deus*, 123.

quoted—of what it means to be human. "Dying for the right cause is the most human thing you can do."

Yet another illustration of the question "What is real?" comes from Donald D. Hoffman, a Californian Professor in cognitive science, in his work on the nature of perception, consciousness, and reality.[72] In it he questions the very existence of space-time objective reality, that what we see through the optical side of our brain is not necessarily what is there, but rather what our consciousness imagines it to be. He refers to icons on our computer desktop, which look like a blue rectangle. But the contents of that file, within the computer, will be neither blue nor rectangular, but something completely different. The icon is simply all we need to know if we are to make use of the reality within the file. Certainly, he suggests, we can take our perceptions seriously, but we should not take them literally. He also refers to the stimulated reality in the film *The Matrix*, and suggests it is our conscious minds that evolve what we think we see from the reality of what really is. He bases this on the work of neuroscientists who are seeking to unravel the mystery of how our brain works and what our consciousness actually perceives. Maybe our consciousness feeds into our brain what we need to know in order to evolve/survive, rather than what actually is; maybe our consciousness reconstructs reality to suit our own needs.

So, defining reality and humanity through intelligence, through what our eyes see, is apparently more of a mystery than we first thought. Developing knowledge in the life sciences is increasingly teaching us that it is extraordinarily difficult to define exactly who we are, what makes up our human identity. We know we are an evolution of particles, a combination of smaller, simpler parts that ceaselessly combine to make up a human being. But is that all we are? Do we have a spirit or soul that cannot be physically located, and yet give characteristics that make up our individual identity? Do we have a source within us, from which values, beliefs, beauty, and love creatively emanate?

So, life sciences are extending our understanding of the complexities of the brain and of the ways in which we perceive reality, even if they are not so clear on wider sources of our individuality. It is becoming clear that we are not straightforward individuals.

It is more that our individuality, actions, and personality arise out of a complex interaction between all the different parts of body and mind (nature) together with our living context (nurture). For example, Daniel Kahneman researched and identified the existence of "two selves" that lay behind our individuality. He called them our "narrating self" and our "experiencing

72. Hoffman, *Case Against Reality*.

self"[73]—separate but interlinked—that both contribute in different ways to whatever action we finally take. Our experiencing self remembers our moment-by-moment experiences, whereas our narrating self takes the longer view, the calculated assessment, through using stories, past memories, and crucial decisions. It can then go on to offer evaluations and action plans.

Whereas the former is often spontaneous, passionate and inspiring, it is the latter from which key decisions are drawn. Our narrative self is the one which shapes who we are, what we do, where we hope to go. However, the research also shows that even the narrative self doesn't take everything into consideration before coming to a conclusion. It primarily works on the peaks and the final remembrances of any particular event, taking the best parts and the conclusion, then averaging them out to bring about a final position. On this basis a computer algorithm, taking absolutely everything into account, would actually come to a more accurate conclusion! Ultimately our thoughts and actions will reflect a mix of narrative and experience, but for most people it will be the narrative self that is the most influential.

However, a further twist in the tail comes when computer power is linked up to the workings of the brain. When computer and brain are linked up, the two parts of our self can often be seen to have two different responses. Research in the American military has shown that when our brain is linked up to a computer-connected, transcranial helmet, our deepest subconscious thoughts and feelings can be very different from our surface reactions.

A similar reflection about who we are comes from David Baddiel concerning, for instance, the way social media posts are used by young people. He writes about "the reflex distortion of the self online."[74] Referring to Erving Goffman, a distinguished sociologist and social psychologist, he reminds us that there is an element of performance in all our relationships with other people. However, such performance can be very marked in postings and blogs on the internet. In effect we can create, through those postings, an idealized persona which could actually be very different from our real selves. A further extension to this is that we can easily begin to believe that we are truly the image we have posted for others to see: we want to believe we are the person of our dreams, rather than the person whose body we inhabit. All of this research, discovery, and reflection contribute to the discussion on who are we really/what do we really think/who is our real undivided self/what is human consciousness?

As we have seen in chapter 1, an even greater complication has been given to the concept of what is human by the comments of Stephen Hawking

73. Kahneman, quoted in Harari, *Homo Deus*, 342.
74. Baddiel, "How We are All Becoming Cyborgs," 71.

and Martin Rees on the possibility of a superhuman upgrade. They cite the potential enhancement of people through the editing and manipulation of genes. They go further to consider the possibility of life beyond DNA: the cloning of mechanical and electronic algorithms, which could evolve at a greater speed than could be matched by slower human biological limitations.

### 3.3.1 Virtual Reality/Augmented Reality

Now in addition to the complexity and uncertainty of human identity, there is alternatively an ever-expanding reality of the virtual world: from the augmented reality of games such as *Pokémon Go* to 3D vision, from avatars to sci-fi films, from virtual relationships through the internet to virtual sex with robots. Virtual interaction with computer software turns us all into cyborgs!

Virtual reality was conceived in the 1950s and realized first in the 1980s. Now it has joined, at affordable prices, the ever-lengthening list of must-have tech toys. Although at present VR comes through special headsets, Jaron Lanier of Silicon Valley prophesies that ultimately the flat screen in our living room will be replaced by VR "caves," within which we will experience a whole new world of entertainment.[75] As the Silicon Valley giants invest heavily, VR productions and programs will extend from video games to sports events, concerts and so much more. Just as with singularity, molecular manufacturing, and genetic enhancement, the holy grail being chased is haptic technology—a sensory feedback system between machine and user whereby the user is able to play things into existence. Between human participation and the machine, Lanier suggests, we will be able to expand creatively our whole human experience; opening up a fuller sense of what is deep down within us.

A rather different experience of virtual reality is depicted on screen by Joi, the digital love interest of Agent K in *Blade Runner 2049*. Virtual sex can now be a reality for anyone, with the growing trade in sexbots. In Europe, there are brothels dedicated to sexbots, replacing traditional prostitutes. Tech development investors see an opening here, expecting an incremental growth in the lifelikeness and attractiveness of these robots. For a variety of reasons, increasing numbers will take to this leisure pastime, hinting at the question, is sex with humans a thing of the past? Already flirting is being superseded by internet apps such as Tinder, Grindr, and Snapchat, so there is no reason why this virtual reality sex might not become popular. What three-dimensional pornography says to young people—especially those

75. Lanier, "Dawn of the New Everything."

who already find face-to-face relationships difficult—raises social and ethical implications that are now being fully debated.

## 3.4 THE DARK SIDE

In the midst of many discussions about change and the future, reference is often made to the dark side. Looking for prosperity and advancement can easily provoke negative as well as positive aspects. Sometimes this dark side refers to technological development in general, sometimes to that emerging new tribe, Silicon Valley, and sometimes to the internet itself.

## 3.4.1 Technological Development and Values

In this debate we recognize that what is needed are values and principles to guide development, to put focus at the heart of the debate, delineating between what is constructive/acceptable from what is more destructive/ unhelpful. To find and agree upon such values and principles takes us back to our presuppositions, our different worldviews. Therein lies the inherent difficulty. Our wide-ranging worldviews include rational humanism, market capitalism, Christianity, state capitalism, Islam, Hinduism, Buddhism, and so many others. Behind these wide-ranging approaches lies the vexing question of where it all began, the big history of everything, the origin story of sapiens.

Do we start by believing that particles came together by chance, bootstrapping themselves to kickstart evolution and create greater forms of substance? Or do we start from the presupposition that existence emerged out of a givenness, the other: a creator being who enabled evolution to evolve into substance, a humanity held together through relationship, a purposeful creator recognizable from the order and purposefulness of creation? Are we assuming society is being developed through survival of the fittest or through the purposeful wholeness of humanity, both strong and weak? Do we expect to achieve our aims through an eye for an eye, or by turning the other cheek, through coercion and competition or through collaboration, through tyranny or transformation, through a winner-takes-all policy or through one that says victory is achieved when we are all winners, through power that emanates from force or through power that arises out of vulnerability, through the bottom line of profitability or the bottom line of community and societal enhancement, or, alternatively, as Dalio has put it, "a double-bottom-line," of both together?[76]

Surely the starting point of any consideration of ethical considerations within technological development is to acknowledge and engage with each other's different assumptions. Only then can we hope to identify together a dark side and seek to harness or defuse it. From such a togetherness we could work toward agreed-upon values, norms, objectives, meaning, and direction that should advise global tech development, that can act as a guide to those who are already running that development—the innovators and investors of Silicon Valley. Only then can we integrate the output, the substance of our hard work, with a healthy relational ethos of societal development. Only then can we identify benevolent foundational principles that work positively to minimize malevolent elements which might threaten our children's future.

## 3.4.2 Disruption

One point that needs to be acknowledged is that disruption, interwoven so often into technological development, could be seen as embedding violence into tech culture. Innovation is constantly disrupting the equilibrium of the present, thereby threatening past achievements. Moreover, motivation behind innovation/disruption can easily be accentuated by personal greed rather than altruistic objectives. These two traits behind disruption can then encourage destructive change, leaning more toward tyranny than toward transformation, more toward monopoly and coercion from innovators than toward collaboration between innovators and established institutions.

On the one hand, disruption is crucial if innovation is to be advanced. Jesus was a radical disrupter, living and working outside the mainstream, challenging the dominant religious institutions and practices, ministering among the marginalized, and embodying a complete revolution in faith and practice. On the other hand, disruption is potentially destructive, and needs to be handled with care. Disruption often involves the promise of high returns for some, together with the end of the road for others, leading quickly toward inequality. It seems that when the rewards of disruption are privately owned, inequality will almost always follow, though it is true that some of those rewards can be redistributed altruistically through philanthropy, on a benevolent grace-and-favor basis, which has its own disadvantages.

---

76. Dalio, "Why and How Capitalism Needs to Be Reformed," 14–15.

Going further than the negative effects of disruption is the view that toxic tech is building up in a number of forms.[77] As well as violence being associated with disruption, the author, Trevor Phillips, indicates how sexism and racism can so easily be built into computer algorithms, which dominate the way data is procured and used. Kate Crawford—Microsoft researcher and MIT professor—told a White House symposium on AI, "sexism, racism and other forms of discrimination are being built into the machine learning algorithms."[78] And as Trevor Phillips then pointed out: "Supposedly dispassionate artificial intelligence aren't neutral at all, they are adopting their master's prejudice . . . Biases built into these virtual decisions carry real world consequences for tens of millions of citizens."[79] Many researchers infer that the whole field of tech development is staffed by a preponderance of nerdy white males who, possibly subconsciously, allow their prejudices to infect the system.

## 3.4.3 Silicon Valley

It is not a big step to move from digital technological development in general to the innovation, investment, and production firms centered around Silicon Valley, California, and its associated global spin-offs. Narrowing that view further, we can see how five or six Western giant corporations, together with China's Baidu, WeChat, Tencent, and Alibaba, dominate the whole sector. Even without Google's figures, the other four are said to "account for 10 percent of the value of the entire Standard and Poor's 500 Index."[80] If you accept that, behind five or six corporations and their venture investors, supported by the big four accountancy cartel, lies computing power and data-extraction facilities—doubling every two years—of a phenomenal nature, then it is not difficult to conclude that this small elite group of organizations is in the process of reprogramming society through their mantra of "monetize first, moderate later."[81] Surely this is behind Brian Appleyard's description of them as "old fashioned robber barons in trainers."[82] That dominance is increasingly being extended worldwide, as their mastery of computer code develops into a global surveillance system that encompasses all markets, bringing profits back into a very small group of investors.

77. Appleyard, "Not OK Computer," 1–2.
78. Phillips, "Help," 19.
79. Phillips, "Help," 21.
80. Phillips, "Help," 21.
81. Arlidge, "Humans Aren't Working," 15.
82. Appleyard, "Facebook, Amazon, Google, Twitter," 24.

The significant question is, surely, how has twentieth-century capitalism morphed into surveillance capitalism? Is it that innovation, disruption, and financial incentive have caused this accumulation of power and wealth amongst a very small group of people? Or is it that this accumulation was not inevitable, but that it was allowed to happen by the lightly regulated nature of the contemporary Western economic model? With hindsight it is becoming clear that the speed of technological development is such that government debate, legislation, and economic policy consistently falls behind the pace of innovation, enabling those who are quickest off the blocks to have a decisive advantage over those who follow. It is not, therefore, innovation as such that has led to growing inequality, but rather the overall management and development of that innovation. The ethos of monetize first, moderate later, the emergence of a winner-takes-all mentality, and the resultant race for power and control is what appears to have led to an increase of inequality within our Western and indeed global society.

The scenario of a robber baron elite controlling a huge underclass of serfs has to be a retrograde and unhealthy step for civilization in the long term. To attempt to mitigate these extremes by introducing a redistribution of wealth through a UBW may enable the market system to continue to function, but does nothing to enhance our understanding of/vision for human life. Human dignity and aspirations are the greatest losers.

As matters stand at present, governmental authority and democratic processes appear powerless to keep pace with the direction of innovation/ technological development and the aggregation of the resultant monopolies of power. As has been noted by a British commentator, reflecting on those five global corporations, "They strive to disrupt everything excluding themselves."[83]

A second public concern that has been given considerable media coverage concerns the misuse of data; highlighted by the case of private data being released by Facebook to Cambridge Analytica during the 2016 US presidential campaign, data that was mined, analyzed, and used for political and commercial purposes. This has been repeated in a number of cases since then. Self-regulation appears inadequate and government regulations are struggling to keep up.

The same is true with regard to fake news and bots. Although the media giants are at pains to explain how they are doing their very best to eliminate these from their platforms with great speed, Silicon Valley insiders such as Jaron Lanier claim that this is only window dressing. Fake news and bots will always keep coming until the underlying algorithms in the networks are

83. Appleyard, "Not OK Computer," 9.

changed, and that will not happen because it is those algorithms that sustain the commercial viability of the organization.[84]

### 3.4.3 The Internet

There is no doubt that the internet, like the printing press before it, has brought massively increased information levels right into the heart of many people's lives. It has opened up horizons, minds, aspirations, and participation in life. It is ever expanding, and consequently empowering more people to contribute to the advancement of humanity.

It is, at the same time, also being acknowledged as having a dark side which varies depending on the angle from which you view it. It certainly attracts criticism from all sides, from those who note its vulnerability to cyber-attacks to those who consider it a colossal scam or a "giant culture devouring vampire squid,"[85] from those who think it is a time-waster that is corrupting children to those who are frightened by its portrayal of pornography and by its potential for encouraging terrorism and organized crime.

However, it is important to acknowledge the rich variety that makes up the internet itself. It is an illustration of innovation, developed through CERN in the 1980s with academia, for a way of sharing information and research between universities and the like. At the same time, it was quickly picked up for military communications. In the 1990s, it expanded and developed through commercial interests, and as a communication network connecting working teams in the private, public, and voluntary sectors. The world wide web was created in 1989, using the internet as an information space where documents and resources became instantly available. That has now developed with the huge presence of business and commercial interests, together with the whole social media phenomena.

Whereas to begin with the internet was centered around an information-sharing concept, it has now become a network for all forms of communication, predominated and interlinked by commercial advertising and social networking. Many aspects of the internet are funded by advertising, promoting some of the key corporations of our global economy. It is true that Apple and Microsoft make products, but Amazon—and now Instagram—sell the products of others, with Google, Facebook, and other social media sites living off advertisements. And although we often conceive of the internet as something that serves us, increasingly its unfettered algorithms are subtly redesigning our world, primarily for the benefit of the

---

84. Lanier, Review of *Ten Arguments*, 42.

85. Appleyard, "Not OK Computer," 8.

organizations who dominate it. In the process they draw, from people and personal data/choices for their own benefit. Drawing on our interests, purchases, and social facts of life enables the large corporations, described by Jaron Lanier as "behavior modification empires,"[86] to target us more specifically. The attaining and analyzing of vast amounts of data allows corporations to design their products to suit our needs, and to mold our needs to suit what they have to offer. Lanier suggests that they can manipulate our online behavior through pervasive surveillance and data harvesting, leading to targeted advertising, and feeds that reflect and exacerbate our prejudices. So corporations can use the internet to extract more than we actually realize, without us recognizing the power and influence of the medium itself.

Undoubtedly the internet remains a source of information and an effective method of communication: we can browse search engines and Wikipedia about every subject under the sun. We can email, Skype, WhatsApp, and chat. We can share photos of every occasion. We can take for granted all the connections that can be made at speed, regardless of time and space, at our fingertips. But the flip side of that is the way the internet draws us into itself.

The internet can also act as a mirror, reflecting back and endorsing interests indicated by our search and browsing history. It can act as an amplifier of our own opinions and impulses, and confuse everybody by publishing fake news. It can feed in other opinions through a kind of filter bubble, offering insights that appear normal, but in fact come in coded language from a particular underlying slant. This all gives the impression of constructiveness, and yet hidden below the surface, it is subversive. Added to all of that, such platforming potential can encourage the growth of minority groups who express extreme views under the cover of apparent acceptability. The internet also breeds its own form of inequality. It uplifts those who have learned to master it, those who have access to fast broadband speeds and state-of-the-art devices, whilst at the same time disfavoring those who struggle with electronic devices, or who have poor digital connections.

The internet steals our time, chasing subjects and objects not necessarily central to our lives at all. It can exhaust us without taking us out of our chair. We spend less time face to face with other people, less time imagining, less time creating something original and personal to us, less time thinking of the lives and needs of others. As the Silicon Valley critical insider Jaron Lanier reflected "You have to be somebody before you can share yourself."[87]

Others describe the internet as both a cure and a poison. It has been a major source of information, but it can also fill our minds with banal

---

86. Lanier, Review of *Ten Arguments*, 42.

87. Lanier, in Appleyard, "Not OK Computer," 8.

machine-readable triviality. It can reduce our very selves to a shallow shadow of the person we could be. Many would argue that the internet amplifies many of life's problems. The question for future generations is whether it can contribute to the solution. What the internet takes from us is, of course, up to us. As consenting adults, we have the choice to become absorbed into it, or alternatively to resort to it only when necessary.

However, some of the strongest criticism of the internet comes from those who fear its influence on young children, saying that it is not an appropriate medium for young children. It is amazing how young children have been absorbed into the clutches of screen-watching. It is said that 21 percent of three- to four-year-olds have tablets or games consoles, and that 83 percent of children between the ages of twelve and fifteen have smart phones. Statistics suggest that children may spend up to six hours screen-watching. Certainly, it is the concern of many parents. YouTube Kids is described as the new child's dummy. Many also fear for the shortness of children's sleeping hours. Phones, always to hand, are worse than the TV being continuously turned on. Social media has replaced chatting on the way back from school, or meeting up on a Saturday morning.

There is no doubt that those who make the programs and games know how to extend, *ad infinitum*, the viewing times of children. Reward loops, trailers for the next program, losing what you have just achieved if you switch off now, different elements built into many games, all try to stop children switching off. For many young children the key word is "again." They do not have the adult self-control to think enough is enough, so life for many children consists of both their real life and a screen life on social media. Life on Snapchat, YouTube, and Instagram has taken the time and place of watching TV. Personal interaction on social media apps such as Instagram are clearly seen in positive terms by the postmillennial generation; it fills out so much of their time, lifestyle, and friendships. However, negative aspects of this medium are increasingly being felt. The easy availability of videos on self-harm, eating disorders, and even suicide, have been quoted as having the potential to be a devastating influence on vulnerable teenagers. Information can be as equally "real" as it can be "fake," it can be slanted or memed—from personal details to the lives of celebrity stars, from world news to fake news. Often the news tab, on a number of popular apps is where many teenagers find out about what is going on in the world, leaving daily papers, BBC/ITN news programs, Radio 4, etc. of little interest.

For teenagers to spend so much time on these apps has led them towards learning a different view of reality. "Always connectivity has transformed our world into a never-ending flow of potential information rewards."[88] In teenagers such addictive behavior may well have implications later. Tech requires us to "exact more self-regulation—to bring our own boundaries—than we had to in the past."[89] To be engulfed with any form of information, and not having the width of experience or willpower to be able to say no could have serious implications in later life.

Screen time is clearly an issue before you even get to the question of content. Possibly the most frequently mentioned issue of content is pornography, particularly amongst teenagers and millennials. The center of internet porn is said[90] to be Pornhub, a global, $100-billion industry, with more visits per year than BBC, CNN, and Amazon combined. Its target audience is millennials—aged 18 to 34—who make up 63 percent of its users.[91] It claims that its videos were viewed fifty-five billion times in 2016.[92] Other groups of viewers include prepubescent and teenage youngsters, who are said to learn all about sex from the internet, as virgins, before they have actually experienced it for themselves. To them the sexual norm is the fantasy they watch, rather than the experience that they will later encounter. Often this can lead to the real experience unsettling them and causing them anxiety. They watch the video, try to emulate the porn stars, and then find it is far less exciting than they imagined. Porn in effect becomes a template for what they should expect to experience, and what is socially and sexually acceptable. This can easily lead to adolescent introspection, anxiety, and a sense of inferiority.

Rather than containing the level of porn content, stars, producers, and distributors are constantly having to provide more graphic and extreme variations. They introduce more violence into sexual encounters just to sell their product, leaving young people in greater turmoil with increasing risk of nonconsensual sex or rape, and further violence of a sexual nature. Although pornography is in no way limited to under-18 viewers, what teenagers learn there, and what twenty- to thirty-year-olds continue to experience, will have a continuing effect as their lives develop into maturity. Although porn has been with us since the start of civilization, there is no doubt that technological development, such as the laptop and the smart phone, has, as with every other subject, amplified porn and made it far more easily and freely available than before. The internet cannot be blamed for the existence

88. James Williams, in McChonnachie, "Wired Generation," 23.

89. James Williams, in McChonnachie, "Wired Generation," 23.

90. Pogrund, "Clear Browsing History?," 37.

91. Pogrund, "Clear Browsing History?," 37.

92. Pogrund, "Clear Browsing History?," 37.

of porn and increased sexual violence, but their expansion on the internet can be regarded as contributing to the image of its dark side.

## 3.4 ADDRESSING DIFFERENCE

Digital technological development has speeded up, intensified, and amplified questions, uncertainties, and differences that arise out of continuous change, complexity, and paradigm shifts; it has thrown up differences of opinion and culture that have led to different forms of violence. Although the days of mass carnage experienced in the First World War and culminating in the atomic explosions at the end of the Second World War have not been repeated, the existence of difference, and the threat of resolving differences by resorting to violence, is just as prevalent as it has ever been. One only has to look at the Sudans. In the South they have been in civil war since achieving independence in 1956—with the exception of the 1980s—leading to the resolving of differences by resorting to the AK-47. It has been wired into the consciousness of young people in each following generation.

---

**RESOLVING DIFFERENCES**

At the heat of the civil war, Joseph Marona, a bishop committed to reconciliation and one who had encouraged the rebel Southern People's Liberation Army to have chaplains amongst its troops, was himself a victim when his son-in-law, an army soldier, had a family argument and then resolved it by opening up with his AK-47 in the family compound.

---

Of course, methods of war have changed considerably. Instead of the carnage of face-to-face conflict on the Somme, we now have suicide bombers creating individual carnage on the streets. It is said that Peter O'Toole playing T. E. Lawrence in *Lawrence of Arabia* was depicting a dramatic change in the conduct of warfare. Instead of the impossibility of defeating the Turks head-on in Arabia, Lawrence realized a more effective strategy would be to disrupt their supply chain, hence the bombing of the rail lines. Today, al-Qaida, ISIS, and so many other insurgent groups follow suit.

However, an alternative approach to resolving differences has been put forward in Sun Tzu's *The Art of War*. The central figure in the modern Denma translation of this Confucian-age text is described as a Sage Commander, who sees achievement of purpose as the prime goal, with fighting the enemy as the least preferable option. Fighting causes casualties on both sides as it encourages resentment and hurt in the vanquished, and creates over-inflated egos in the minds of the victors. A far better result, from the

Sage Commander's position, would be that, if the enemy's strong and weak points and his own army's strong and weak points were analyzed clearly, then barriers might be bypassed and alternative routes explored, rather than engaging in binary destructive conflict. The stronger force would achieve its objectives, but in such a way that the weaker force didn't lose face.

Today we are growing into a winner-takes-all culture. We are becoming accustomed to an elite dominance from data barons over a resentful majority of neoserfs. Although this is the twenty-first century we are moving towards a repeat of the Middle Ages. The wisdom of the Sage Commander, compiled over 2,500 years ago, offers moral, practical, and contemporary challenges for today's society, engrossed as it is in technological development and divisively distributed rewards.

## ENDNOTE

Having looked in part 1 at the practical details of digital technological development and some of the questions/implications arising from that paradigm shift, part 2 turns our attention to the development of the Christian church down through the centuries and through changing contexts.

As we have seen in part 1, many of the questions and issues emerging from and embedded in radical technological development raise serious dilemmas and diversions for a traditional Christian understanding of society and humanity. What part 3 will address is how the church might reframe its approach in the light of such challenges. To what degree should it accommodate itself contextually to this paradigm shift; and to what degree should it speak counterculturally, with alternative, faith-based proposals, to this reenvisioning of humanity and its environment by technological development?

But before that, part 2 needs to remind us of the church's journey so far, of how that journey has led the church to its present state. That should then equip us with a base from which to consider and chose an appropriate way forward.

# PART 2

The Journey of the Church
and its Faith

## INTRODUCTION

From the heart of the Cotswolds, Seven Springs, Coberley, and the Thames Head spring near Coates, all compete with each other for being the source of the River Thames. Through green fields, with sheep drinking and children paddling, they meander down to the trout fishing stretches at Fairford before reaching Lechlade, where the Thames begins in earnest for the leisure cruisers, where, in the old days, barges were filled up for transporting goods up to the London ports. With busy river traffic competing with the rowing eights of Leander at Henley, the river moves slowly to its culmination in London, with the city ports, water taxis, flood defenses, and then Tilbury docks, before flowing out towards uncharted sandbanks and English Channel shipping lanes.

Such an image, with its four main stages, could be used to equate to four eras in the life of the Western church. First, the sources of the Thames and the tiny streams that flow through sheep fields could be seen to represent from the birth of the Christian church at Pentecost, through times of persecution, all the way to when Emperor Constantine legalized the faith/church in Rome in AD 313. Second, the busy, jostling river, with leisure craft and rowing boats travelling to and fro, from Lechlade onwards, depicts the expansion of the church between the time of Constantine all the way to the period of the Renaissance/Enlightenment. Third, the great wide river that meanders slowly through the suburbs, the center, and then the city of London, through to the flood defenses at Tilbury Docks, relates to the rise of individualism, the Renaissance in art and culture, and the emergence of the life sciences and Enlightenment thought. Finally, the flow through the estuary, and on into the busy shipping lanes of the Channel, represents the uncertainties/complexities of the millennial digital age—the context in which the church now finds itself.

This division of Western church history into four sections, from Pentecost to Constantine (chapter 4), from Constantine to the Renaissance/Enlightenment (chapter 5), from the Enlightenment to the Millennium (chapters 6 and 7), and then finally the churches of the twenty-first century (part 3) illustrate key paradigm shifts in the life and growth of the Christian faith. These four divisions link in with the previous theological approaches that divided church history into epochs/eras, but takes them further into the new era of the twenty-first century. The previous approaches have been well documented by David Bosch in his seminal work on mission.[1] He introduces both the six epochs identified by Hans Kung,[2] and also James Martin's breakdown into four eras that relate to Kung's analysis. For my own part, I have condensed these previous analyses

---

1. Bosch, *Transforming Mission*.
2. Kung, quoted in Bosch, *Transforming Mission*, 182–3.

into three eras, and then added a fourth era to describe our time from the millennium onwards. It is important to refer to these epochs/eras because they have significant bearing on how we arrived at where we are. How the contextual engagement and countercultural activity of those eras was enacted could have a bearing on how we contextually and counterculturally engage with society in this postmillennial period. As Bosch put it: "We need the perspective of the past in order to appreciate the scope of the present challenge."[3]

My own approach is to see the development of our Christian faith growing through the four eras, from which certain thematic roots can be distinguished that have relevance to the context of the fourth era in which we find ourselves. The first era, chapter 4—following Kung and Bosch— flows from New Testament times to Emperor Constantine, from message and movement through to institution, from sodal to modal. The second era, chapter 5—again following Kung and Bosch—is from Constantine to the end of the Middle Ages, from a primitive to a societal belief, fully integrated into state structures. The third era, chapters 6 and 7, covers from the Enlightenment through the ecumenical and postcritical periods to the millennium. Then the final era—part 3—really looks toward the third decade of the twenty-first century, from hierarchical structure and survival mentality towards networking complexity and a posthumanist future: "Progress, the God of the enlightenment, proved to be a false God, after all."[4]

These same four stages of church history can be illuminated by reflecting on similar stages of development in early Judaism. First, Pentecost up until Emperor Constantine could be reflected in the time between Abraham's call and the establishment of the Jacob/Israel/Joseph dynasty. Second, from Constantine to the Renaissance/Enlightenment could be reflected in Moses's life from the bulrushes to becoming Pharaoh's son, inhabiting the royal palace. Third, the period between the Enlightenment/secularization debate and the millennium is reflected in the wilderness experience. Fourth, today, facing the twenty-first-century agenda could equate to the Israelites entering Palestine, with Joshua facing the whole range of new complex choices.

Yet another shorthand way of identifying these four stages of church history is to describe them as from diversity to unity, from persecution to power, from power to exclusion, from exclusion to a fresh opportunity.

Beginning with this first period in chapter 4, we can discern how the church grew and changed; between the bestowal of the Spirit, through the Orders of Ignatius, to the official recognition of the church as an institution by Emperor Constantine in AD 313.

3. Bosch, *Transforming Mission*, 188.
4. Bosch, *Transforming Mission*, 189.

# Chapter 4

## From Encounter to Institution

The emergence of the Christian church was born out of a coming together of three distinct elements. The foundation base came first from its Jewish heritage: Old Testament writings which assumed the God-created nature of the universe, and humanity's place within it; that the Other, the Father of everything, created both the world (substance) and humanity (relationship); that this givenness of faith undergirded Judaism's understanding of everything. Second, it came from the understanding that God the Father had sent the long-expected Messiah, his son; born from a miraculous encounter between a young girl and the very spirit of God. The unseen builder of the universe showed his real presence through this woman having a baby without the assistance of her husband. The third element that activated the church was a third given, which was the appearance and experience of wind and fire overwhelming first a household, and then a global collection of pilgrims visiting Jerusalem.

That multiracial crowd of thousands who were soon going to disperse in every direction at the end of their holidays, were overwhelmed by a transformational experience, by an ability to understand each other regardless of language and heritage differences, by a sense of being drawn together by this shared event, by a personal sense of God's presence that was entirely new. This historical event of empowerment was inexplicable but real nonetheless. The events of that day were followed by pilgrims returning home travelling along every road out of town—north, south, east and west—to Syria, Lebanon, Turkey, Greece, Rome, Gaza, Egypt, Ethiopia, Caesarea, and eventually to India through Thomas. Every road the Romans had built between Rome and Jerusalem, every crossing of the Mediterranean, every caravan route to Egypt and the south, became lines of communication upon which this encounter, this annunciation of global significance, this inclusive experience of a life-changing nature, exploded instantly, and was carried out into the then known world.

## 4.1 THE MOVEMENT

This occurrence, this meeting between the Other and ordinary people, multiplied amongst the friends of Jesus, in frequently mundane circumstances. The first witness to this was Stephen,[1] who suddenly faced a conservative backlash, and died for his honesty and transparency. Philip went north to Samaria, and south, hitchhiking toward Gaza. The encounters became infectious.[2] Peter travelled to Lydda, Joppa, and Caesarea on the coast, and was surprised by the inclusiveness of this Spirit.[3] Meanwhile, travelling north to Syria through the Golan Heights, a conservative, terror-driven, Jewish fanatic, intent on murdering believers, encountered a spiritual roadblock as he neared Damascus, where the very person of Jesus returned to speak to him. After that shock encounter, he was led into the town where he was visited by a very frightened Christian leader who proceeded to heal him of his blindness and then welcome him into the Christian fellowship—the people he had vowed to exterminate. Such was the impact on Saul that, after a time in the Arabian desert, he travelled continuously[4] under the name of Paul, as a person transformed by this roadside encounter, to Lebanon, Turkey, Greece, Cyprus, and ultimately to Crete, Malta, and Rome.[5] In some instances gatherings had already been established,[6] united by the message of Jesus and the transforming power that had been bestowed upon them. Contagion was the one word that conveyed the explosion of those first few months.

From that point onwards these new believers formed communities in each place. Clearly Jerusalem was formed first, then Antioch on the Lebanese coast, then in towns wherever the faith spread, including Ephesus, Corinth, and Alexandria. Within the established Roman Empire, the movement spread like wildfire with a radical revolutionary core, causing fear and

1. Acts 7.
2. Acts 8.
3. Acts 9–10.
4. Acts 13–26.
5. Acts 27–28.
6. Acts 19–21.

persecution from the establishment, both civil (Roman) and religious (Jewish). The new movement spoke a new language of love, affirming it with involvement amongst the poor, sick, prisoners, and slaves. They touched both spiritual and physical worlds in a holistic way, more through social transformation than political movement. They were empowered in this task through personal experience, a sense of community and an expectation of their Lord's return.

> The New Testament witnesses assume the possibility of a community of people who, in the face of the tribulations they encounter, keep their eyes steadfastly on the Reign of God, by praying for its coming, by being its disciples, by proclaiming its presence, by working for peace and justice in the midst of hatred and oppression, and by looking and working towards God's liberating future.[7]

In those early days the core centers of the movement were Jerusalem, Antioch, Ephesus, and later, Alexandria. As Bosch[8] points out, the Jerusalem church became what appears to be the institutional center, following a more apostolic approach, consolidating the establishment of a new faith. The church in Antioch, on the other hand, had a far more spirit-led approach, with a pioneering outlook that led to expansion along the trade routes to Turkey, Greece, and Cyprus. At an early stage there were already signs of tension between those who wanted to develop a firm base for an institutional approach, as compared to those saw ministry as expansion, evangelism, and missionary zeal.

Tony Bradley[9] describes New Testament development in somewhat geographical terms. He sees the Antiochene model built around a circular model of shared leadership, the Markan world reflected in the Alexandrian church, built around the master/disciple, protomonastic model, a Johannine world reflected in the Ephesian church, built around a center/periphery minster model, and a Matthean model reflected in the Jerusalemite church, built around a dominant leader/bishopric model, from James onward.

A somewhat different view comes from Anthony Hanson.[10] He argues that ministry in this earliest period is one of a pioneering church. He describes this "Pioneering Church" as emerging from the apostles and disciples, and he identifies it as the "Remnant of the Faithful" in Israel, who responded to Jesus Christ. The apostles and disciples, "were the Remnant and

7. Bosch, *Transforming Mission*, 54.

8. Bosch, *Transforming Mission*, 51.

9. Bradley, *Guidelines for the Ministry*.

10. Hanson, *Pioneer Ministry*.

therefore the first Church," and he adds that "the apostles are the ministry because they are the first Church."[11] So he concludes that "Ministry is the pioneer Church," and "the Church in nucleo."[12] Hanson goes on to suggest we learn that "the task of ministry is to serve the Church, but to serve it by itself living out the suffering and redeeming life of Christ in the world, in order that the Church as a whole might do likewise."[13] So the early concept of pioneer church ministry developed into the Pauline doctrine of ministry.

We can begin to recognize that a transition takes place between the earlier period of evangelism and expansion—where boundaries are crossed through life, grace, and movement—toward a more established, settled order consolidated on law, doctrine, fixing boundaries, and establishing institution, when "white hot convictions, poured into the hearts of the first adherents, cooled down and became crystalized in codes, solidified institutions, and dogmas."[14] The first is typified by the Antiochene model, and the second by developing the Jerusalem model. So, between New Testament times and Ignatius, ministry develops away from the pioneering ministry, from the description of teaching, preaching, guarding, shepherding and protecting—Eph 4:11-13. Instead it turns towards the Ignatian model of a "settled ministry of Bishops—or elders—and deacons,"[15] away from the "dynamic of movement" toward "becoming an institution,"[16] away from ministry as "the Church in nucleo," towards a view of ministry that exercised a certain priority over the church,[17] away from the "dynamic generative activity of the ecclesia," and toward "the necessary moments of stasis, consolidation and forming of networks and functions of endurance."[18]

However, this move from expansion to consolidation, was not necessarily clear-cut and straightforward. Bishop Michael Nazir-Ali has pointed out that, during this New Testament/early church tunnel period, two differing forms of ministry were existent, working side by side with each other. One was the local ministry of presbyter/bishop, and deacon, with an emphasis on *kenosis*, self-emptying (Phil 2:7). The other was a wider, often itinerant ministry of apostles, apostolic delegates, prophets and teachers (Acts 13-14) with more of an emphasis on *plerosis*, the filling of the Holy Spirit,

11. Hanson, *Pioneer Ministry*, 63.

12. Hanson, *Pioneer Ministry*, 115, 86, 94.

13. Hanson, *Pioneer Ministry*, 62.

14. Bosch, *Transforming Mission*, 53.

15. Hanson, *Pioneer Ministry*, 51.

16. Hanson, *Pioneer Ministry*, 51.

17. Pickard, *Theological Foundations*, 82.

18. Pickard, *Theological Foundations*, 83.

leading to outward mission (Acts 4:8, 31 and 13:9).[19] The former developed into a caring, sustaining, nurturing structure, whilst the latter was far more about creating, inaugurating and innovating. But although these two approaches were existent together early on, by the fourth century it was the former that had taken control, with the latter approach being picked up only later by the monastic movement, in their itinerant, mission-oriented way.

There were fundamental reasons for this transformation from a primitive faith towards an institution of size and influence. First, whereas in Paul's time Christians appeared to meet in households, with worship and church life influenced by peripatetic preachers, by Ignatius's time membership was much larger, with many household congregations coming together to worship. This worship was then led by a group of elders headed by a senior elder, a bishop, and assisted by deacons. So, as the numbers grew, the voice and role of the membership became subservient to an institutional order, an organizing class, emitting "form, boundaries, and symbols of endurance."[20]

Second, the church's Jewish-oriented faith was strongly centered around the historical Jesus, an apocalyptic and eschatological faith expectant of the Lord's imminent return. As time passed however, the need arose for the church to find its place in a more Greco-Roman world, working out doctrinal articulation that could hold its own in a Hellenistic-thinking world. As a consequence, the emphasis switched from thoughts of Christ's return and the Spirit's empowerment towards thoughts of eternity and the exalted Christ, toward building up the sanctity of the church. The Spirit was seen less in terms of individual blessing and more in terms of grace conveyed through the orders of the church. The unity of the faith was being threatened by doctrinal differences that emerged, threatening the unity previously derived from apostolic tradition. So, as Bosch points out, in the writings of Ignatius and Cyprian, a reliable antidote was put in place that encouraged believers to follow the directions of the clergy and bishops in particular, who then became "the sole guarantors of the apostolic tradition and the ones endowed with full authority in matters ecclesiastical."[21] From Cyprian onwards the Episcopal role became an administrational office, with a strong jurisdictional role over a "quasi sacred" diocesan area.[22] Cyprian also developed the Synodical structure, encouraging the participation of the laity in the legislative process. With such developments the width of ministry was constrained for the benefit of order and orthodoxy; freedom of

19. Nazir-Ali, *Shapes of the Church*, 4–5.
20. Pickard, *Theological Foundations*, 83.
21. Bosch, *Transforming Mission*, 468.
22. Pickard, *Theological Foundations*, 179.

spiritual expression was limited by the need for discipline and control, and for protection in the face of persecution.

Third, the context and position of the church changed dramatically. Instead of being a minority faith in a pluralist world, a *"religio illicita"* within the rule of a malevolent state, it gradually became an accepted faith with special dispensation from a benevolent state after the Edict of Milan in AD 313; it became a religion that was tolerated. That changed again in AD 380 with Emperor Theodosius, who then proscribed all religions except Christianity, throughout the empire.

Fourth, the faith was transformed from one that exhibited itself primarily through "the exemplary lives of ordinary Christians," with "love on their lips,"[23] expressing a gospel of love and charity, towards a church committed to vigorous intellectual discussion, determined to hold its own in the relative, syncretic, and fatalist Hellenistic milieu, towards a clear relationship between altar and throne. Having emerged out of a backwater of the Roman Empire, it found it had to articulate a sustainable identity in Roman society, which itself was beginning to disintegrate.

## 4.2 STABILIZATION THROUGH ORDER

The pre-Byzantine church realized that a serious transition was required. As we shall see, this transition gave rise to negative as well as positive outworkings. But as Lesslie Newbigin has pointed out,[24] they probably had very little choice. So, between the second and fourth centuries, the faith became less centered on the ministry of the baptized and more on the representative ministry of the Ignatian Orders.

However, the empirical issue of ethos, structure, and shape established between the time of Ignatius and the fourth century has never been fully accepted. In Europe, as we shall see, the Anabaptists and Pietists both rebelled against the Roman pattern. In England, the Augustinian monastic movement clashed with the Celtic monastic tradition of Columban, Aidan, and Kenelm, the former bringing the liturgy, rules, and stability of Rome, the latter bringing the itinerant evangelists and monks from Ireland. These two very different approaches clashed head-on at the Synod of Whitby (in AD 664) where the Roman order prevailed over the more charismatic Celtic approach.

---

23. Bosch, *Transforming Mission*, 191.
24. Newbigin, *Foolishness to the Greeks*, 129.

Then again, these two differing approaches have been illuminated through the work and writings of Roland Allen[25] and Vincent Donovan,[26] together with the rise of the charismatic movement in late twentieth century, and in the inherited church/fresh expressions dialogue of this present century.

---

### ROLAND ALLEN

Roland Allen, an Anglican missionary in China in the early twentieth century, pointed out how St. Paul's approach to mission on his missionary journeys was very different from the way the Anglican missionaries sought to share the faith and build the church in China. Rather than having confidence in the newly baptized believers, leaving them to establish and build up the church in their own place, as Paul did, the Anglican missionaries settled into each place and never moved on—building up a mission station approach that reflected English culture as much as the Christian gospel. Consequently, new converts immediately became dependent upon and subservient to the incoming missionary hierarchy, with English culture being absorbed as part and parcel of the Christian faith.

Roland Allen's understanding of Paul's strategy and Vincent Donavan's ministry strategy in Tanzania were based on such passages as Ephesians 4:11–13, describing the variety of gifts that can be expected to emerge from the body of Christ. "To prepare God's people for works of service, so that the body of Christ may be built up," indicates, surely, that the whole of the church, rather than the ordained, are to participate in such an expansive ministry.

---

Allen's key point was that that ministry changed from Paul's time to the time of Ignatius, that, bearing in mind the expansion and growth of the church in Paul's time, maybe we should be returning to the model operated by Paul. He initiated the contemporary debate between a church life centered around the functional role of a priestly ministry as compared to a church life emanating from the ministry of the baptized.

More recently, picking up on the sociological differences between the first and second centuries, Brian Capper gave further insight into the issues raised by Allen and Donovan.[27] Capper's main thesis is that order and ministry changed radically from Paul's method to Ignatius of Antioch's model of monarchical bishops, that the social nature of the churches changed dramatically during that time, that whereas the ministry of the baptized was central in Paul's time, by Ignatius's time order rather than fragmentation, orthodoxy rather than heterodoxy were increasingly central to

25. Allen, *Missionary Methods.*
26. Donovan, Christianity Rediscovered.
27. Capper, "Order and Ministry."

the Ignatian model, that the leadership and inspiration of church life and growth changed from being led by a peripatetic, mission-oriented group of apostles, prophets, and evangelists, to a more settled, threefold order of bishops, priests and deacons.

Capper's reading of 1 Corinthians 12 and 14 leads him to conclude that in Paul's time ministry is not the preserve of the leading officers of the congregation, but the service which the Spirit inspires in each believer (1 Cor 12:4–6) and that "the manifestation of the Spirit is given for the common good" (1 Cor 12:7). But by Ignatius's time, Capper sees the church as being "defined by the threefold order of bishop, elder and deacon and in which it would be difficult to imagine the lay person having a prominent place or public role at all," and where "a clergy class had abrogated to itself all authority and public expression of the gospel in the act of ministry."[28] Ignatius described the episcopal role as that of the lyre, the presbyteral role as the strings, and the laity as the choir.[29] So, by the second century, transition toward a different form of ministry was achieved.

## 4.3 ANNUNCIATION TO INSTITUTION

Both Taylor[30] and Bosch[31] clearly articulate this subtle change in the life of the church from rapture to rules, from a first-generation to a second-generation church. Originally, the church emerged, spontaneously reflecting its joy and release: "its white hot convictions poured into the hearts of the adherents,"[32] its source of new experience was "unmerited grace," it was "risk-taking" by being committed to the poor and widows around them, it was reveling in expansion and growth. However, the church of succeeding generations took on very different attributes. It became solidified through the drawing of boundaries, through the rules and unreasonable prohibitions to enforce purity and unity. As it consolidated in this way, through order and moral control, it

> cooled down and became crystalized codes, solidified institutions and petrified dogmas. The prophet became a priest, establishment charisma became office, and love became routine. The horizon was no longer the world but the boundaries of the local parish. The impetuous missionary torrent of earlier

28. Capper, "Order and Ministry," 1.

29. Hanson, *Pioneer Ministry*, 113.

30. Taylor, *Go-between God*.

31. Bosch, *Transforming Mission*.

32. Bosch, *Transforming Mission*, 53.

years was tamed into a still flowing rivulet and eventually into a stationary pond.[33]

The movement had become an institution. The pioneering spirit of Antioch, of grace, of crossing boundaries, had been replaced by the consolidation, law and boundary-fixing doctrines of Jerusalem: "The mobile ministry of the apostles, prophets, evangelists, were replaced by the settled ministry of bishops, elders and deacons."[34]

## 4.4 INSTITUTIONALIZATION OF THE HOLY SPIRIT

Another illustration of the differences between the first-generation New Testament movement and the more settled, ordered institution of Ignatius's time, comes from Taylor's analysis of how the church understood the work of the Holy Spirit during those first two centuries. To begin with it was clear that the fullness of the Holy Spirit was the birthright of every baptized Christian: the Holy Spirit was seen to "transform and intensify the quality of human life."[35] It was an annunciation experience within the lives of new converts, illustrating the transforming gift of the Spirit in each person giving rise to the assertion of sonship and liberty. Together with that fullness of the Spirit came the ministry of preaching and healing—handed down by Jesus himself—to the emergent, first-generation, New Testament church.

However, as the second-century church developed, there was a gradual move for this gift of the Spirit to be centered into a more institutional form. Taylor describes how, by the time of Origen, Tertullian, and Cyprian, "a greater priestly control of this charismata"[36] was recognized, and that "by the fifth century the priest alone was permitted to anoint."[37] Taylor concludes that there was a "determined attempt to institutionalize the Holy Spirit in the life of the Church. Instead of being the creative lord and initiator of all communal responses of the Church, he is treated as a thing—a force to be manipulated, a fluence to be placed at the disposal of Bishops and Priests and dispensed sacramentally," developing a "spiritual aristocracy in the midst of an unenlightened fleshly majority."[38] This clerical monopoly over the gifts of the Spirit, as Taylor goes on to say, had the effect

---

33. Bosch, *Transforming Mission*, 53.

34. Bosch, *Transforming Mission*, 51.

35. Taylor, *Go-between God*, 199.

36. Taylor, *Go-between God*, 208.

37. Taylor, *Go-between God*, 208.

38. Taylor, *Go-between God*, 208.

of separating this "life of the new creation, and its hallmark of freedom and strength of love,"[39] away from the normal life/witness of the whole church membership, and towards the status and authority of the Episcopal Orders.

Quite possibly it is in this transition that the delineation described by Oliver O'Donovan begins to establish itself. O'Donovan writes about the church having both an outer and an inner identity. The outer identity consists of its order and leadership, its rules and boundaries, its visible structure, whereas its inner identity comprises its sources: the biblical text, the gospel of Jesus, the inner lives of individuals influenced, molded, and empowered by those sources.[40]

During the New Testament period therefore, it was that inner identity that dominated, reflecting the nature and identity of the Christian faith. But by the time of Origen, Tertullian, and Cyprian, an outer identity of leadership, rules, and boundaries had become the dominant expression of the church. Ever since then, it can be argued, the outer identity has tended to dominate as the modal norm, with the inner identity seeking to reestablish its importance through reformation when the opportunity arose, often in the form of a sodal movement.

## 4.5 MODAL/SODAL EXPRESSIONS OF CHURCH

This empirical disjunction between the New Testament church and the consequent generational church, between the vibrant, exuberant, personalized expression of faith, and the more regularized, institutional order, has the habit of reappearing regularly. Rediscovery of the Spirit's personal touch on every believer regularly challenges the traditional assumption, that the church is the primary conduit of God's grace, by highlighting the Holy Spirit's direct impact upon the lives of individuals. The list of large-scale breakouts would be endless, but they would include, Monasticism, Anabaptists, Pietists, Methodism, Pentecostalism, the Missionary Movements, Salvation Army, Basic Ecclesial Communities, the Charismatic Movement of the twentieth century, and many fresh expressions/community churches in the twenty-first century. This disjunction is also highlighted in the present Anglican church, through the way, even in the last seventy-five years, there has been no resolution to the dissonance between the ministry of the baptized, and the representative orders of ministry (the representative orders have precedence, even as the two approaches to ministry still flow along side

---

39. Taylor, *Go-between God*, 209.
40. O'Donovan, "What Kind of Community?," 186.

by side, like river and canal) with no significant move towards unifying the two approaches of ministry.

Maybe the clearest way of understanding these two different approaches in the contemporary church can be illustrated through the terms "modal" and "sodal," articulated by George Lings, following Dr. Ralph Winter.[41] The modal form of expression is seen in the Ignatian threefold order which can be followed right through to the institutional, established churches of today. On the other hand, alternative sodal expressions of faith break out from the traditional structures to form personal expressions of faith that gel into movements such as those mentioned above. These sodal expressions seek to rearrange and rejuvenate the existing structures. Sometimes they do effect real change: sometimes they get reabsorbed into the existing institution; sometimes they become new institutions themselves. These sodal movements act as catalysts to the institution, seeking the reinvigoration of the faith from the outside—sometimes from the inside—of official structures.

## 4.6 NARRATIVE AND EXPERIENCE

Interesting support, acknowledging these two different approaches to ecclesiastical development, comes from social and psychological research, which has identified similar traits in the human psyche. As we have previously noted, Harari refers to Daniel Kahneman's research on the existence of the "two selves" within us:[42] the "narrative self," and the "experiencing self." The experiencing self is "our moment-by-moment consciousness," which experiences everything but remembers very little. On the other hand, our narrating self "retrieves memories, tells stories, and makes big decisions."[43] Although both aspects are part of our brain as a whole, it is our narrative self that has predominance, making decisions and activating them.

These two sides of our personality have an uncanny link up with the way we engage in religious expression. The narrative self appears to accord with a more historic, linear, planned, structured approach to church development initiated by Ignatius. Whereas the experiencing self seems to rejoice in the here-and-now experience of, say, being filled with the Spirit, of recognizing healing miracles. It would be more likely to align itself to the spontaneous movements of spirituality that burst sodally from the modal institutional church.

41. Winter, *Two Structures*.

42. Harari, *Homo Deus*, 342–48.

43. Harari, *Homo Deus*, 343.

An interesting illustration of these two identities can be seen in the Sudan and South Sudanese Episcopal Churches. On the one hand, the outer Anglican identity is upheld in the Episcopal and Synodical structures, with considerable pomp, status, and Western financial support. An advantage of this structure is membership of the Worldwide Anglican Communion, together with the status accorded to the archbishops, enabling them to engage with the presidents/governments on both human and Christian rights issues. However, there is, on the other hand, another self-sustaining, experiential, confident, inner identity of faith and belief, in the vibrant Sunday church celebrations in the mud and corrugated iron roof churches of rural areas, in the shanty town churches of greater Ondurman, North and South Khartoum, in the fearful congregations of the Nuba Mountains and Dafur. More often than not, they are upheld by the vitality of the Mothers' Union rather than the Diocesan administration, living out that unforgettable Sudanese Christian phrase, chanted throughout the decades of oppression: "But God is not defeated."

## 4.7 DWELLING AND SEEKING

This linkage between narrative planning/modal institution and the spontaneous, experiencing self/sodal charismatic movement running throughout the history of the church is endorsed further by work done by F. LeRon Shults on Christian spirituality.[44] He quotes David Schnarch, a couples' therapist,[45] who puts forward the concept that within the spiritual life there is both a cycle of spiritual "dwelling", and also a growth cycle of spiritual "seeking". The dwelling state relates to the sacred in ways that feel familiar, comfortable, and safe, connecting to "a spiritual community and tradition that legitimize certain rituals and spiritual practices, and provide a sense of continuity to spiritual experience."[46] On the other hand, the growth cycle of spiritual seeking can arise from a transformational experience of spiritual awakening that is often both exhilarating and destabilizing. The research appears to suggest that some believers remain content, happy, and at peace with a settled ritual and order, whereas others can become bored with that and look for much more exciting, expanding, thrilling, and personal experiences of faith.

Both Harari and Shults's ideas indicate that the human person may have, built into their psyche, a natural affiliation towards one or the other approach. Whereas some will be attracted to an ordered, patterned, regulated

44. Shults, *Transforming Spirituality*, 32.

45. Schnarch, *Passionate Marriage*.

46. Shults, *Transforming Spirituality*, 32.

church, others will be drawn towards a more experiential, personal engagement with faith. In contemporary terms these two approaches would equate to those who prefer "inherited church", and others who would prefer "fresh expressions".

This idea is endorsed by Carl Jung's sixteen personality types and the Myers-Briggs training that has resulted from it, which is used extensively in training by many churches today. From this analysis it can be argued that certain personality types are attracted toward an institutional, cerebral belief and faith, while other types are far more likely to prefer intuitive, experiential, community-based, contemporary spiritual approaches, and indeed would be put off and bored by more traditional, authoritarian styles. As an example, it has been said anecdotally that virtually all the diocesan bishops of the British Anglican Church exhibit two particular personality types—J being Judgmental, and T being Intellectual. J has a preference for facts, concrete data, permanence, tradition, and ordered structures, whilst T uses intellect rather than feelings as criteria for making judgments and decisions. These two traits in particular blend into the leadership criteria of a traditional, institutional organization. On the other hand, other types—who value intuition more than facts, who work on feelings rather than cerebral thinking, who perceive ways forward without clear cut reasoning—might find themselves far more in tune with experiential, participatory, free-flowing worshipping communities that go with the flow rather than following prescribed rules and structures.

## 4.8 PARTICIPATORY DEVELOPMENT THEORY

One final contribution to this debate between more structured, ordered modal forms, and more experiential, charismatic sodal approaches, comes from a secular source. From the 1960s onwards, many countries gained independence from their former Colonial masters. As these countries sought to grow—with few developed resources and little administrative capability—they looked to the West to offer development aid. Quite quickly a similar disjunction developed between those who were expected to offer assistance, and those countries who expected to receive that assistance. The former had the knowledge and resources, and believed they knew how to distribute them, emphasizing their role as generous benefactors who could dictate the terms of the gifts. They were the modal institutions, offering to share their largesse with the freshly emerging sodal independent countries. However, these newly emergent independent countries were not happy at all about how this aid was being offered. They had very different ideas about how it should be distributed and received. Established structure was challenged by more spontaneous, innovative, personalized expectations. And so commenced a debate that continues to this day.

---

**PARTICIPATION DEVELOPMENT THEORY**

From a village in Upper East Coast Ghana, a group of men put it this way: "The one who rides on the donkey doesn't know the ground is hot." In other words, "The rich man cannot know or feel a poor man's problems unless he gets off the donkey and walks on the ground, or unless he asks the poor man."[47] Out of this thinking, both in the developing and developed world, emerged the concept of Participatory, or People-Centered, Development, where the starting point of development was to be the lives of people in need, rather than the professional expertise of the top-down, capital-intensive, high-tech, centralized contributors. "People come before things; and poorer people come before the less poor."[48]

This concept began to take root deeply and comprehensively in international development, until Nelson and Wright[49] and then Cooke and Kothari[50] shook the whole strategy with devastating criticisms, claiming that these participatory methods were not living up to their claims, that there were major flaws in the approach. Ever since then those criticisms have been widely debated. A major response to these criticisms has come from Hickey and Mohan,[51] which sought to work through the criticisms and find a constructive way forward.

---

This contemporary secular debate illustrates again the different attitudes expressed between those who see themselves controlling/administering one centralized organization, and the attitudes reflected by a receiving, spontaneous, diverse, innovative, freshly formed society. Again, this is a theme to which we will return later.

## 4.9 FROM IGNATIUS TO EMPEROR CONSTANTINE

Returning to Ignatius's move to establish the threefold order of ministry, to undergird church leadership through order, stability, and authority, we find the central focus of the church began to move from Jerusalem to Rome. Later Cyprian in North Africa followed the Ignatian structure and added a

---

47. Dogbe, in Chambers, *Rural Development*. 97.

48. Chambers, *Rural Development*, 241.

49. Nelson and Wright, *Power and Participatory Development*.

50. Cooke and Kothari, *Participation*.

51. Hickey and Mohan, *Participation*.

more jurisdictional element. Gradually the concept of dioceses, under the leadership of a bishop, began to form. So Episcopal rules encompassed not only ministerial leadership but also the implementation of rules and boundaries of both practical administration and doctrinal orthodoxy, confirmed later in England by the Synod of Whitby in AD 664.

The relationship between the church and the Roman state authorities also changed during this period. Initially the church was persecuted, not only by the Jewish leadership, but also by the Roman State. Christians lived in hiding, fearing for their own lives in the caves and catacombs of the city of Rome. Officially the Roman Emperor was seen as a god, and as such, was expected to be worshipped. Refusal to worship the emperor as god had led to martyrdoms. But this situation gradually eased so that, by Emperor Constantine's time in AD 313, an agreement was struck between church and state. A benevolent relationship developed all the way through to the Renaissance.

A distinct change in the ethos of the church began to take place. In the earlier period Christians were seen as revolutionaries, opponents of the state, bands of zealots, outcasts, and marginalized, often centering around communities of the poor and ostracized. Later, with more middle-class adherents, and with an organized structure of leadership, they became more accepted as a class within society, with the state accepting their existence. Gradually the church leadership's association with civil power and state authority began to emerge. In England, this was first illustrated when Augustine was sent by Rome to evangelize England. One of the first things he did, on arriving at Dover, was to establish a deal with the King of Kent. From that moment on, the seeds of the concept of an "established church" of England was born; with the King or Queen being entitled "Defender of the Faith." Today's situation can trace its roots all the way back to that first relationship with Emperor Constantine, that close liaison between altar and throne.

We now need to look, in chapter 5, at how that relationship developed, all the way through European church history and the Reformation to the Enlightenment period, when there was another dramatic disjunction, this time between church and state, when altar and throne were distanced by modern science, art and culture, individualism, and modern science.

# Chapter 5

## From Constantine to the Renaissance/Reformation

The journey in this second era begins with the agreed-upon liaison between state and church, initiated by Constantine, continuing with its power-centered association with the Roman Emperors until the collapse of the Empire and the period of Barbarian rule. It expanded throughout Europe and traveled with the voyages of world discovery, an era that concluded with the Protestant Reformation, the rise of individualism, and the Renaissance/Reformation movement. By the time of the Enlightenment—the rise of modern science and humanism—the church had begun to lose its position of power and its close association with national and state leadership. This loss of position will lead us into the third era which will be the subject of chapters 6 and 7.

This second era, from Constantine to modern Europe and beyond, can be illustrated again by the valley of the Thames between Lechlade and the outskirts of London. The river takes on so many fellow travelers, including coarse fishers, transport barges, luxury leisure cruisers, international rowing teams, and even the adventurous houseboat. They all use the waterway, growing and developing as the river itself is enlarged by more tributaries and canal networks.

This second era also brings to mind the growing development of God's plan within the Old Testament. Following on from Abraham's call and the rise of the Jacob/Israel Dynasty—which got stuck in an Egyptian swamp—we come to the time of Moses, saved as a baby in a floating basket amongst the bulrushes, up until when he becomes established as an adopted son of

Pharaoh, resplendent in Pharaoh's palace. Moses, as it were, comes out of nowhere, dependent on God's plan alone to become a potential inheritor of central power in a world super-state, before climactically losing it all in his defense of a fellow Hebrew, which leads to his self-imposed exile in the Arabian desert.

So what are the salient features of the church's journey from the gaining and wielding of power and influence, to the sudden feeling and realization that it, the church, was about to be written out of the equation?

## 5.1 JOINING A SOCIETY IN DECAY

The Western expansion of the Christian faith—out of Jerusalem and towards Rome, Constantinople, and North Africa—had led to the establishment of a more stable relationship with the Roman authorities in the west, but in the east it was having to face up to the oncoming arrival of the Arab Islamic Movement. However, just as it received the accommodation of the Roman state, the whole empire collapsed following the fall of Rome in AD 410 to Alaric and his Barbarian hordes.

Before that collapse the church did set a direction of travel that it followed all the way through the barbarian period right through to the Enlightenment itself. It decided to anchor itself in the Hellenistic intellectual climate of the day, a distinctive paradigm shift away from its Jewish/Hebrew roots. But equally importantly, it decided to adapt from being a church at odds with the authorities, to being a church that benefited/stabilized itself through an endorsement from the state, which then morphed into an expanding Europe. Such a direction of travel was welcomed by the state, which was able to claim that God was legitimizing its existence. So this collusion legitimized the Christian faith in the eyes of the state, and correspondingly, the church legitimized the state in its hour of need. So the church benefited from this societal crisis by being in the right place at the right time, building itself up into a position of authority and power within that society, morphing itself from a tiny movement in an eastern backwater of a vast Empire through the turbulence of Barbarian times towards expansion into Northwestern Europe. From thence it would travel alongside the discoveries and the colonization of other continents in the expanding known world. Only with the Enlightenment and the arrival of modern science did this strategy of societal influence gradually become diverted from the mainline of civilization into the siding of personal belief.

As both state and church saw the potential of this liaison, they penetrated and permeated each other. The church contextualized itself in the stability of state order, in an organizational, structural system, in intellectual, Hellenistic thought patterns. This increasingly gave rise to a clear articulation of orthodoxy, through which debate could take place. A result of this realignment was that gradually the Christian faith took on the mantle of civilization, as the pagan barbarian northern tribes came to sack Roman structures and society. The church sought to instill an indissoluble unity of interest for both church and state, becoming both a stabilizer in a disintegrating structure and offering a challenging ethical faith for the future, seeking to contextualize itself in the predominantly Hellenistic Roman society, yet simultaneously offering a radically different transformational faith in Christ and belief in God. As fatalism and despair took hold with the waning of the Greco-Roman Empire, the Christian faith was in the right position "to fill the vacuum—and the citizens of the Empire responded."[1] As Bosch has poignantly noted, "no mass movement into the Christian faith has developed in a culture that was stable and rich in content, but always only in societies that have lost their nerve and were disintegrating."[2]

The church therefore took advantage of this opportunity and grew into the heart of empire society, leading to an increasing influence of power over that evolving society. As we shall see later, that role may not have been appropriate for the primal message of Jesus, but it did install the church into a key political and social role as the nation-states emerged in Europe.

A perceptive reflection on this move from the pre-Christendom era to the Christendom era comes from Alan Kreider of the Anabaptist/Mennonite tradition. He writes of eight ways in which the church changed at this point in time. He sees this shift towards Christendom as moving the Christian faith,

> from the margins of society to the center: buttressing Christianity's appeal with imposing and attractive incentives; moving the Church's reliance from divine to human power; changing the Faith from a voluntary movement to a compulsory institution; losing the Faith's capacity to be distinctively different; seeing the examples of Jesus as applicable to only a minority of 'perfect' Christians; turning gatherings for worship into grand assemblies; altering the focus of the Church from mission to maintenance.[3]

It is interesting to note an endorsement of Kreider's viewpoint, from another tangential commentator, with reference to this particular paradigm shift in

1. Bosch, *Transforming Mission*, 193.
2. Bosch, *Transforming Mission*, 193.
3. Kreider, Beyond Bosch, 59–69.

the faith/church's development. Harari, an Israeli atheist historian, reflects on this new relationship between church and state, between the medieval popes and the Donation of Constantine (AD 315). Harari emphasizes the political and social power bestowed upon the church leadership from that point in time; a position of power that they never really relinquished until it was mainly taken from them during the Enlightenment period.

The Donation of Constantine was a document signed by Constantine "granting Pope Sylvester 1, and his heirs, perpetual control of the western part of the Roman Empire."[4] Harari goes on to point out that "The Popes kept this precious document in their archives and used it as a powerful propaganda tool whenever they faced opposition from ambitious princes, quarrelsome cities, or rebellious peasants."[5] He suggests that, as kings and emperors were given great weight in medieval society and seen as God's representatives, it left the church in a very powerful position just as Europe was coming into being. This document, Harari claims, "was an important cornerstone of papal propaganda, and of medieval political order."[6] However, Harari gleefully goes on to point out that, despite the fact that it was regularly referred to by the church authorities during that medieval period, in actual fact in 1441 it was discovered to be a forgery by a Catholic priest, Lorenzo Valla—having been forged in the eighth century.

Such a document, particularly if it was a forged one, would suggest that the church put great store in the moral authority of ancient imperial decrees offered by Constantine and later Emperors. The church in practice certainly sought to hang on to that influential support, despite the fact that it didn't sit easily with the intention, message, and practice of Jesus—who spent a considerable amount of his life attacking the rules, status, and practices of the Jewish authorities. As we shall see, this position taken by the church to ensure its future position continued from before the fall of Rome, through Barbarian times, and on to the stabilization of Northern and Western Europe. Lesslie Newbigin has argued that one shouldn't criticize the church too strongly for this course of action, as they had no real alternative if the church was to survive. However, if the church did indeed resort to and depend on an apparently forged document simply to shore up its position of power and authority, it might be more appropriate to acknowledge that this attempt by the church to hold onto worldly power and position for its own sake is indeed a travesty of what Jesus Christ actually stood for. It will be argued that herein

4. Harari, *Homo Deus*, 223.

5. Harari, *Homo Deus*, 223.

6. Harari, *Homo Deus*, 223.

lies the seeds of today's disjunction between the structure of the church and the message and purpose of its founder—to which we shall return later.

## 5.2 KINGS, PROPHETS, AND BISOCIATION

This identification of divergence between the structures (outer identity) of the organization and its core message (inner identity) in the early stages of the Christian faith's development is of considerable significance for the future image of the church. The danger of such deviation from a message could be illustrated by one of the features included in modern cars. In such cars, if you inadvertently veer towards the hard shoulder of a motorway, or cross the white lines dividing fast and slower lanes, a beeping noise will remind you to turn back into the lane you were in. It is a warning to remind you to drive in a straight line, within the limits of the lane you have chosen.

Such warning signals have also been noticed in the Old Testament, when the rule of kings began to veer away from the primary purposes of God. In those instances, the warning sounds came to the royal establishment from the prophets, as in the case of Ahab and Jezebel being warned by Elijah. John Taylor highlights this prophetic role within the mission of God, the Old Testament journey of faith. Taylor[7] refers to Amos, Hosea, and Jeremiah as having a vision of God's purposes and plans, far beyond the minds of the kings, and indeed the Jewish society of their day. It is as though the prophets can see, through God's inspiration, to what might be, as compared to the normal national leadership seeing only what is.

---

**BISOCIATION**

Taylor takes this from Arthur Koestler's *The Act of Creation*, where Koestler describes the vision of an artist as a process of bisociation, "the ability to perceive . . . some unsuspected link between two completely unrelated objects or ideas . . . sometimes emerging from the subconsciousness in dreams, which places side by side two facts which no one else had previously seen together."[8]

---

So Amos uses a plumb line, Hosea his own marriage, and Jeremiah the despair felt in refugee centers along the banks of the Euphrates—or is it the Nile?—to draw attention to the true purpose of God as compared to the actual situation in which the people found themselves. Finding themselves surrounded by what is, these prophets have the vision to discern what

---

7. Taylor, *Go-between God*, 72–73.
8. Taylor, *Go-between God*, 72.

might be. Their closeness to the Spirit of God enables them to criticize and protest against the norms of the day. Maybe the metaphor of the car's beeping mechanism is a contemporary illustration of O'Donovan's point that the inner identity of the Christian message should continuously refine and reshape its outer shell.

Now this crucial prophetic role appears to have been absent as the church developed such a close and powerful association with the state authorities. It failed to see the disjunction between its structural position and its message that was beginning to emerge. It became deaf to the Holy Spirit pointing out "what might be", because it had become so tempted into associating with the state's implementation of "what is", that it lost sight of the personal promptings of God's Spirit, as it was attracted by status within the state authority. This close association between altar and throne made the role of prophet almost impossible to fulfill.

As the church leadership chose this association with the state, implementing it through coercion, they lost sight of the annunciation of the Holy Spirit. They downplayed the unique personal-life witness of love and forgiveness that had so characterized early church life. By earthing the faith's reputation in Hellenistic intellectualism they moved towards a more cerebral articulation of orthodoxy. By gaining power and status from the state, they lost Christ's identification with vulnerability, suffering, and ostracism. In the process of attaining safety and stability, they failed to follow the one who entered willingly into suffering, and who ultimately ended up on the cross.[9] And to recall from part 1 the contemporary insights of Dee Hock concerning today's hierarchical institutions, the faith subsumed itself in the structures of the day at the expense of the very purpose, meaning, and example of its founder.

## 5.3 EXPANSION TOWARD THE EUROPEAN RENAISSANCE/REFORMATION

This church/state partnership continued throughout the Middle Ages, as civilization continued to spread into Northern and Western Europe, following those same countries as they expanded through exploration and colonization into the hitherto-unexplored extremities of the planet. It had clear foundations from Eusebius of the Byzantine church who "constructed a system in which church and state were united in harmony,"[10] where a new synthesis developed between "monotheism and monarchy," "where

9. Bosch, *Transforming Mission*, 513–14.

10. Bosch, *Transforming Mission*, 205.

all measures were taken to assure the indissoluble unity of the interests of Church and state,"[11] building on Augustine of Hippo who, "compromised the Church to the state and to secular power . . . (causing) the Catholic Church to become a privileged organization, the bulwarks of culture and civilization and extremely influential in public affairs."[12] It even got to the situation whereby Emperor Charlemagne wrote that his task was to "defend the Holy Church everywhere against the assaults of pagans and the ravages of unbelievers."[13] By this stage both emperor and pope "knew that each needed the other."[14]

However, as the Middle Ages developed, a significant cultural change was emerging that encouraged the church to adapt itself, once again, to a changing context. Having just adjusted itself to engage with the classic civilization of "city based, literary, intellectual and technological tradition"[15] and orthodoxy, it now found itself having to adapt itself to the primal world of the "circumstances of peasant cultivators and their harsh uncertain lives,"[16] from the orthodoxy of the empire state it had to invent the concept of a "Christian nation." Instead of dealing with decrees of emperors, it had to come to terms with local and national "customs," and had to realize that custom was "binding upon every child born into a primal community, and that non-conformity to that custom is simply unthinkable."[17] This meant that each community would have a single custom and that, if faith was to progress, it would need to become the faith of that community as a whole— a theme picked up by Vincent Donovan in his ministry to the Maasai.[18] In turn, as communities related to each other, a Christian nation was born, "bringing once again, nation and Church coterminous in scope."[19]

Bosch notes the same cultural shift facing the church when he refers to appropriate texts for each cultural context in which the church operated. In looking at the Greek patristic paradigm, he sees John 3:16 as epitomizing the message "that whoever believes in him shall not perish." However, when it comes to the Middle Ages, he suggests the church's message would be best

---

11. Bosch, *Transforming Mission*, 205.

12. Bosch, *Transforming Mission*, 212.

13. Bosch, *Transforming Mission*, 212.

14. Bosch, *Transforming Mission*, 212.

15. Walls, *Missionary Movement*, 19.

16. Walls, *Missionary Movement*, 20.

17. Walls, *Missionary Movement*, 20.

18. Donovan, *Christianity Rediscovered*.

19. Walls, *Missionary Movement*, 20.

described by Luke 14:23 "make them come in."[20] Bosch concludes that by the time of the High Middle Ages,

> the structure of human society was finally and permanently ordered, and no one was to tamper with it. Within the divinely constituted and sanctioned order of reality, different social classes were to keep their places. God willed serfs to be serfs, and lords to be lords": an "immutable, God given 'natural law' ruled over the world of people and things. Everybody and everything was taken care of . . . the monopoly of the Church . . . was undisputed.[21]

When it came to the Age of Discovery—the colonization of Africa, Asia, and the Americas by Western Europe—the same held true. As Bosch articulates: "Colonization and mission, as a matter of course, were interdependent; the right to have colonies carried with it the duty to Christianize the colonized."[22]

So, as the paradigm shift between Roman Empire and the wider European Middle Ages took place, the church adapted itself accordingly:

> It moved from being a small persecuted minority into becoming a large influential organization . . . from harassed sect to oppressor of sects . . . (with) an intimate relationship between throne and altar . . . membership of the Church (becoming) a matter of course . . . dogma (being) conclusively fixed and finalized.[23]

It moved conclusively from being a faith based on personal experience through the individual touch of the Holy Spirit on individual lives, to a large, comprehensive, continental organization, engaging at every level of society from king to serf through a priestly, institutionalized understanding of the grace of the Holy Spirit.

As has been noted, Newbigin has questioned whether the faith had any other option other than to "go with the flow."[24] However, despite positive outcomes that are clearly recognizable, it is the dark side of the church's liaison with authority, control, power, and persuasion that becomes the object of the Enlightenment's critique of the altar/throne relationship. It is also a dark side that still continues, to a lesser degree, even up to the twenty-first century.

---

20. Bosch, *Transforming Mission*, 236.

21. Bosch, *Transforming Mission*, 225.

22. Bosch, *Transforming Mission*, 227.

23. Bosch, *Transforming Mission*, 237.

24. Newbigin, *Foolishness to the Greeks*, 129.

But before moving on to the Enlightenment period, there is still one further element of transition within the Constantinian/Enlightenment paradigm to mention: that of the Protestant Reformation.

## 5.4 PROTESTANT REFORMATION

One significant fact of this whole period of church reformation in Northwestern Europe lies not in what it did introduce but in what it left untouched. For all their antagonism to Roman Catholic tradition, Reformation leaders, in the main, did not reject that organization's alignment between church and state. When certain areas fell into Protestant control, the Lutheran, Reformed, and Anglican leadership simply accepted the Christendom framework of the church/state liaison,[25] and made no attempt to question these sociopolitical structures of the day. It was only the Anabaptists, Pietists, and Moravians during this early Reformation period who clearly rejected that church/state relationship. As Bosch notes, "Anabaptists insisted on absolute separation between Church and state and on nonparticipation in the activities of Government."[26] The Pietists expressed their opposition by developing a dualism between the "civic" and the "religious," between the "profane" and the "sacred,"[27] restricting their activities to the latter in each case. The Anabaptists, however, were, at heart, against the whole Catholic Christendom tradition. They recognized the paradigm shift that was crystallized in Constantine's time, and sought to return to that earlier New Testament pre-Christendom pattern. "Their project was not the reformation of the existing Church, but the restoration of the original early Christian community of true believers."[28] We shall see how this ideal synchronized with later similar expressions from Roland Allen and Vincent Donovan.

One other significant feature of this period is the way in which—following the seed thoughts sown by Jesus, Paul, the early church, and some medieval theologians[29]—the Renaissance saw the flowering of the individual. Whereas the Middle Ages remained primarily centered around local communities and nation-states, the individual was gradually coming to claim center stage. Bosch's text to summarize the Reformation period as a whole is Romans 1:16, "where the Gospel is described as 'the power of God unto

---

25. Bosch, *Transforming Mission*, 240.
26. Bosch, *Transforming Mission*, 246.
27. Bosch, *Transforming Mission*, 255.
28. Bosch, *Transforming Mission*, 247.
29. Siedentop, *Inventing the Individual*.

salvation to everyone who believes."[30] Luther, and those who followed, all turned away from the corporate nature of faith, coercive conversions, and the close association between the institutional/sacerdotal grace emanating from the church's hierarchy/authority. Instead—influenced by Renaissance individuality—they pointed out that the Christian faith could be understood and accepted by each individual, who could become justified simply through their own personal response. As the individual was able to read the vernacular text of what Paul had written, that individual would become free from the controlling centrality of the priestly, pontifical tradition, and be able to respond personally. The reformer's emphasis lay in the "local encounter of man with the Word of God."[31] This emphasis on the significance of the individual, and the individual's ability to make choices for themselves, was a theme that would ultimately come to fuller fruition in the Enlightenment a century later. But suffice it to say, the pendulum was beginning to swing back from the predominant role of institutional grace/power centered in the church authorities, and from communal decisions/mass responses, towards the particular consciousness of an individual's decision, and their application of such faith in their lives.[32]

## 5.5 PRE-ENLIGHTENMENT WARNING SIGNS

As the Enlightenment approaches during the seventeenth century, one can see with hindsight the warning lights go on for the future of both the Roman Catholic and Protestant wings of the church. But at the time, both the traditional and reformed church failed to see those signs. Although the ongoing Roman Catholic Church managed to turn a blind eye and significantly ward off the Enlightenment movement at this time, the newly emerging Protestant churches began to struggle with what was to come.

The church, firstly, failed to recognize the disjunction between their altar/throne liaison and the core message, purpose, and practice of Jesus Christ: it rested its case on power, status, and substance—whilst Jesus had decried authorities, rejected power alliances, and made personal relationships amongst the most vulnerable. The church didn't realize that such action would make it vulnerable to the charge of hypocrisy.

Secondly, the church assumed that by aligning itself with rulers and kings it could retain a preferential position of leadership/authority on

---

30. Bosch, *Transforming Mission*, 240.

31. Walls, *Missionary Movement*, 21.

32. Walls, *Missionary Movement*, 21.

matters social, spiritual, and ethical, illustrated up until recently by the Irish Roman Catholic hierarchy's influence over both government and society.

Thirdly, the church failed to recognize the growing threat of cosmological discoveries, and the possibility of these undermining its own explanation of creation, and of a God-given purpose for being.

Fourthly, the church was slow to comprehend that the rise of individuality/knowledge could seriously undermine the pronouncements of a hierarchical clique of erudite theologians, who claimed to dispense *the theory of absolutely everything*.

Fifthly, it failed to recognize the possibility of progress/personal aspiration, separate and distinct from the realm of the church.

For all these reasons and many others, the church was ill-equipped to recognize and face the next paradigm shift in Western society. This time the shift was going to occur through circumstances far beyond its control: through the advancement of cosmology and the life sciences, through discovery and progress centered around those who, unconvinced by explanations of faith and belief, grounded their thinking on reason and fact—what we would now call secularization.

In effect, the church's authority, the whole Christendom framework, that had dominated Europe for more than 1000 years, was beginning to crumble. As this new paradigm shift took hold, the Protestant churches particularly would have to spend the following centuries working out a response—which will be the subject of chapters 6 and 7.

# Chapter 6

## From the Enlightenment
## to the Millennium

This third era is dominated by the way Enlightenment thinking overshadowed the Christian faith in the west; culminating with postmodernism and the technocentric fourth era of the millennium period. As Bosch states, this third era is described as being when "The unshaken massive and collective certitude of the Middle Ages has indeed entirely vanished,"[1] and then he notes that "Its dominant characteristic . . . is its radical anthropocentrism."[2] The church is no longer the prime source of meaning: it has lost its position of power and status in society to the emerging life sciences/humanist explanations that followed.

Following our earlier image of the River Thames flowing from its sources to the channel, this era can be identified as the river which passes through London from Richmond to the Woolwich tidal flood defenses before it enters the estuary and the channel.

Following the second image of the early Old Testament story, this era could be likened to Moses leading Israel for forty years in the desert before Joshua and others enter and engage with the promised land.

So what are the key attributes/issues that arise as this era leads us into our own time and the challenges of this fourth era? Others have identified the main issues of the Enlightenment, but I would like to draw attention to four issues/disjunctions in particular that will then gain increasing

1. Bosch, *Transforming Mission*, 268.
2. Bosch, *Transforming Mission*, 267.

significance over this period. I will then follow these four issues/disjunctions into the fourth era (the chapters of part 3).

The first issue centers around the concept of power—and key elements of the Christendom project—and the association of the church with the institutional, political, societal, and philosophical powers of the day, as compared with Jesus' insistence on the power of vulnerability and suffering.

The second centers around the hierarchical structures of the church as compared to the networking digital communication medium of the information age, and the differences between a cerebral, reasonable articulation of orthodox faith and the more experiential, intuitive, innovative, personal, and diverse expression of faith often seen in contemporary life.

The third issue is the disjunction between the traditional, hierarchical, threefold order of ministry, and the diversity of the ministry of the baptized, the personal experience of the Holy Spirit, and the blossoming of local community networking faith groups.

The fourth issue is the balance between the church being contextual and being countercultural, between the faith/church being contextual to every different culture within which it exists, as compared to the countercultural prophetic role which the gospel ought to reflect to any surrounding addressing a critique that the church lacks confidence in this prophetic, context; countercultural role.

This chapter will follow these four issues through enlightenment liberal humanism, the Industrial Age, postmodernism, and on into our own digital age of information, uncertainty, and complexity.

## 6.1 THE CHRISTIAN FAITH AND THE ENLIGHTENMENT

The Middle Ages saw the establishment of nation-states. The church, with its purpose-giving God and its Christendom framework, enhanced the legitimacy, stability, and status quo of these nation-states. Those relationships were to change dramatically with the rise of the individual, the advent of the life sciences, and the cumulative effect of secularization, urbanization, and pluralization. Society began to change from being theocentric towards becoming anthropocentric. As Bosch points out: "God was largely eliminated from society's validation structure."[3] This gradual change both took the church by surprise and caused its leadership and academics great fear and concern. As we have seen, the church had put great store in its close relationship with power and authority, its strong influence over societal

3. Bosch, *Transforming Mission*, 263.

behavior. Now that position was being eroded through the rise of science, which often refuted belief as the explanation and meaning of everything. "Individualism threatened the communal basis of religious belief and behavior, while rationality rendered many of its beliefs implausible."[4]

This new philosophy marginalized belief in the biblical creation story, as the life sciences introduced the concept of evolution. It displaced a theocentric ethos in favor of a rational anthropocentric consciousness. It placed great emphasis on knowledge-based scientific fact and the power of human reason to develop it (i.e., when Descartes said, "I think and therefore I am"). It declared that God was a product of the human imagination, and was therefore superfluous in the face of scientific fact, that God might have provided stability/order for society in the past, but that now he was no longer essential, that religious belief was a perfectly reasonable way of thinking for individuals, but that it should no longer be granted a central role in societal development. From evolution, discoveries, inventions, and achievement the Enlightenment drew out belief in consistent progress, leading to confidence, hope, and expectation for the future of humankind. Such progress envisaged emancipation from the past through the benefits of education, leading to enhanced rationality for all.

The dethroning of God, the Christian faith, and a theocentric concept of reality highlighted acceptance of the principle of cause and effect—one primary evolutionary event leading to another. This alternative approach was made possible as the value-free facts of scientific discovery/rational thought began to replace the values of a theocentric mindset and, in that view, unsubstantiated human belief. In this way Enlightenment thinking began to undermine and repudiate the church's view that society was all ordered and unchangeable in accordance with God's purposes, that it should not be tampered with, that the size of the pizza was set, that Christian values were there simply to rearrange the distribution and size of the slices and choice of toppings. The Enlightenment alternatively proposed, in the light of scientific discovery, that the overall size of the pizza could be increased through progress and modernization, that these concepts had nothing to do with God and everything to do with human potential, that the poor and the weak would be catered for not through God's bias for the poor, but rather from the crumbs from the rich man's table / trickle-down theory, that tradition and dogma—factually unsubstantiated beliefs—could be replaced by knowledge in its multitude of expressions. All of this emphasis on facts and reason and the consequential downplaying of religious values meant

4. Davie, "Europe," 74.

the emancipation of the autonomous individual as central to life, and the demotion of God's controlling influence to the sidelines of private belief.

Behind all of this lay a difference in presuppositions that had been there from the very beginning: the difference between the Jewish/Christian tradition and the Greco-Roman-Hellenistic thinking as they developed over centuries. These different worldviews, already referred to, became much clearer as Enlightenment thinking became the dominant philosophy of Western society. On the one hand, the Jewish/Christian tradition understands that all reality is based on relationships between the constituent parts of the whole; it is not the individual atom that is significant but rather the relationship between the constituent parts of it. Try splitting them up and you will soon find out: truth is seen to emanate from the relationship between a creative life force—the Other—a created universe or multiverse, and humanity. The Enlightenment, on the other hand, follows the Greek emphasis that "the human individual conceived as the autonomous center of knowing and willing, is the ultimate constituent of society,"[5] that truth emanates from knowledge derived from this empirical factual starting point.

### 6.1.1 The Enlightenment

But perhaps the most significant clash of all, between presuppositions, lay in the differing views on the source of existence, where it all began, the primal spark. Up until the Enlightenment it was a given that God revealed himself to humankind through his self-revelation in creation; through his self-revelation in the incarnation, ministry, death, and resurrection of his son; through the continuous stream of transformations amongst his son's followers, attributed to his spirit; through the expression of love, goodness, and unmerited grace that was witnessed in the life of the early church; through the articulation of all of this in the Bible, the basic source document describing God and his purposes.Please start a new paragraph here

With the coming of the Enlightenment, a completely different view of a brief history of time/everything—as articulated now by such as Yuval Harari and David Christian—was described. It understands that the universe came into being through providence, chance, through the bootstrapping effect of one molecule building upon another. This led to the centrality of the human being, who evolved via the animal kingdom, who was answerable to no other primal force, and who was not dependent on outside or other assistance. So, the starting point of the Christian faith and fully fledged Enlightenment thinking could not have been further apart, despite the argument

5. Newbigin, *Gospel in Pluralist Society*, 172.

already quoted that the original seedbed of the staunchly secular, liberal ideology lay, not in the Italian Renaissance, but rather in the revolutionary identification of the individual by Jesus, Paul, and the early church, and continued by such eminent scientists as Copernicus and Newton.

The clash between these two distinct worldviews lay at the heart of the debate, which returns into clear focus, as we shall see, with the advent of technocentricity and the crisis now facing humanism and capitalism.

## 6.2 THE RESPONSE OF THE CHURCH

The Christian faith in the form of the Western church found therefore that, rather than being in a close mutual relationship with the powers that be, it was instead being deposed and sidelined by a new philosophy that was overwhelming Western society. Whereas in the main the Roman Catholic Church continued on regardless, up to the Second Vatican Council,[6] the Protestant churches faced up to this head-on clash of views during this period, a period which ultimately led to the rise of postmodernism. During this time, Enlightenment thinking came not only to dominate society as a whole but also to seriously influence theological development. The church's theologians were forced to work at ways of accommodating to its message in order to survive. It was the next major step in contextualization, as the church faced a philosophy that had turned on its head the relationship between faith and reason. Until then, faith had priority over reason. The Enlightenment argued that reason supplanted faith as a point of departure, that ultimately "God owed his existence to human feelings."[7] Within the early stages of this era the church struggled to contextualize, and had little confidence to express any possible prophetic or countercultural contribution to the ongoing debate.

As time went on, a number of responses to this societal philosophy and to the church/state relationship arose. The Holy Roman Empire began to crumble and individual European states took its place, developing in different ways. The Divine Right of Kings came under extensive threat from Cromwell's Commonwealth, the French Revolution, and Holland's move to becoming a republic, all of which resulted in a reversal of previous church-state relations—beautifully depicted in a phrase some have attributed to Voltaire on his deathbed that the last king should be strangled with the guts of the last priest.

---

6. Bosch, *Transforming Mission*, 262.

7. Bosch, *Transforming Mission*, 269.

So the Enlightenment period saw the end of a close relationship be-tween church and state, leaving the church in an ethos of uncertainty. Its previous ally was deserting it, as societal thinking was being transformed all around through the advancement of modern science. Its authority, as a stable core belief for the nation, was disintegrating in the face of this grow-ing philosophy based on human discovery, understanding and knowledge, and a rational approach that required no dependence on God as a source of existence.

## 6.3 THE RESPONSE OF THE CHURCH OVER TIME

Over the next two or three centuries the Christian faith responded generally in one of two different ways. It either veered toward assimilation with the new philosophy, developing a new orthodoxy in tune with rationalism, or, alternatively, it reacted against that philosophy by reemphasizing the cen-trality and absolute nature of God within the reality of life. As Peter Berger put it, "rejection and adaption are the two strategies open to religious com-munities in a world understood to be secularized."[8]

But it is at this point in history that a wider perspective needs to be taken into account. The story of Western Christian faith can be likened to the journey of the River Nile as it enters the Mediterranean Sea. Having entered Egypt as one large, slow-flowing river, it dissipates into a whole se-ries of different channels, a huge, vast estuary as it exits into the sea itself. Similarly, the Western church, having grown out of Jerusalem and Rome and expanded into the whole of Western Europe, as well as North Africa, then went on to widen out over a period of two centuries or more into a series of globally diverse channels, all reacting to the differing contexts in which they found themselves.

As we have referred to, and to which we will return, the primary re-sponse in Western Europe took the form of three reactions. First, the Prot-estant Reformation sought to adapt and assimilate itself with the prevailing Enlightenment culture. Second, other parts of the church reacted by reject-ing what the Enlightenment stood for by returning to a pre-Enlightenment, theocentric approach centered around an absolute Creator God who was the source of all meaning and the focus of all behavioral response. This second response was epitomized by the series of evangelical awakenings in America and Europe. The third European response came from the Roman Catholic Church, which, similar to the second response, reacted strongly against any relationship with the Enlightenment, and turned in on itself.

8. Berger, *Desecularization of the World*, 2.

This was epitomized by the First Vatican Council of 1870, which proclaimed the infallibility of the Pope, even while the Enlightenment-influenced Victor Emmanuel I and his army entered Rome and marginalized the Vatican. That stance continued all the way until the Second Vatican Council of Pope John in 1960, which sought to open up the Catholic Church to the winds of change. However, this was soon constrained by the more conservative Pope John Paul II. At the present time, Pope Francis is once again seeking to open up that church to wider horizons.

At the same time as these movements developed in Europe, the Christian faith grew by following exploration and global expansion into the remaining continents: South America, Africa, India, the Far East, and Australasia. In Russia and China, the growth of the church was forced underground through persecution at the same time as the New World continents saw an incredible expansion of faith. Walls has described this birth of the modern missionary movement as "the autumnal child of the Evangelical Revival."[9] The expansion of the worldwide church, which continues with us today, has predominantly emerged from the more anti-Enlightenment European church, developing into Pentecostalism and more traditional approaches. Now Christian membership in Africa alone far exceeds the European source from which it grew. In China, the Christian population has grown from 700,000 in 1949, when Western missionaries left, to 46 million—official figures—in 2018. Were unofficial churches to be included, some have postulated that this figure could rise to 100 million by 2020. By 2017, the Bible Society were distributing four million Bibles per year to 60,000 churches, with one being printed every second in 2018. Chinese Christians have themselves an aim to send out 100,000 missionaries to other countries in the next ten to twenty years.[10]

This divergence of the New World churches from the parent European church is of particular significance through the way the child has so flourished at a time when the parent body is languishing. This twin perspective of growth over the past 200 years highlights the issue of secularization, which we will need to refer to in chapter 10. But for the time being let us return to the Western Protestant church's reaction to the Enlightenment.

To begin with, the strongest current in this particular estuary channel flowed through the church, attempting to hold on to a kind of Christendom framework/maintenance model by assimilating itself into the new Enlightenment project. This was epitomized by the Latitudinarian "broad church" in England, which came to align itself with rationalist Enlightenment

9. Walls, *Missionary Movement*, 79.

10. Bible Society Journal, "Salt and Light," 4–5.

thinking. This accommodation continued later, through the Victorian Age, to the centrality of biblical criticism, the rise of the social gospel, the secular city/honest-to-God debates, and to the liberal radical constructivism of the twentieth century.

The alternative channel in the estuary expressed a more countercultural approach, a more outward-looking mission model compared to the maintenance model of the establishment. These more pietistic movements arose with a return to the centrality of God: an alternative to the anthropocentric ethos of the day. Whereas the former "orthodoxy emphasized the *objective* criterion of what God had done, and what the Bible taught; Pietists and separatist groups stressed the *subjective* criterion of personal spiritual experience."[11] This strand continued into the ministry of the Wesleys and George Whitfield, and the emergence of the Methodist and Evangelical revivals. This Second Awakening, at the end of the eighteenth century—following on from the First Awakening in the USA, from 1726–1760—was strongly influenced by the theology of the Presbyterian, Jonathan Edwards. He sought to combine both the objective emphasis on what God had done together with the personal, subjective, spiritual experience of faith. He "knew that Scripture without experience was empty, and experience without Scripture, blind."[12] This was carried into the English Revivals, where Methodism particularly offered an alternative to the enlightenment-influenced central Latitudinarian church body. It emphasized the need for spiritual transformation, but at the same time—as with the Moravians earlier—was deeply rooted in a commitment to serve the disadvantaged.

These themes continued on into the Anglican Evangelical Revival, which offered a more spiritual alternative, combined with the social action of Wilberforce against slavery, and Shaftsbury against child labor/harsh working conditions. All in all, at this time these revivals reflected an approach that diverged from the established church, which had aligned itself more closely to the philosophical framework of the day—the spirit of rationalism. This alternative "represented a fairly effective opposition, in some respects even an alternative, to the Enlightenment frame of mind."[13] That state of affairs continued on through the more solidified and static Victorian period up until the twentieth century. There the more Enlightenment-influenced social gospel approach vied with a more rigid evangelical party, with both being influenced by the Enlightenment framework far more than they realized. That was all to be put in disarray by the disarming of

11. Bosch, *Transforming Mission*, 277 (emphasis mine).

12. Niebuhr, *Kingdom of God in America*, 109.

13. Bosch, *Transforming Mission*, 281.

Enlightenment thinking and by the questioning of humanism through the arrival of postmodernism and relativism.

## 6.4 "TOMORROW IS ANOTHER COUNTRY"

Many in the Christian faith, having assimilated themselves into the accepted philosophical framework of the day, now found themselves in an embarrassing position as postmodernism began to deconstruct so many of the central tenets of the previous era. The faith/church found itself in the midst of a major paradigm shift within which we still exist. Having adjusted to the Enlightenment framework, the faith found that many of that framework's principle elements were being torn up, having made the effort to assimilate itself with Enlightenment perspectives, the faith found that the presuppositions of that era were being replaced through the continuing forward movement of knowledge, innovation, and achievement. Once again, the faith/church had been surprised and nonplused, as the furniture in the house that it thought was permanent was being thrown out of the window and replaced by new items and designs it had never before encountered.

With hindsight it is now possible to discern that this period of postmodern development has been as significant and far reaching of a turning point as the Enlightenment before it. We appear to be in the midst of a radical transformation of our structures of organization, technological abilities, anthropocentricity and our modus of thought and consciousness; a transition to techno/datacentricity.

By the mid-twentieth century, the mainstream liberal position of the churches had acknowledged the Enlightenment emphasis on scientific knowledge and reasoning. At the same time, the evangelical movement clung onto the absolute and objective base of the biblical text. Both approaches, however, were in for a shock. The primary tenets of the postmodern framework were that there is no single worldview, that no truth is absolute, that the individual is less significant than community.

The emphasis on the relative nature of truth cut to the heart of Christian thinking, which can be popularly illustrated by the refereeing of a football or rugby match. Take the example of two imaginary football games, one before and one during the World Cup 2018 in Russia. Before going to Russia, Harry Kane plays for Tottenham. He is fouled in the penalty area and the team calls for a penalty. The referee sees the action but doesn't award a penalty. Later, in the *BBC Match of the Day* program, his action is reviewed by the football pundits. The referee had decided from where he stood that it was not a foul. However, the pundits reviewed video footage from five different camera angles and decided it was a foul. So was it a foul or not? Well it all depended on from where you were looking. Now travel to Russia, where all the games had a VAR (Video Assistant Referee). If Harry Kane, the England captain, appeared to be fouled, the referee, from his viewpoint, might wave play on, rejecting any appeal. But his decision might not be accepted. The VAR team, in the stands, having access to all the different camera angles, might overrule the pitch referee and call for a free kick to be given. The first example illustrates the objective decision of absolute fact taken by the referee. "It was not a foul." But in the second example the original decision taken by the referee was overturned. After viewing all the different subjective camera angles, the action was determined to be a foul. One action, but two very different conclusions, all depending on where you stood.

So all sides of the Christian faith found that, what they once considered to be the objective foundations of their religious framework, were now being deconstructed by differing subjective viewpoints. For those who like long words, the first approach was termed objectivism, propositional absolutes, naïve realism, and the second was termed radical constructivism, radical perspectivism.

In the light of this dilemma, theologians came up with a response, not unlike another sporting example, this time taken from a real incident that occurred during the Rugby Lions tour of New Zealand in 2017. In the second test, Sonny Bill Williams of New Zealand seriously fouled a Lions player and the referee considered giving him a red card. The referee consulted his two linesmen, and then the video referee—TMO—who in effect gave conflicting and inconclusive advice. In the end the French referee, having considered all this advice, decided to give the red card—the first time an All-Black player had ever been sent off in a test on home soil. After the game there was a huge debate about the action taken, but in the end most people agreed that the referee's decision was correct. That event illustrated the response some theologians, such as Tom Wright, Walter Brueggemann, and Middleton and Walsh[14] have given to the dilemma they faced. Having considered all the different views and options, they settled on an intermediary way between the absolute and total relativity, veering between an emphasis on objectivity (critical realism) on the one hand, and on a more subjective approach (perspectival realism) on the other.

Such a viewpoint does accept that there will be a variety of camera angles interpreting differently what actually happened, whether it be in the smallest detail of a football stadium or radio waves from beyond the solar

14  Middleton and Walsh, *Truth is Stranger*.

system. However, within the context of evolutionary time, the viewpoint also has an understanding of God's overarching presence as a referee, which exceeds our imagination and our conscious thought processes, our own personal camera angles. This viewpoint believes that it is possible to hold these two truths together in the same way as light being seen to travel in both waves and particles. There are indeed many camera angles catching the event on the field, together with pundits offering the different individual opinions, but at the same time there is also one referee who makes a decision that stands forever once the final whistle has been blown.

Another significant postmodern issue that the Christian faith has had to contend with relates to the issue of time. Because technological innovation is developing so fast, the present is seen to be far more significant than the past or future. We are of the "now" generation: the past is irrelevant and outdated, the future is impossible to discern; both can be discounted; neither what happened in the German goalmouth in 1966, nor whether the next World Cup will be played in the searing daytime heat of Qatar, is of interest. The only fact we really know is that France are world champions now. That is all that counts in the here and now. We are called to live the consumerist dream, because that is what surrounds our present experience.

Now interestingly, whereas on the issue of relativism the theologians discovered a middle way that sought to take account of both its tradition and its new context, on the issue of time, Walter Brueggemann[15] has come up with a more countercultural response. Instead of acknowledging that the past and the future were of less significance than the present, he argues that, instead, we should always frame the present within the context of the past and the future. Rather than absolutizing the present, we should show appreciation to the past and future. Brueggemann has consistently emphasized the rich biblical past, with its emphasis on the created order, the significance of the individual, and the central role of the community. By taking on such biblical insights, Brueggemann sees the here and now as taking on a fresh complexion.

As well as an emphasis on our past biblical heritage Brueggemann, together with Jurgen Moltmann,[16] have also highlighted the significance of the future, stressing the inevitable consummation of our present world order; that God will not quit until God has had his full way in the world. They see hope and promise constantly expanding the horizons of the present. Therefore, as we learn to trust how the fullness of God's promises in the past, have led to transformation in people's lives, so too we can expect that

15. Breuggemann, *Texts Under Negotiation.*
16. Moltmann and Leitch, *Theology of Hope.*

biblical promises of hope, within the future, will be fulfilled, as the present continuously unfolds.

So, as the Enlightenment framework crumbled in the face of post-modern relativism and pluralism, the faith once again had to adapt to very different presuppositions, arising out of exponential technological develop-ments, and an explosion of pluralism resulting from "the first ever massive voluntary migration of population to other lands, creating a heady mixture of customs, beliefs, foods and religions."[17] This time the response to the paradigm shift in society will need to discern a more appropriate balance between becoming contextual, and outworking the responsibility to be counter-cultural.

However, what also needs to be acknowledged is that, whereas the existing church views postmodernism's relativism, the primacy of the pres-ent, and the negation of any concept of a single universal worldview, from the security of its past traditional, Christendom context, today's Generation Z and following generations do not have the benefit of such a theological background. They are growing up in a post-Christendom age, where post-modern tenets are the norm, with little opposition to them. This generation has to understand and articulate their faith to friends, family, and associates as they live their lives in a post-Christendom age, totally surrounded by postmodern presuppositions. In many ways they stand in a similar position to Christian believers in the first century. They have to articulate and of-fer their faith to a population totally devoid of any Christian framework or understanding, people who don't accept the Bible as an authority, who put no store in the church as an institution or the services and beliefs it seeks to sell. Their position—that of the postmillennial—is therefore very different from the average church congregation of today.

## 6.5 ENGAGING TOMORROW'S WORLD

Although society today exhibits considerable affinity with postmodern trends, there are ways in which today's society is moving on from the heady initial impact of postmodernism in the late twentieth century. It may be more difficult to articulate and detail, but the millennium and our lead up to the third decade presents once again the church with a fresh context with which to acclimatize itself, to address fresh questions and dilemmas, and to discover appropriate countercultural contributions. Being in the center of this exercise, it is hard to identify how the church is responding. However, before making reference to areas with which the church should engage, it

17. Cundy, *Tomorrow is Another Country*, 9.

might be worth reminding ourselves of the key postmillennial issues that could well influence our future dramatically.

At the millennium, Bill Joy, then Chief Scientist at Sun Microsystems, in his famous article in *Wired*,[18] suggested that, in the light of Moore's Law, computers would be one million times more powerful by 2030 than in 2000. Today, after eighteen years, Moore's Law appears to continue to hold, implying that computer power continues to multiply exponentially. Bill Joy highlighted three key areas of significance in this developing climate: genetic engineering, nanotechnology, and robotics. We are already a long way along these roads, with considerable practical and ethical questions unanswered. Genetically modified crops are still in their infancy. They bring huge advances in food production, but fears of uncontainable pandemic side effects still remain. Hawking and Rees' imaginings of human enhancement leading to superhumans is clearly only a theory. Nanotechnology, in its primary meaning—the technique of molecular construction—is still not yet in sight, despite its presence in biological life forms, but it remains a very achievable target in the minds and pockets of a number of major investors. Were it to be achieved it would have an unimaginable effect on production, labor, and on society as a whole. In robotics and artificial intelligence, huge strides have already been taken, with many benefits gained, with machines, in an increasing number of instances, becoming more intelligent than humans. The holy grail of having a sentient, conscious computer—artificial general intelligence—remains more of a dream than a reality. Again, wherever or whenever this breakthrough takes place, it will have a monumental effect on practice and ethics on a global scale.

As these achievements and their potential development interact and amplify each other, the questions of "out of control replication" and "grey goo" become increasingly vibrant. The question of the ethical aspect of every potential development is referred to, but very little appears to be done. As well as referring to Moore's Law, Bill Joy also refers to Murphy's law—"If anything can go wrong, it will." He infers and reminds us that once Pandora's Box has been opened, no idea can ever be put back inside. He suggests that ethical debate is not keeping up with technological capability, that even in 2000—quoted earlier—"we are being propelled into this new century with no plan, no control, no brakes."[19] As we have seen, this comment in 2000 has been reiterated in the recent House of Lords Report on artificial intelligence.

What makes new ethical guidelines hard to establish is the dethroning of the Enlightenment's emphasis on universal rationality/norms.

18. Joy, "Why the Future Doesn't Need Us."

19. Joy, "Why the Future Doesn't Need Us," 13.

Postmodernism has veered away from a one-size-fits-all approach, empha-sizing instead more of the local, the relevant, the particular aspects found in pluralist societies. Agreeing to a definitive code of conduct is therefore much harder to achieve. Universal truth, and in consequence universal eth-ics and morals, could be compared to catching a goldfish in a goldfish bowl.

With regard to the issue of continuous growth—central to the whole capitalist enterprise—many would argue that increasing the size of the pizza is not sustainable in the long term. Even now it comes at considerable eco-logical cost which the planet cannot afford; it comes at a cost of increased inequality that appears uncontainable, where the proceeds of growth are consumed by a rich minority at the expense of a poor majority. It perpetu-ates the myth that accumulating substance and possessions is the primary way of achieving happiness and contentment.

A further point, already referred to, involves the clear move from an anthropocentric society towards a technocentric society. Thoughts of the future will always include questions concerning the centrality of the human individual as compared to the intelligence and capability of the machine. Uncertainty, already present in postmodernism, has multiplied in the search for empirical human identity. Relativism continues to raise the question: "What is real?" Witness, for example, the popularity of films such as *Blade Runner* and *Blade Runner 2049*.

These questions of ethics concerning "Who is able to apply the brakes?" concerning the difference between benevolent and malevolent develop-ment, covering the issue of unexpected consequences, are all matters that face the church as it seeks to swim in the torrent, away from the safety of real river banks. They flag up a torrential paradigm shift that shows no hint of calming down. As well as having to acclimatize contextually, the Christian faith has to search to discover the enormous possibilities of a countercul-tural contribution in this melting pot of technological development.

In its 1996 workbook on postmodernism, *Tomorrow is Another Coun-try*, the Anglican UK Board of Education referred to having "an aspiration to universal standards of meaning and truth."[20] It criticized postmodernism for its "provisionality and awareness of our historical, social and cultural positioning."[21] It called instead for a reiteration of the belief that a base truth of the Christian faith was that "the meaning of God is inseparable from a sense of the totality of life."[22] This key presupposition lies at the heart of any desire to discover meaning and truth amongst all the questions being raised.

20. Cundy, *Tomorrow is Another Country*, 19.
21. Cundy, *Tomorrow is Another Country*, 19.
22. Cundy, *Tomorrow is Another Country*, 19.

It challenges postmodernism's dilution of the concept of universal truth and knowing. It offers a significant perspective on both progress and relationships as technology opens up wider horizons. It should form the basis of any countercultural contribution to a society that is still dependent upon a humanist philosophical framework. It should spotlight the existence and the nature of the relationship between the creator and the created as an alternative to the headlong pursuit of progress, prosperity, and growth through any form of innovation that technology can provide. It should question worldviews based on individuality, substance, and possession, as compared to those based on relationships between the creator and the created, between person and person, between humanity and its environment. It must insist that the "Thou" of Martin Buber's "I-Thou," which may be beyond human comprehension, is actually resonant with our inner being, endorsed by the view that "the unity and dynamism of the expanding universe are given coherence and symmetry by the forcefield of God's covenantal care."[23] It should affirm such a framework as a viable alternative to the view that we are simply here through providence, through chance, through molecules bootstrapping themselves into greater organisms. It should affirm that any way forward for humanity needs to provide for all of its inhabitants, and not just for a privileged few.

Through each era, as has been illustrated, the Christian faith has attempted to stay close to the organs of power in society. It has rubbed shoulders with emperors, kings, rulers, and philosophers, in order to maintain a close proximity to power. In doing so, it has diluted its contribution to meaning, hope for the future, and fulfillment for humankind, with the 1980s exception when the church took on an opposition role against Maggie Thatcher's policies and the effect they were having on the disadvantaged. It needs to recognize, in this latest paradigm shift, that, once again, the center of power has shifted. Having moved from emperor to king of nation-states, to philosophic enlightenment, it is now in the process of moving toward Silicon Valley giants, the controllers and manipulators of data. Investors, innovators, producers, and profit-takers are increasingly circulating around the big five or six distributors and their economic, accountancy shadows, the big four together with their Chinese counterparts. The Christian faith has, therefore, not only to engage contextually, but also to fearlessly discover a countercultural and prophetic role. Instead of being seduced by power and substance, the faith/church should rather critique development from the point of view of human identity and equality, from the point of view of relationships between people, from the point of view of someone above and

---

23. Fowler, *Faithful Change*, 195.

beyond human knowledge and possessions, from an infinite horizon rather than from the limits of finite imagination and innovation.

It should involve itself in the turmoil within society, affected and transformed by technological development, drawing attention to the significance and relevance of Jesus' two commandments to love, to the guidelines for life expressed in the Ten Commandments; to the "fundamental condition of trust and loyalty, mutual regard and ethical sensitivity required for human conditions to flourish"[24] supremely exhibited and visualized in the life of Jesus Christ.

24. Fowler, *Faithful Change*, 196.

# Chapter 7

## A Tsunami of Threats

In part 2, we have gone back historically, and then journeyed with the history of the Christian faith up until the present day; noting its strong attempt to contextualize each step of the way, with weaker attempts at a more counter-cultural approach. This journey focused on the development of faith, particularly in relation to power and the power brokers, of society in each era.

As we follow this through to the end of the twentieth century, the primary theme continues but is joined by a number of other related issues. This period could be described as a crisis of identity. Up until this time the faith/church were just about holding their own, though admittedly in a minority position. However, by the end of that century, the church was facing a tsunami of threats, seen more clearly in the Anglican scene but present elsewhere in different forms. They involved a crisis of central funding, increasing difficulties in sustaining a professional ministerial workforce, overheads for building maintenance, and an imbalanced age demographic spectrum. Underneath the headlines lay three major issues, each with deep historical roots, some of which we have already touched on.

The first root relates to what the church has accumulated down through the centuries—a close association with authority, status, power, wealth, property, and substance. The second root lies in its dependence on a professional functional ministerial leadership, originating from the Ignatian threefold order, at the expense of making full use of the ministry of the baptized—seen clearly in Roman Catholic and Anglican circles but also present in other authority structures. A third root returns to the theme of contextualization. The church has indeed contextualized, in each century;

however, the church is now struggling to contextualize with this new era, leaving it out of touch with emerging generations.

All of these roots lead up to the trunk of the tree: a question of identity. Is the faith/church prepared for the third decade? Does its image, its structure, its outer identity, its forms of ministry and communication, its relevance, truly reflect its inner identity, its message? Can it confidently respond to the Marshall McLuhan dictum that the medium is the message?[1] Is it really capable, in its present form, of harvesting a crop of faithful believers in an era when hierarchies are being undermined by networks, where innovation starts at the perimeters, where place and plant are less significant than streams of connectivity, where relationships are being threatened by algorithms?

There is a pessimistic view that, at this point in time, the church is so drawn to KTLO—keeping the lights on—that it cannot reach out into the future, that it is so survival-oriented that it is paralyzed like rabbits caught in the oncoming headlights. Both George Lings and Andrew Walls[2] warn that, despite sodal alternative breakout movements—such as fresh expressions—regularly arising, there remains a real danger that the mainline modal institutional train is fast closing in on the buffers. Walls goes on to point out that often, it is only facing up to these significant and distinct cultural changes in cultural context, that energizes the church to change course: "indeed on several occasions this transition took place only just in time, that without it the Christian faith must surely have withered away."[3] So, with that warning in mind, let us focus on both the roots and the surface of our present landscape before going, in part 3, to consider possible ways forward for the future.

## 7.1 ROOTS IN THE PAST

First, the church is facing a crisis with the power and status structure that it still maintains within its place in society, cultural traditions, and ethical norms. That structure has been accumulated ever since the time of Constantine in AD 313, through its position in relation to the state, the status quo, tradition, and Britishness; through its dedication to stability, orthodoxy, and unity; through its accumulation of capital wealth, property, substance, and prestige. That position, despite secularization, continues to confer some degree of status and position in society even though it grows weaker as time goes by.

1. McLuhan, *Understanding Media.*
2. Walls, *Missionary Movement*, 22–25.
3. Walls, *Missionary Movement*, 22.

Secondly, the church remains wedded to a hierarchical/authoritative controlling image, a status identity, a traditional presence. Maintaining this hierarchical structure, that in the past provided it with considerable benefits, is now becoming out of place in a digital world. The upkeep of this and its governance structures involves responsibility for a vast array of historical and expensive-to-maintain buildings, a collection of the nation's architectural treasures, a dependence on church buildings as a tangible evidence/witness of faith itself. All of these have now become a millstone around the neck of a dwindling and aging membership. The deep roots of this accumulation now make it virtually impossible for many established denominations to extract themselves from their present predicament without a disintegration of their core structures.

The third root concerns the ministry of the church. From the second century, the church decided to follow the path of a formalized leadership structure. In doing so it put on one side its earlier strength and dependence on the direct ministry of its membership—the baptized. That representational, elite-trained ministerial order has taken center stage, and in the process has deskilled the rest of the body of Christ. The dependence on those orders of ministry is now being highlighted by the inability to select, train, and pay for them, and by the fact that the laity are ill-equipped to take over that ministry and witness.

The fourth root concerns contextualization. During the second and third era, already described, from Constantine through the Enlightenment to the late twentieth century, the church's hierarchical structure was developed in the light of its context. Hierarchical order suited the ethos of those centuries. However, this fourth era of the information and digital age has seen the demise of top-down hierarchies at the expense of more lateral horizontal networking operations. Now, the church is struggling to contextualize yet again with this fresh networking context. As a result, not only is it top-heavy, not only does it struggle with grassroots innovation and networking, but it also fails to connect with young people, whose lives center around mobile, digital networking social communications. The church's roots in stability, control, and orthodoxy are out of kilter with peripheral innovation, instant decision-making, and creative participation—the hallmarks of the third decade.

So now let us look in greater detail at the tsunami of threats facing the church under the two headings of "A Crisis of Structure" and "A Crisis of Ministry."

## 7.2 A CRISIS OF STRUCTURE

As the church struggles to maintain its positioning in this challenging century, it continues to be daunted by and bombarded with a whole range of structural burdens that restrict its mission and ministry. This preoccupation has distracted it from having a fundamental reappraisal of its *raison d'etre*. In the light of these demanding overheads, there are already signs of an ordered retreat into suburban areas of strength, at the expense of areas of high population and need such as inner cities/outer housing estates, and lowly populated rural areas. These overheads include large, expensive administrations that far exceed the requirements of a small, aging, and diminishing membership: responsibility for a huge number of expensive-to-maintain historic buildings; a shortage of running costs to cover central administration; and an overdependence on a shrinking cadre of expensive professional operators. All of these are before one gets to the age spectrum of the membership, and the extraordinarily difficult ethical questions thrown up by the oncoming era.

### 7.2.1 Structure and Purpose

Perhaps the greatest baggage of all can be found in the church's *raison d'etre* concerning their image and purpose. As previously mentioned in part 1, Dee Hock[4] stresses that the purpose and principles of an organization need to be addressed long before the concepts of structure and implementation. However, very often the structure of the church appears to totally overshadow the original purpose and message of Jesus Christ. Structure is, as it were, acting as an overwhelming and overweight carapace that engulfs the shrinking human membership lying within it. The predominant feature of the church is that its structure dominates the purpose, while the medium (outer identity) is not reflecting the message (inner identity).

    The structure itself can be very hierarchical, centering around a top-down clerical administration which is delivered through order, power, control, and coercion: "through the right of some to lord it over others by means of power, wealth sharing and titles."[5] The hierarchical structure is overwhelmed by its responsibility for its professional workforce, its administration of a large number of buildings, and a significant financial portfolio. These tasks are very much at odds with the kernel of the Christian faith: a band of believers, inspired by Christ, empowered by his spirit, spreading

---

4. Hock, *Birth of the Chaordic Age.*

5. Wink, *Engaging the Powers*, 112.

good news and enfleshing a kingdom vision for humanity. On the basis of that comparison, the medium does not reflect the message, and the structure does not reflect the purpose. As we have seen with the previous two eras, the church continues to identify itself with power, and hesitates to follow Christ's example of identifying with vulnerability, suffering, and the marginalized, opposing powerful structures and authorities in the process.

Walter Wink, as quoted by Lesslie Newbigin, has pointed out

> The victory of the Church over the demonic powers which was embodied in the Roman imperial system, was not won by seizing the levers of power: it was won when the victims knelt down in the Coliseum and prayed in the name of Jesus for the Emperor. The soldiers of Christ's victorious army were not armed with weapons of this age; they were martyrs whose robes were washed in blood.[6]

These illustrations of the serious mismatch between a hierarchical structure maintained by order, domination, and coercion, and the purpose/message of Christ, highlight a strong hint of hypocrisy. The church insists its message is one of love and sacrifice, yet the outer structure speaks a very different language—one of order, authority, control, and sexual abuse. Such a mismatch can be hypocritical to younger enquirers, and off-putting to humanists and atheists, who easily see through this moral disjunction.

## 7.2.2 Hierarchies and Networks, Stages of Development

As the church considers engaging with this changing context it has begun to realize that within the church as a whole there are very different interpretations as to what it means to be church. In his book, *Church in Every Context*, Michael Moynagh makes a clear distinction between "inherited church" and emerging "fresh expressions" of church. The former are happiest in more traditional forms of worship, while the latter seek new forms of worship, new structures, new ways of relating to the local community. These can include issue-centered groups as distinct from locality-centered groups.

This identification of two fairly distinct approaches to being church takes us back to some earlier research undertaken by James Fowler.[7] Although his work was primarily addressed at the development of individual faith, it is not difficult to transpose the analysis into different faith communities and church life. Just as individuals develop a life of faith, so too

6. Newbigin, *Gospel in a Pluralist Society*, 210.

7. Fowler, *Stages of Faith*.

church communities develop in a similar fashion. And just as individual believers react to change in different ways, so too church communities can react differently to change in a similar fashion.

What makes Fowler's research relevant to this discussion is the way it can be seen to foresee the different responses to change depicted in inherited and fresh expressions attitudes.

Reflecting on how individuals and communities engage with change, he identifies six stages that individuals go through that deeply affect how they view their beliefs, and how those beliefs then embed themselves in particular forms of institutional church. He identifies these stages, practices, and attitudes in day-to-day church life. These stages reflect the various reactions to change that both individuals and church life exhibit in relation to personal preference for particular forms of worship and activities. Such an analysis fits into the context of change, that of a hierarchical organization seeking to come to terms with a networking society. It also relates to situations where top-down central order is challenged by bottom-up innovative diversity and by fresh questioning arising from technological development. Fowler bases this work on Carl Jung's sociological and psychological approach. His analysis of these stages of change can be seen to synchronize with the concepts of organizational change described by Cassels, Alberts and Hayes, and Charles Handy. His later stages also correspond to the principles adhered to by Dee Hock in his establishment of Visa International. The area of Fowler's work that meshes into the present position of the church is found in his description of stages three to six in faith development.

## STAGE THREE

This "Synthetic-Conventional" stage is related to an external faith expressed in many traditional churches today—Michael Moynagh's "inherited church." The faithful, and the churches they support, are hierarchical in nature, dominated by a top-down established authority and structure; deeply held traditional convictions; and a place of order, conformity, stability, and equilibrium where members feel at home. They are confident and certain about the basis of their faith, but have difficulty facing vulnerability and in communicating their faith to anyone outside their cultural bubble.

## STAGE FOUR

Those individuals and churches, described as "individualistic-reflective" on the other hand, are far less confident and certain. They are not constrained by authority; they feel challenged by complexity, by issues of change and questions of faith raised by society that aren't easily answerable; they want to personally engage with and respond to pluralist social circumstances; they realize that truth is not tied down to traditional symbols, that complexity needs to be thought through; they want to move forward but are uncertain as to how to proceed. All of these attitudes threaten a stage 3 organization. This might lead them to breaking away from a stage 3 church, or, on the other hand, develop what might be described as fresh expressions, within that stage 3 church, thereby creating a mixed economy, a two systems-one organization structure. But all of this leaves a stage 4 mindset uncertain and unsatisfied, with their previous simplicity of faith being confronted by the complexity of life. They struggle with growing into a more mature faith.

## STAGE FIVE

Fowler sees this stage as being about "conjunction," Jung's term—following Nicholas de Cusa—for "being able to hold opposites together in a single frame."[8]

Conjunction can be illustrated by the definition of light. In the past, light was just seen as passing from its source to a person's eye at a speed of 186,000 mph. Now it is recognized that light not only travels as particles, but also as waves—simultaneously. In terms of straight-line, cause-and-effect rationality, this is simply impossible. Yet at the same time scientists believe it to be true. Believing in both methods of travel indicates that truth is stranger than it used to be. Conjunction is about being at home in a world where apparent opposites/divergences can be held together within a single frame of understanding.

Individuals and churches, seeking to hold apparently opposing viewpoints in tension rather than through polarization, would come under Fowler's stage five. They personally experience and accept the existence of complexity, and feel drawn to engage with it. They realize that truth is not absolute and can relate to experience. Although this approach might separate them from stage 3 individuals/churches, they are more likely to be drawn into the communities within which they reside. They don't need to exist in their own cultural bubble because they are happy living in the complexity surrounding other people's lives. They may also have experienced pain and suffering along the way as they grappled with the dark questions inhabiting stage 4. It will be that grappling experience, that seeking after conjunction, that acceptance of paradox being part of truth itself, that will better

8. Fowler, *Faithful Change*, 174.

equip them to stand upright and be committed to justice despite the complex questions/experiences surrounding them.

## STAGE SIX

This stage is about those who have learned to hold diversity in tension themselves, and at the same time encourage others to participate. They have a wish to take their transforming vision of the world, and turn it into the single mission of their lives; it is a stage that is often accompanied by suffering, and in some instances may lead to death. Names of such charismatic people are often on our lips, from Ghandi to Florence Nightingale, Oliver Tambo to Helen Suzman, from Mother Theresa to Trevor Huddleston, from Oscar Romero of Recife, Brazil, to David Sheppard in East London and Liverpool.

In a later book Fowler takes these six stages further. He likens the later stages to the key stages of development in Western society, which can in turn be linked to the different stages of church and individual development. In stage 3—"orthodox temper"—Fowler believes, churches and individuals owe their strength to pre-enlightenment conditions and understandings of truth. He sees their faith based on absolute truths, legitimized by church or biblical authority. They resemble pre-Enlightenment modes of thinking and experiencing . . . (adhering to) an implicit, tacitly held ideology . . . explicit formulas and slogan . . . (and) not likely to have a critically reflective conceptual grasp on the worldview they espouse."[9] He sees such churches as deeply hierarchical "with leadership elites enjoying the same implicit sanction of natural or divinely ordained authorization.[10]

Stage 4 individuals and communities, Fowler suggests, are more at home with the Enlightenment framework, where traditional authorities are being questioned through objective criteria and a scientific mindset. They are suspicious of the authority of traditional leaders or texts. Rather they,

> reserve the right of individual review and personal revision of received traditions, based upon experience, reason, and coming to terms with new circumstances and continually changing conditions.[11]

9. Fowler, *Stages of Faith*, 165.

10. Fowler, *Stages of Faith*, 167.

11. Fowler, *Stages of Faith*, 169.

If certain sacred cows of a stage 3 mindset have to be sacrificed then so be it. Fowler then goes on to identify stage 5 with the conjunctive thinking encouraged by Jung—"the ability to hold opposites together in a single frame."[12] He sees this as being more appropriate to a postmillennial society dispensing with hierarchies in favor of more networking forms of organization. Fowler describes this millennial time as being on a "watershed in the evolution of cultural consciousness."[13] He sees both the orthodox—pre-Enlightenment, stage 3—and the progressive—Enlightenment, stage 4—approaches as being under threat and somewhat inappropriate for the complexity and plurality of the millennial mindset. He therefore espouses this more conjunctive approach—stage 5—as being more appropriate to the networking communications, economic interdependence, plurality of cultures, growing ethnic conflict, and ecological red flags of our present century.[14]

---

### FRANCES YOUNG

As the millennium approached, Frances Young wrote *Face to Face* as a theological reflection on her relationship with her disabled son Arthur. In doing so she offered a living illustration of a conjunctive approach to the complexity of life/humanity, raised by her son's handicap. In seeking to come to terms with her son's severe mental disability and the resulting question of what it means to be human, she became very aware of "how society copes with anomalies and ambiguities,"[15] which lies at the heart of pluralistic and postmillennial experience.

Young herself illustrates conjunctivity within her own personality. By profession she was Professor of Theology at Birmingham University, a widely acclaimed scholar of international repute who was also an ordained Methodist minister. At the same time she was the mother of a disabled child. She was a "social worker's client, the recipient of social benefits, and a vulnerable patient—or at least the parent of one."[16] She had two very different personae that she did her best to hold together—illustrated in the book in question. Her search for understanding began with challenging questions arising from her two very different situational experiences/environments. It led her toward recognizing a number of paradoxes in how she saw the very nature of God. She realized she had to hold in tension— in conjunction—both, "the love and wrath of God, the 'now' and the 'not yet,' divine initiative and human responsibility." She understood that she had to "live with the fact that Christ is human and divine, that the Scriptures are the product

---

12. Fowler, *Faithful Change*, 174.

13. Fowler, *Stages of Faith*, 172.

14. Fowler, *Stages of Faith*, 173.

15. Young, *Face to Face*, 171.

16. Young, *Face to Face*, 217.

of human history and culture, yet the word of God, that Christ is the fulfillment of God's promises and yet there is still sorrow and sighing," that God's being was both "personal yet beyond the personal, passionate yet beyond the passionate."[17]

Young resonates with Fowler's stages 3 to 5, describing them as interveners (God's hand everywhere), rationalizers (responsibility rests with us), and inbetweeners (sheer complexity allows for diversity).[18] She describes the latter as a "garden run wild" where "we have to live without total explanation."[19] She epitomizes this in her description of the nature of God, who is in one sense an,

> ocean of love that can absorb all the suffering of the world and purge it without being polluted or changed by it. And yet at the same time in Christ He subjected himself to personal involvement in pain and anguish, so that in some sense He genuinely knows what it feels like to be a victim and shares in our experience of suffering."[20]

Young experiences this tension as a personal struggle similar to that experienced by Jacob when he fought with a man at the ford of Jabbok. Like Jacob, she is looking for a blessing, as she seeks to come to terms with her son's mental and physical disability.

The journey of Young's search for a wholeness to humanity reflects the empathy she developed with Arthur. Despite the fact that society would highlight the clear distinction between her full humanity and his distinct handicap, she concluded "Arthur is a whole person as much as I am. I am a handicapped person as much as he is."[21] Not only was Young conjunctive in her own person but she was also able to bring that to bear with both her empathetic and emotional relationship with Arthur, as well as in her rarified academic, theological exploration into the nature of God. Her ultimate peace of mind surely indicates a blessing equal to that bestowed on Jacob at the ford of Jabbok.

Such a framework, put forward by Fowler, questions the adequacy in today's response of having separate elements within a mixed economy, those who emphasize an orthodox, inherited approach, and those who present a more progressive, fresh expressions questioning approach. Such an approach could be seen as a staging post, but not as a satisfactory end-point. Instead Fowler points out the watershed nature of the postmodern/millennial

17. Young, *Face to Face*, 235.
18. Young, *Face to Face*, 226.
19. Young, *Face to Face*, 227.
20. Young, *Face to Face*, 239.
21. Young, *Face to Face*, 107.

paradigm and calls for a more conjunctive approach that can live with, handle, and contribute to the complexity, plurality, and global/local nature of our emerging world culture. But more of that in part 3.

Interestingly, Fowler's approach is not all that dissimilar to two other writers, one writing before him and one writing after him. Before him, Frederick von Hugel describes three stages of Christian development: institutional (where we start our journey deeply influenced by others beside us), critical (as we mature we begin to criticize certain aspects of that institution and question its beliefs and practices), and thirdly mysticism and spirituality (centering around a deeply considered prayer life). After Fowler, Brian McLaren, from an emerging church movement perspective, describes an approach of generous orthodoxy, not all that dissimilar to Fowler's conjunctive stage 5. He writes about going beyond the false certainties of modernism and the uncertainty of pluralistic relativism toward a third alternative—emergent models of Christian growth.[22] But here he appears less clear as to what might comprise this third way.

## 7.2.3 Personal Preferences–Individual Bias

A further aspect within the dynamic of structural change between hierarchies and networks lies in a differentiation between an institution, which develops out of intellectual thought, analysis and orthodoxy, and a community, centered around a mutual experience of personal faith, networked through the interaction of individual lives. John Taylor illustrated this with the phrases "knowing *about* Mt Kilimanjaro" through pictures, videos, and books, and "knowing *of* the mountain" by climbing it.[23] As has already been mentioned, Taylor[24] goes on to differentiate the "cerebral" from the "experiential." Harari[25] similarly describes the differences between the "narrative" side of the brain and the "experiential" side. The intellectual, narrative, knowing about emphasis, leads on to organizational structure, orthodoxy, and rules, whereas knowing of Christ through a personal individual experience is less likely to be taught by a traditional church and more likely to be caught by a networking community.

Similarly, as already mentioned, the research work carried out by F. LeRon Shults and Steven J. Sandage on the "crucible model of transformation" suggests that there are two components to our spiritual journey, that

22. McLaren, *Generous Orthodoxy*, sec. 287.

23. Taylor, *Go-between God*, 13 (emphasis his).

24. Taylor, *Go-between God*, 220–22.

25. Harari, *Homo Deus*, 342–48.

of "*dwelling*" and that of "*seeking*."[26] Our first step centers around a "cycle of spiritual dwelling that involves relating to the sacred in ways that feel familiar, comfortable and safe . . . (including) connection to a spiritual community and tradition that legitimizes certain rituals and spiritual practices and provides a sense of continuity."[27] This would equate to our understanding of being part of an established, traditional or inherited stage 3 church. A different step would lead us on to a "cycle of spiritual seeking . . . An experience of spiritual awakening . . . That is initially destabilizing . . . (and which) can feel scary to question one's community and tradition"[28]—Fowler's stage 4. These two steps are depicted as an inner and outer circle, which are interconnected. These circles depict that we can begin with an inner experience of dwelling that gives us safety and security and is comparatively inward-looking. We can then take steps to move out toward the outer circle, that of seeking. This circle looks outward to others and seeks wider, fresher, and more intense experiences of faith that can lead to a more deepened spiritual intimacy. It is both possible to remain in this cycle or to return to the dwelling cycle, refreshed by the seeking experience of faith.

This illustration of there being two possible elements to spiritual development ties in with the contemporary mixed economy analysis of church life as being inherited or fresh expressions, the first centering on a traditional structure (stage 3), the second veering toward fresh personal experiences of faith that empower people to look outwards (stage 4).

An allied connection to this research work can be found in the development of Jung's work on personality types by Myers and Briggs.[29] Although not popular with the scientific community, it is used extensively in training programs to develop leadership and management skills. Certainly, by identifying their four main types, they show how people view the world from different perspectives—how they gain energy, take in information, make decisions, and approach life. This can not only help people to identify their own innate preferences, but also enable them to understand how others might approach similar situations, with very different perceptions and consequent reactions.

When it comes to the nature of a mixed economy church, two different models can be identified. The first is a traditional, structural, hierarchical, cerebral narrative body. The second is an intuitive, experiential, innovative networking form of association. It could be argued that traditional

---

26. Shults and Sandage, *Transforming Spirituality*, 32; italics mine.

27. Shults and Sandage, *Transforming Spirituality*, 32.

28. Shults and Sandage, *Transforming Spirituality*, 33.

29. Hirsch and Kise, *Introduction to Type and Coaching*.

Ignatian-based hierarchical, inherited, cerebral, modal church structures are more likely to attract those who think factually "T," and make judgments 'J,' according to proscribed boundaries. Whereas more experiential fresh expressions, networked, sodal, ministry of the baptized, community-based faith groups are more likely to attract those who react intuitively "I," with feeling and perception, and "P," from the heart, rather than from the head.

These two areas of research, if put together with both Taylor and Harari's points, might suggest that anthropological and psychological aspects exist within the very nature of church. They might suggest that whereas some are innately drawn to an inherited, dwelling, cerebral, traditional stage 3 church, others are more easily attracted intuitively to a perceptive, experiential, seeking, heart-oriented, relational stage 4 approach to faith and belonging. Such a division does not discount the possibility of moving beneficially from one to the other.

However, such an analysis does not necessarily mean that hierarchy has to give way to networking, that the cerebral give way to the experiential, if the faith is to contextualize into the twenty-first century. All forms of activity and belief need some form of structure. The explosion of faith in New Testament times would always have needed some form of structure as it evolved with second- and third-generation Christians. The alternative to structure is anarchy, which in the long term leads only to other structures. Both Ferguson,[30] in his description of Sienna society as an interaction between the tower and the square, and Taylor,[31] in his articulation of "fusion" between the cerebral and the instinctual, "towards an integration of the two,"[32] both insist that the one needs the other, that a synthesis needs to be sought. Taylor suggests that "the Spirit of Truth, the enlightener, the bearer of discernment and understanding" is every much a part of the Christian faith as the "Creator Spiritus, the bracing energy, the rushing mighty wind sweeping along all the subterranean corridors below consciousness."[33] Such thinking leaves today's churches with a very real challenge: not to see how hierarchy can be deposed by networking, but rather how both hierarchy and network can so fuse together—in the principle of Sienna—to form alternative structures that do justice to both the networking ethos of the twenty-first century and also to the fullest understanding of the Trinitarian relationship between Father, Son, and Holy Spirit. Taylor suggests that this will come about only when human defenses are down, "broken either by

---

30. Ferguson, *Square and the Tower*.

31. Taylor, *Go-between God*, 220.

32. Taylor, *Go-between God*, 221.

33. Taylor, *Go-between God*, 221.

intense joy or by despair," that our shameful humiliation as Christians is a "prerequisite of a renewal of the Holy Spirit."[34] Just as the word "humiliation" is derived from "humus," soil, dung, so too fusion between structure and network can only truly be built from the bottom upwards.

## 7.2.4 Property and Buildings

Allied to the crisis of structures lies the future of buildings owned by the church and the crisis of central funding for the administration. Both of these issues are most clearly seen in the Anglican Church, but they still relate to all institutional churches in one way or another.

But to take the Anglican situation as an example, we see that buildings take up a great deal of organizational responsibility. Strong substantial pressure on church life concerns the cost/effort required to prevent so many historic, grade-one- and grade-two-listed buildings and churches from falling into rack and ruin. The report of the Church Buildings Review group has highlighted the depth of the situation. In rural areas, where only 17 percent of the population live, 91 percent of the churches are listed buildings. Concerning all grade-one-listed buildings, the Church of England is responsible for 45 percent of them, of which 75 percent are in rural areas.[35] Overall 78 percent—12,200—of Church of England churches are listed.[36] The task of building upkeep for these communities and congregations is unsustainable and totally burdensome for the clergy with primary responsibility for them. For the report to suggest that the only single solution for these maintenance responsibilities is for the church to grow seems ludicrous. Small congregations in low-population areas, with the existing upkeep responsibilities hampering them, have very little opportunity to address spiritual renewal and mission.

Although such tasks could be somewhat alleviated by reducing red tape, encouraging/facilitating multi-purpose usage, and enabling building maintenance to be handed over to community bodies, long-term sustainability—particularly with the reduction of clergy—can surely only be relieved by intervention from government and historic buildings authorities. The government's review on the sustainability of English churches and cathedrals has indeed presented their vision:

34. Taylor, *Go-between God*, 128.
35. Church Buildings Review Group, *Church Buildings Report Summary*, 1.
36. Taylor Review, *Sustainability of English Churches*, 11.

to create a more sustainable future for the buildings of the Church of England by empowering and assisting congregations to do even more to involve local communities in enjoying, valuing, using and caring for their Churches; introducing greater strategic oversight of maintenance and repair work.[37]

The report argues that responsibility for upkeep has been[38] and should continue to be[39] jointly held by government funding and local church communities. However they hope, in the long term, government funds will be reduced.[40] They describe a Future Funding Model, including Major and Minor Repair Funds, and a network of Community Advisory and Fabric Support Officers, as assisting local communities in the task of maintaining these buildings following on from the results of proposed Pilot Schemes.[41] However, their concept of reduced government funding, and their expectation that local communities will continue to "tirelessly commit their time and expertise . . .,"[42] together with the added responsibility of filling the gap left by reduced government support, appears to many as hopelessly unrealistic.

Both reports provide excellent analysis of the situation but appear to offer limited, inadequate, and dreamlike responses to the size and sustainability of the task at hand. The most likely result, therefore, will be that clergy and congregations will continue to be exhausted, depressed, and diverted from their primary function—that of pointing towards the crucified Christ and his empowering spirit.

Addressing this elephant in the room is certainly a huge issue to face. Church buildings have, for so long, been not only the substance of the church's place within the community, but also a symbol of its mission and ministry to the community. To walk away from those buildings would signify a departure from that part of the church's identity, which goes back to a centuries-old chain of witness. To hand over those buildings to the government or the community to sell them or allow them to crumble into rack and ruin, would take a great step of faith and reenvisioning. It would need a large imagination to believe that there is life after owner-occupancy. The substance identity of bricks and mortar would need to be replaced by

37. Taylor Review, *Sustainability of English Churches*, 12.

38. Taylor Review, *Sustainability of English Churches*, 17.

39. Taylor Review, *Sustainability of English Churches*, 17–18.

40. Taylor Review, *Sustainability of English Churches*, 18.

41. Taylor Review, *Sustainability of English Churches*, 19.

42. Taylor Review, *Sustainability of English Churches*, 19.

a new Christian identity, based on a Christlike quality of relationships between believers in community. Contemplating such a paradigm shift might benefit from the wisdom of the Umoja project—described later—from East Africa. Being released from church buildings would be like giving birth to elephants. "It takes time, requires a competent facilitator, can be unsettling for the existing leadership"[43] according to the Umoja website.

Together with that experience arising from East Africa, a linguistic point can be made from Spanish and other languages. Whereas English has only one word—"church"—to describe a building, a community, and a religious belief and culture, Spanish has a whole range of different words to describe each of these three different aspects of the one English word. What is lost when one physical aspect of identity, denoted by the word "church," is lost, can become the springboard to discover and relish other aspects of church identity waiting to be celebrated and owned.

## 7.2.5 Funding

The second element in maintaining present church structures lies in the area of central church finance, provision of running costs for the central administration of the organization. Over both of the twentieth and twenty-first centuries, statistics suggest that there has been a gradual reduction in those attending church. This reduction has been uneven in its distribution. Deep rural and inner-city areas have seen considerable decline, whilst suburban and city churches have remained comparatively buoyant—with popular commuter villages holding their own. The surveys normally cover numbers and may not do justice to the quality and depth of faith of those who attend. It is difficult therefore to say from the statistics that the faith itself is on the decline. In certain areas there is real evidence of growth.

However, the image of decline is strengthened when it comes to measuring the health of church structures. Large church structures often struggle as they expect diminishing memberships to cover increasing costs of plant maintenance, pay, and minister pensions. Weighty hierarchical structures regularly resist calls to be slimmed down. Of course, the central church organizations have considerable historic funding, but that has to be targeted increasingly to support urban ministry who struggle for lack of glebe/historic resources.

There is also anecdotal evidence that the burden of fundraising is increasingly being carried by the suburban churches, where numbers are holding up, so that they and the commuter villages are asked to cover and

43. Njoroge, et al., *Umoja Facilitator's Guide*, 30.

support the declining rural and inner-city congregations. Greater stress is added by some larger suburban and mega-city churches having strong theological positions which are frequently at odds with traditional central church attitudes. These churches often prefer to target their giving towards outreach and mission activities rather than towards the maintenance of self-perpetuating organizational structures.

Overall there is continuous disquiet from congregations having to pay increasing central and ministerial costs. Reflecting on this grassroots disquiet makes one realize that congregational members are, on the one hand, expected to give generously of their money and time to maintain the organization and its buildings. On the other hand, when it comes to the growth of spiritual life, faith, and belief, the vast majority of the laity are seen simply as consumers and recipients with no expectation of spearheading the church's spiritual mission to the world. Their contributions toward spiritual growth remain subservient to the professional clergy, who dominate both the spiritual and physical nature of the church.

## 7.2.6 Organizational Structure

The third element to all of these structural areas lies in the church's response to the issues that have peaked since the millennium. Most denominations and community church organizations face, to a greater or lesser degree, the challenge of organizational management interfering with, and distracting from, the spiritual and mission-oriented objectives/activities of the church: allowing the upholding and sustaining of the existing structures to take precedence over the empirical responsibility to witness to a transformed way of living; protecting the substance of the organization rather than focusing on the primary objective of relating to people on a face-to-face basis; concentrating on improving management skills rather than equipping the saints to live out and share the good news. Although there is much talk of fresh expressions, ordained pioneer ministers, focal ministries, church planting, and other sodal movements, the background assumption is centered around the professional ministry doing their best to uphold and reinvent a groaning home base. Such approaches raise the question as to whether focusing on management and ministers is the real and underlying issue, and whether or not it offers a realistic answer for the church's present dilemma.

Other ways of addressing crisis issues within the church have led authorities in a number of denominations to look at John Kotter's leadership and management approach, a dual-operating system described as "two structures-one organization."[44] Kotter argues that it is perfectly possible to formulate a two-tier system of organization, with order and policy being authorized at one level, and with implementation/innovation being encouraged at a different level. But the cohesion, trust, and communication required to make such an approach successful would be enormous—far beyond the imagination of traditional leadership, who would have to unilaterally relinquish so much of their control. Once again, these illustrations offer different possibilities for a church considering a change of leadership style; but effort, hard work, and trust would certainly dominate such a transition.

This concept above illustrates the possibility of both hierarchies and networks working together but in separate bubbles. It would allow the traditional church management to continue to operate in what has been termed inherited church mode, but at the same time sanction considerable flexibility, networking, and innovation to take place outside of these traditional rules, regulations, and management control. Those differing approaches would include pioneer ministries, fresh expressions, etc., and would allow more contemporary approaches to be developed amongst younger generations.

## FRESH EXPRESSIONS

This movement has been part of the established churches for around twenty-five years, and has grown to become a significant part of church activity in a number of denominations. The start-up rate of these new initiatives has grown since the publication of the *Mission Shaped Church* in 2004, making these church communities the largest and fastest-growing part of the church's presence.

The nature of a fresh expression of church, such as messy church, café church, child-focused church, and church plants, can be extremely varied with average numbers or attendees ranging from thirty-five to fifty-five. They are usually initiated by a small team from a parent church, often from a younger generation. They emphasize open-ended outreach, and a concern to build up faith and maturity, often expanding into areas in which traditional church struggles.

Research[45] on over 1,000 of these communities suggests both strength and growth, together with some frailty. Twenty-eight percent continue to grow numerically and 55 percent have broadly maintained the growth gained. Seventeen percent are shrinking, and 11 percent of those started have since died.[46] A majority of

44. Kotter, *Accelerate*, 5.
45. Lings, *Day of Small Things*, 2.
46. Lings, *Day of Small Things*, 2.

those initiated are now stable, and the overall movement is growing through the establishing of new initiatives.

This movement exhibits the growth of hybrid approaches to being church, with growth coming from innovation at the periphery of the church's influence, with the tradition and rules of the parent church structure being relaxed. The targets of the Chinese church—being self-sustaining, self-propagating and self-financing—are recognized, but not necessarily being met.

Such a movement particularly offers hope for growth amongst young people on the fringes, but doesn't indicate that it is a model appropriate to the whole church. The image of the "Fosbury flop"—a high-jump technique that completely transformed high-jumping methods in the 1960s—comes to mind. It may be an important expression of new ways of being church, but at present there are no signs that it will be a Fosbury flop for the parent organization, thereby transforming it totally.

These ministries have grown considerably over the past few years alongside existing traditional church structures, giving rise to the phrase introduced by Archbishop Rowan Williams of a "mixed economy", where the two approaches run alongside each other, similar to the tower and the square working together in Sienna. But to what degree there is any real fusion, or integration[47] between the two approaches is yet to be seen.

## 7.2.7 The Age Spectrum

The development of this mixed economy approach highlights the difficulties that churches face with the age spectrum of their regular membership. Since the 1960s, as societal attitudes and culture have changed dramatically, the age spectrum of church attendees has done likewise. Since then the average age of clergy and congregations has increased significantly—an Anglican report in 2020 stated that 68 percent of churches have less than five children/young people under sixteen attending each Sunday, with 38 percent having having no children at all. Of those children attending, 44 percent are to be found in just 6.4 percent of Anglican churches.[48] Rural and inner-city churches have aged most with fewer younger people joining. Suburban churches able to provide specific youth ministries have seen a significant increase of faith amongst young people. This is particularly true where peer groups can congregate together, and where a more socially and

47. Taylor, *Go-between God*, 221.

48. General Synod, *Report on Children and Youth Ministry*, 2.

theologically monochrome approach makes for more effective evangelism. Certainly, a clear authoritative proclamation of belief has an attraction for undecided, thinking adolescents and couples with younger families. The growth of consumerism has led to churches who can provide for the needs of children and young people, growing to the detriment of smaller, more limited congregations. Ease of travel has aided the breakdown of traditional parochial structures. So young people do attend, but they tend to congregate in more suburban churches.

However, it is important to recognize the depth of the issue. It is no longer simply a matter of a 1960s-type generation gap. The gap between parents and their Millennial/Generation Z children is on a different scale. Postmodern plurality, complexity, and rationality all create a very different environment/mindset. Fresh expressions and contemporary music/video technology and worship are not necessarily touching the deeper changes that are taking place in society.

In a world of novelty and hybridization—and of having to make sense of changing values, assumptions, objectives, and expectations—the faith journey/traditions of one's parents' generation, based on objective morality/spiritual truth, are becoming increasingly insignificant. The overwhelming ethos of inescapable uncertainty, surrounding complexity and choices, includes hesitancy about the proclamation of an absolute Creator. In Luther's day the technology of the printing press benefited the spread of the gospel, but today's technology could well have more negative effects. As David Kinnaman[49] has pointed out, enabling and encouraging the faith to flourish in the third decade requires far deeper thought than just changing the styles of worship. It is that which we will address in part 3.

## 7.2.8 Sodal Offshoots

Down through the centuries new approaches have regularly emerged out of traditional church structures. Dissatisfaction with the modal norm has resulted in sodal offshoots, as illustrated by the Anabaptists, Pietists, Moravians, and Mennonites in Europe, together with the Methodists, Baptists, and Congregationalists in England. A more contemporary illustration of these offshoots is that of many restoration/community churches, such as New Frontiers—established fifty years ago under the leadership of Terry Virgo—which are growing and expanding today. However, it is interesting to note how, after leaving the traditional structures of existing denominations, that organization has established its own structure that increasingly

49. Kinnaman, *Faith for Exiles.*

appears to resemble the inherited church structures it left, with spheres instead of dioceses, and apostolic leaders in place of bishops. The question of authority remains a key issue. Despite its separation from established denominational traditions, it retains a commitment to authority, even if that authority is more biblical than tradition centered. But although it was assumed that such a change of direction would solve everything, that is not necessarily proving straightforward.

## NEW FRONTIERS

New Frontiers is a well-established group of community churches, led by Terry Virgo, arising out of the charismatic upsurge in the sixties and seventies. Upon Terry Virgo's retirement in 2012, the centralized leadership pattern was disbanded in favor of a more decentralized approach: multiple leadership. It has been described as a father handing over to his sons—as Paul did with Timothy—with about five established groups of churches (spheres) developing somewhat independently of each other, with no central organization maintained. There was also an international aspect to it, with about twenty leaders in that worldwide movement.

The result of that decision was that these five spheres diverged along different paths, leading to the following questions: Is this the end of New Frontiers? Has this movement run its course? Divergence led to other issues. The unity that was present before dissipated, and different attitudes, opinions, and actions developed, causing distance to be put between the groups. Then, in 2015, the five leaders decided to meet up again. The result was that they discovered a new mutuality in the faith and began to meet regularly on a relational rather than a structural basis. The present UK New Frontiers Apostolic Leaders Team emerged as a result. It was like teenagers having left home to go away to work, returning back to their old haunts, and then developing new relationships with their old associates.

Now the leadership team is fourteen or more and working on fresh ways as to how to engage together in the faith. In the meantime, New Frontier churches have doubled in number globally, and a new day has dawned in local church experiences. Their underlying purpose is closely aligned to their heartfelt beliefs, with wide ownership of both faith and growth, and increasing numbers being caught up in mission and the vision. With an increasing number of these spheres, together with their sense of vision, there is now a new relational, creative, expansive, and outward-looking commonwealth.

Clearly the expanding apostolic team realizes that such steps are in their early days of reimagining of what it means to be a second- and third-generation church organization. They are encouraged by what has happened. But having already experienced doubts and uncertainties since the end of the more centralized, father-dominated existence, they are well aware that there will undoubtedly be new questions asked and new issues to face as they sail together into uncharted territories. They know they haven't reached their destination, but there is clearly excitement, expectation, and confidence experienced in their journey.

Certainly, the central leadership has devolved from one person to an apostolic team which has released a fresh expansion of vitality and growth. To what extent this decentralization has trickled down from the apostolic team to the eldership teams, and then on to the church membership itself, is less clear. It appears that decentralization in the form of interdependence was undertaken at the senior leadership level, but fear of too much diversity and dilution of authority may well be inhibiting and restricting development/participation at the base church membership level. As with the established church, order and uniformity of belief can so easily constrain risk-taking, and allowing the influence of the spirit to work freely amongst the membership. Such potential diversity can be seen to be a threat.

The journey described of New Frontiers offers an interesting reflection—from the restoration/community church movement who have begun this decentralizing process—to the established church as it considers such a move. It illustrates that, on the one hand, decentralizing is both risky and exciting; it can lead to expansion and growth as individual churches discover their own independence and potential. On the other hand, there is the fear that the whole exercise will get out of hand, that the expansion, growth, and diversity will become uncontainable; that the authority of the pastors and eldership will be lost if free reign is given to the membership. The dilemma that faced the early church, between Paul's New Testament times and the Ignatian period, is clearly repeating itself, as can be seen in the diversity of institutional/experiential, cerebral/intuitional, and dwelling/seeking church patterns.

### JEB

A similar, more personal example can be taken from a sodal offshoot from 1900: the Japanese Evangelistic Band initiated by my grandfather, Paget Wilkes, and Barclay Buxton, around Kobe, Japan. Although it was based on biblical rather than Anglican traditional authority, the status of minister, the "sensei", was, and remains today, paramount and absolute. The authority structure operating between the authorized minister and the membership of the church remains sacrosanct, all in the name of uniformity to a biblical norm.

## 7.3 A CRISIS OF MINISTRY

Perhaps the most significant issue facing the church today revolves around the subject of ministry. In practice how does the church effect its mission and ministry as it strives to express the mission of God and encourage the kingdom of God to grow?

Traditionally, ever since the second century, ministry in the church has been primarily fulfilled through a professional, functional, ordained ministerial class arising out of the Ignatian threefold order.

However, such an approach is now being questioned both theologically and practically. The theological question, as we have seen, has been around for some time, but the practical side is now increasing in intensity and can no longer be disregarded. The practical questions center around the shrinking numbers and the spiraling costs of a trained, full-time, professional clerical ministry. These difficulties facing this representational ministry strike at the very heart of the church's existence. Bosch eloquently described an earlier generation in a way that is still relevant today:

> The Church remains a strictly sacral society run by an in-house personnel . . . (with) the clergyman-priest, enshrined in a privileged and central position, remaining the lynchpin of the Church . . . (and) with the increasing specialization of theological training, the elitist character of the 'clerical paradigm' was further enforced.[50]

As that series of statements strikes a chord, the number shortage and the cost of upkeep challenge the very heart of the church's being and its future continuation.

The intransigence of these practical questions is forcing the church back to the original theological question as to whether the church's ministry should primarily arise from the traditional and functional threefold order, or from the New Testament approach, centered around the ministry of the baptized. Although up to the last century the traditional model remained center stage, the latter part of that century saw a serious questioning of that predominance, and the calling for a rebalancing of these two approaches.

The main difficulty the church is facing in its ministry—within itself and outward towards society—is one that has been with it for a long time. The difficulty is rooted in the duality separating the traditional orders approach—what Moberley[51] has called the "representational ministry" of the professional clergy—and the growing significance of the ministry of the

---

50. Bosch, *Transforming Mission*, 470.

51. Moberley, quoted in Pickard, *Theological Foundations*, 53.

baptized that arises out of the New Testament book of Acts and the Epistles. The duality rests in what lies behind these two concepts of ministry. On the one hand, the orders were instituted primarily to bring stability, order, teaching, and unity, following a time of rapid expansion and growing heretical factions. On the other hand, the ministry of the baptized centered around the idea that someone's baptism into faith incorporates the idea of being ordained to fulfill the ministry of the church through the residency of the Holy Spirit within the heart of the believer. Such a priesthood of all believers, through the spirit's presence and power in every member, brings with it diversity, innovation, celebration, expectation, and open horizons— very different from the ordered pattern that developed from Ignatius and that which is still present in today's representational ministry.

---

### SERVING TOGETHER

This duality has been similarly illustrated by the views expressed in an Anglican report. It describes the church as having two streams of thought that run side by side, like a canal running alongside a river, sometimes merging, but mostly running along parallel lines. On the one hand, it recognizes a church which "cares deeply about retaining a sense of corporate discipline and accountability." On the other hand, it sees a church where "individuals are asked to involve themselves in an organization that cares deeply about deepening their unique and individual spiritual life."[52]

---

This ingrained inconsistency, this illustration of a canal running alongside a river but rarely merging, lies at the heart of the difficulties faced by the church today as it struggles to maintain sufficient professional clergy to sustain existing structures. Within the church today there is sufficient potential for both to be achieved if the ministry of the baptized could be released and encouraged to flower. However, such a release is constrained by the dominant dynamic and control of the representational ministry, that fears losing that order and control in favor of allowing diversity, innovation, free-flowing expansion, and excitement that such a flowering might produce. The fear is that the order and structure now present would dissipate in favor of a free-for-all, uncontrolled diversity of doctrine, belief, and practical leadership.

---

52. Scott et al., *Report of the Lay Ministries Working Group*, para 2.2.

## 7.3.1 From Then to Now

The journey from strict adherence and order toward diversity, from control to freedom, from hierarchy toward the spirit's empowerment, has begun. But it remains in its infancy, primarily due to fear and uncertainty as mentioned above. In modern times this journey of ministry has been illustrated by the example of George Herbert's parish priest,[53] and then by that example being adapted to urban life, with the emergence of the professional clergy class serving the growing parish system in Victorian England.

That settled pattern was then questioned, when it was imposed by missionaries, upon the fledgling church in China. Roland Allen[54] seriously questioned such a crude transposition, but was later rebuked by the then Bishop of Burma, in no uncertain terms.[55] However, his message was rearticulated by Vincent Donovan[56] with his ministry amongst the Maasai in Tanzania in the 1980s. Around the same time in England, a movement to widen the concept of ministry from the control of the professionals toward the ministry of the baptized was growing.

The debate is picked up with Bishop Michael Nazir-Ali pointing out that "God's calling is for each of the baptized to be a witness," that there is the "calling of the whole people of God, the *laos,* to worship, witness and work together."[57] As far back as 1991, a Partners in Mission report commented,

> We are still dominated by the false view that the ministry of the Church is confined to bishops, priests and deacons. The whole pilgrim people of God share in ministry, and clergy and laity must be trained for this ministry.[58]

This fresh approach was effectively articulated by John Tiller,[59] but his report to the Anglican synod was never fully owned and implemented. However, the debate stimulated further discussion and was developed in the writings of Anthony Russell, Andrew Bowden, Robin Greenwood, Jill Hopkinson, and many others. This same debate continues with the Anglican publication and implementation of Setting God's People Free ,[60] where the ministry of the laity is brought back into focus. Attention is drawn to

53. Herbert, *Country Parson and the Temple.*
54. Allen, *Missionary Methods.*
55. Paton, Reform of the Ministry, quoting correspondence.
56. Donovan, *Christianity Rediscovered.*
57. Nazir-Ali, *Shapes of the Church,* 4.
58. General Synod, *Report on Partnership in Mission,* 47.
59. Tiller, *Strategy for the Church's Ministry.*
60. Frost, *Setting God's People Free.*

the point that the ministry of the baptized is to the whole of life, rather than just to ways of servicing the needs of the church and filling the gaps when clergy are in short supply. The report calls for a culture change in relations between clergy and laity, indicating that they have complementary roles. It stresses that the creation of a culture of forming disciples is the foundation and enabler of lay leadership. However, it doesn't really go into detail as to how these two complementary roles of ordained and lay should work in a functional way, side by side. There is little mention of a reciprocal basis to their relationship.[61] Although the question of the empowerment of the laity is raised, there is no reference to addressing the imbalanced and dominant power structure of the threefold order that surely limits any move towards true complementarity. And interestingly, the report, Serving Together, points out that when central funding, time, and resources were apportioned to ministry, far greater comparative emphasis was still given to the ordained rather than to lay ministries.[62] Although much of what has just been written is referenced specifically to the Anglican Church, there is a case to be made that the issue also resides in other denominations, and even within restoration/community church structures.

The contributions of Stephen Pickard have highlighted unresolved tensions that these later reports fail to adequately address. He takes this debate further in analyzing that we have a kind of twin track approach (mentioned in "Serving Together") with the "representational ministry" of the ordained, running on a separate and parallel line to "other ecclesial ministries," i.e., "the ministries of the baptized."[63] As long as they remain separate, he contends, there is little chance of genuine collaboration and integration. The approach is dysfunctional, with the latter becoming submissive to the former, with the baptized working under, rather than with the ordained. So Pickard asserts that for a truly collaborative approach to be established, the dualistic relationship between the ministry and the ministries needs to be resolved.

Pickard traces the conflict between these two strands back to their theological bases and the differing roles they have developed over time: "Tensions between doctrines of ministry derived from Christology and Pneumatology are evident and remain unresolved in contemporary Anglican practice."[64] Whereas the former has stressed a somewhat maintenance-oriented apostolic continuity and order, developing a more static and

---

61. See the comments of Stephen Pickard in *Theological Foundations for Collaborative Leadership*.

62. Scott et al., *Report of the Lay Ministries Working Group*.

63. Pickard, *Theological Foundations*, 5, 100.

64. Pickard, *Theological Foundations*, 110.

status-centered approach, the latter has often brought mission-oriented and kingdom-directed vitality and diversity, as well as boundary-crossing preaching, teaching, reshaping, and renewal. This leaves the former, the stable ministerial forms, in danger of ossification, with the latter pointing out that. "The primacy of 'charism' dissolves existing relations and reconfigures the ministries in new and surprising ways."[65]

Pickard's views on these unresolved issues are endorsed by "Serving Together" which mentions repeatedly the "complementarity of lay and ordained ministries,"[66] and also the holding together or merging—the river and the canal—of the "unique and individual spiritual life," whilst at the same time retaining "a sense of corporate discipline and authority."[67] At present, it appears that there is no real appetite or desire to address the underlying issue: that of the disjunction between having a threefold order, over and above the ministry of the baptized. Similarly, the whole fresh expressions/pioneer ministries movement may well have been seeking to move the establishment into a more contemporary direction, but despite all of their efforts, the underlying modal dynamic of the church remains in favor of the controlling representational ministry. Once again it can be argued that, even leaving the established denominations doesn't necessarily resolve the continuing tension arising between the leadership ministry of the apostolic team/church pastors, and the everyday ministry of each and every recognized church member. The new structures still have a tendency to revert to the old, even if different terminology is used.

## 7.3.2 Functional/Iconic

Underlying this unresolved tension between representational and other ecclesial ministries is the fact that between the historic, hierarchical orders and the ministry of the baptized lies the issue of the role of such orders/positions, and their place in the overall life and vitality of the church.

For a long time the Western church has had a divided approach to ordination. Whereas the Protestant view sided with the more functional role of what a priest was ordained to do, following the pattern illustrated by Paul in Acts 20, the Catholic view has seen ordination more in an ontological way, with a priest becoming a different person who, iconically, pointed the church membership towards Christ himself. So the question arises as to

---

65. Pickard, *Theological Foundations*, 114.

66. Scott et al., *Report of the Lay Ministries Working Group*, para. 3.1.

67. Scott et al., *Report of the Lay Ministries Working Group*, para. 2.2.

whether this order is to do what their title suggests or to be, as an icon of Christ's ministry.

We all know what a functionary does. She or he does what they are appointed to do. However, it is worth reflecting on what an icon is. An icon is used to remind us of or draw our attention to something significant. As Bishop Nick Baines has put it, "an icon is an image that invites you, not to look at it, but to go through it to the deeper reality."[68] As we look at something or somebody and dwell on it, we begin to think further about its significance and its implications. What begins with an iconic visual image often leads to becoming an inspiration for us to change and act in a way we had not previously done. The spiritual truth depicted in the iconic image invites us to own, participate in, and activate that dormant potential within us, awaiting the inspiration and empowerment of the Holy Spirit to bring fruit to bear all around us.

In this iconic sense, the role of those set apart or ordained should be to inspire and ignite the whole church to become the church, and grow into the kingdom. The orders should be expressions and illustrations of what the nature of the whole church truly is. They ought to be, therefore, a sign of that nature, rather than a fixed, hierarchical structure that limits the baptized community from fulfilling their true nature. Their present ordained role, which is primarily functional, is actually denying the baptized the opportunity to properly fulfill their intrinsic role, what baptism ordained them to express: to reflect the life and teaching of Christ to the world and to grow God's new order—a point already referred to in the 1998 Lambeth Conference report.[69]

The same could be said for the role of the bishop/leader and his/her area responsibilities. At present that role is primarily a functional one, similar to the CEO of a large commercial company. The bishop/leader heads a hierarchical organization through a structure expressed, in reality, through domination and control. This role is epitomized by the Anglican statement that "the ultimate responsibility for articulating the theological vision regarding the nature of the church and the general direction of its pastoral and missionary task should be located in the House of Bishops,"[70]—together with Richard Roberts's point[71]—and endorsed by the 2014 Green Report's emphasis on improving management skills of senior clergy.

68. Baines, "Notre Dame," para. 19.

69. *Lambeth Conference Report*, 194.

70. *Canons of Church of England*, C18.

71. Roberts, *Religion, Theology and the Human Sciences*, 164.

Stephen Pickard[72] refers to this point as he highlights the difference between the functional, managerial role carried out by today's Anglican episcope, and the iconic, "curing of souls," caring, servantlike role expressed in the ordination and consecration service. On the one hand, the bishop is in charge of a static, substantive structure; constrained by rules, heavy on buildings, short on running costs, with a diminishing workforce, and a dwindling clientele. Of necessity, both bishop and diocese concern themselves with improving their structural management, administration, and personnel management, in order to enable the church to survive and continue. On the other hand, in the preface to the ordination and consecration of a bishop, the archbishop defines the episcopal role as,

> to serve and care for the flock of Christ . . . love and pray for those committed to their charge, knowing people and being known to them . . . preside at the Lord's table . . . feed God's pilgrim people and so build up the body of Christ . . . nurturing God's people in the life of the spirit and leading them to true holiness . . . discern and foster the gifts of the spirit in all who follow Christ, commissioning them to minister in his name . . . have special care for the poor and outcast and those who are in need . . . seek out those who are lost and lead them home rejoicing, declaring the absolution and forgiveness of sins to those who turn to Christ."

Frances Young recounts a similar experience within the Methodist Church: "People feel 'called' to one kind of activity and find themselves thrust into another by the institutional pressures, by the traditional models and functions, by the projections and expectations of other people."[73] Those called by the church to the traditional, relational role therefore find great difficulty in fulfilling both traditional and managerial roles at the same time, often leading to tension, unachievable expectations, and a continuous sense of inadequacy. As Ian Cundy and Justin Welby have put it, "giving a lead to the Church of England is like trying to take a cat for a walk."[74] The management models being recommended by the Green report just do not synchronize with the ordination charge or the purpose and principles of the faith.

Pickard goes on to point out that the underlying systemic difficulty lies with the coercive Cyprianic base of today's leadership approach. Rather than adopting a close relational approach between bishops/leaders and their local churches that would enable the vows to be fulfilled and collaboration

72. Pickard, *Theological Foundations*, 171–72.

73. Young, *Face to Face*, 232.

74. Cundy and Welby, "Taking the Cat for a Walk," 25.

over purpose and principles rethought, the present approach makes the bishop/leader the judicial, authoritarian figure, responsible for the management of her/his territorial and structural diocese, with not only a traditional right to rule, but also a contemporary right to manage image. Such a role might encourage good management, but it is on a different wavelength to encouraging "representational orders" to genuinely engage with the "ministry of the baptized,"[75] in an overall holistic approach to the ministry of the church.

---

### BISHOP–BULLY

The role and image of bishops was recently given significant media coverage over the internet, following Oxford Thesaurus's decision on August 4, 2018, to give the word "bishop" the synonym "bully." This was evidenced by various clergy who claimed to have been bullied by bishops, and supported by evidence of sexual abuse by bishops on young people, subsequently covered up by episcopal authorities.

Undoubtedly the actions of bishops, within their role as CEO of large, often struggling, hierarchical institutions, could well lay themselves open to a charge of bullying, supporting Pickard's view that bishops are doing very much more than simply fulfilling the guidelines articulated in their ordination.

---

## 7.4 MANAGEMENT OF PEOPLE

Further discrepancies arise within the way ecclesiastical structures operate that do not help the overall ministry of the church. As has been described, far too often the ordained clergy operate more as functional managers rather than iconic ministers and pastors, whose primary responsibility is to care and minister amongst people. At the same time, episcopal/leadership roles are increasingly drawn towards the CEO model. Of necessity in today's world, those ordained have to effectively manage a large operation of plant and personnel, vision and policy, safeguarding issues, discipline, and judicial matters. It is a far cry from Christ's primary witness to the people and culture of his day, or even from Paul's advice to Timothy at the end of his first letter.

Whereas this clerical orders approach has led toward a top-down hierarchical model based on domination, by contrast the ministry of Jesus was based far more on mutual engagement. Jesus grew up in a patriarchal

---

75. Pickard, *Theological Foundations*, 116–20.

society. As will be shown in 8.2.5, Jewish society centered around patriarchal extended families whose whole inheritance was built around their land and possessions. The father dominated this whole basic social structure. His word was sacrosanct. Jesus, however, reacted against such an approach. In the parable of the lost son, the father divides his family assets and wealth, handing half of them over to one son. To divide up the family inheritance before the death of the head of the family was unheard of in that patriarchal society. Then when his son returns empty-handed, the father picks up the skirts of his robe and runs to meet him; again, it was unheard of for a father to run, let alone run in such a manner. The father then celebrates his son's return regardless of the fact that he has just thrown away half the total historic assets of the rest of the family.[76] Jesus, in using this example, is offering a very different approach to fatherhood and family leadership, which totally contradicted the Pharisaical teaching of the time. Instead of patriarchal authority and control he offered mutual understanding, love, care, and compassion.

Similarly, Kevin Thew Forrester[77] has pointed out from John 15:15 that Jesus, speaking to his disciples, says, "I no longer call you servants because a servant does not know his master's business. Instead I have called you friends for everything that I have learned from my father I have made known to you." Jesus, instead of accepting the Jewish patriarchal structure of the day, which would make him the master, indicates that his father's will is to bring all his children into one family encapsulated by friendship and love rather than parental authority and control. This was dramatically different from Jewish culture, and envisaged the emergence of a community the like of which had never been seen before. As the disciples soon discovered, the new community was to be centered around a leadership of servanthood and suffering rather than one of power and domination. Jesus allowed himself to lose everything for the sake of that commitment to his disciples.

Forrester goes on to give another example from Jesus' teaching at a Pharisee's luncheon party (Luke 14:1–14) giving two illustrations, both of which broke the norms of the day, and at the same time illustrated the values of the kingdom. Seating arrangements at dinner parties in those days were dominated by everyone trying to sit as close to the A-list celebrity as possible. Jesus' response was to suggest the opposite: "Know your own weaknesses before God and don't try to make yourself more important in the eyes of other people." Later Jesus talked about making up one's own invitation list for a dinner party: "Don't go for reciprocal invitations, where

---

76. Bailey, *Finding the Lost.*

77. Forrester, *Theology of Mutual Ministry.*

you can expect to get an invitation in return, and where your position in society is perpetuated. Invite instead those who can't invite you back. It won't uplift your society ratings but it might reflect a God-given understanding of humanity, and God's particular commitment to the marginalized."

Jesus was not prepared to perpetuate dominating hierarchies. As Walter Wink has put it "these are the words and deeds, not of a minor reformer, but of an egalitarian prophet who repudiates the very premises on which domination is based; the right of some to lord it over others by means of power, wealth sharing or titles."[78] Alternatively Jesus was seeking to encourage throughout his ministry a church that assumes unity, interconnectedness, interdependency, and mutuality as common priorities in governance and visioning.

An alternative approach to traditional episcopal leadership comes from the late Bishop Jim Kelsey of Michigan, USA. He developed a shared ministry that sought to eliminate domination, and enhance at the same time the overall participation and engagement of the whole body of Christ. Following Bishop Wesley Frensdorff of Nevada, he talked about "transforming our congregations from being communities gathered round a minister into becoming ministering communities."[79] This involved moving away from the clericalism, which declared without saying it that the priest is the minister, towards a mutual society where all ministry is Christ's, and where every baptized person, in their daily life, contributes their Spirit-enabled gifts for the benefit of the whole community. Such an approach would continuously offer an alternative to the existing priest/minister-centered model of ministry

This change in leadership style, from domination to mutuality, may indeed be more in tune with Jesus' teaching and life. It may indicate a move away from the weaknesses of a church structure more reflective of Ignatius than Paul. It may reduce control and increase dynamic connectedness. But it does raise serious questions as to what form the leadership of such an alternative structure might take, and how egalitarian a form it should really follow. Hierarchical leadership has led the English church since the synod of Whitby when Celtic influences were minimized, but alternative forms are not necessarily easy to perceive or operate, as we shall see in part 3.

Each of these writers and practitioners illustrates that the continuance of a structure intrinsically based on top-down central leadership dominance rather than mutual engagement, networked horizontally, open to the creative innovation of all the baptized, is at odds with the example of Jesus; it

---

78. Wink, *Engaging the Powers,* 112.

79. Frensdorff, "Dream," para. 11.

is not offering an appropriate countercultural witness to the competitive-, status-, celebrity-, and fashion-oriented culture in which we live.

Jesus' approach to ministry, and toward the structures of Jewish society around him, offers a considerable challenge to today's church patterns. In principle he was a countercultural prophet, offering an alternative to his contemporary society. Surely that in itself is a challenge to the leadership of today's churches.

## 7.5 LAY VOCATION/TOTAL MINISTRY/ MARKETPLACE MINISTRY

When the ordained ministry takes such a functional role in maintaining the structure and worship of denominational churches, reductions in clergy numbers has caused great concern. This in turn has led to viewing the development of lay ministry as a possible way of alleviating the pressure, so that the church's structure and worship can continue to follow their existing patterns. However, such an approach to lay ministry has raised considerable disquiet, and opened up the whole question of lay ministry and lay vocation.

In general terms, Christian witness and ministry is expressed in three main areas: in a person's home and church; where a person spends much of their daylight hours, maybe at work or in education; and within society's culture/structure, and within the world in which we live. Often it is mistakenly assumed that lay ministry is expressed primarily in the first, with little thought given to the second or third areas.

Kenneth Mason, in his book *Priesthood and Society*, has a telling phrase "the ecclesiastical seduction of the laity."[80] He reflects that, far too often, a person's church membership and ministry within it have taken over "personal vocation," and "whatever he does in the rest of society is wholly secondary or remains only as an embarrassment he would like to be free of."[81]

---

**LAY VOCATION**

Bruce Kaye makes an important distinction when he asks what the difference is between "lay ministry" and "lay vocation."[82] He says that so often we only talk about the former but not about the latter. Lay ministry, he suggests, is normally seen as semi-clericalized church work and withdrawing from the world of secular darkness into the well-lit lounge of the church, whereas lay vocation concerns

---

80. Mason, *Priesthood and Society*, 153.

81. Mason, *Priesthood and Society*, 153.

82. Kaye, "Vocation of the Laity."

engaging with the whole of society and its structures that surround and often engulf us. In a personal reflection, Bishop Mark Bryant has commented that "what we need is baptized Christians, with a lively faith, somehow 'being different' and provoking questions in places where they find themselves day by day."

Francis Dewar makes a similar point[83] about lay vocation, stressing that in most cases it will be something expressed in the secular sphere rather than in the church, reiterated more recently in the phrase "whole life discipleship" used by the London Institute for Contemporary Christianity. David Heywood endorses this as he talks about all Christians participating in the "mission of God,"

> We are beginning to see that most of these gifts are to be exercised in the secular sphere, that the Church is called to be an outward facing community, whose ministry is exercised in the world that God created and loves.[84]

He goes on to say therefore that the focus of congregational life, and indeed of clergy ministry, should be on "promoting vocation, and resourcing the whole congregation for discipleship in the world"[85]—getting out of the ghetto and into the real world.

An Anglican report makes this point as one of its key elements in a culture-shift towards lay ministry development. It calls for a "way to form and equip lay people to follow Jesus in every sphere of life,"[86] and quotes from *Towards the Conversion of England* Report: "The Christian laity should be recognized as the priesthood of the Church in the working world and as the Church militant in action in the mission fields of politics, industry and commerce."[87]

## TOTAL MINISTRY

Total ministry refers to the ministry of the baptized, "as the servants of the Church, in and for the world."[88] It sees the body of believers going out to personally express the mind of Christ in their countercultural critique of society and in their mirrored reflection of Christ through every part of their lives. They are to exhibit this through proactive engagement with the emergent issues of the day,

83. Dewar, *Called or Collared*, 56.

84. Heywood, *Reimagining Ministry*, 150–51.

85. Heywood, *Reimagining Ministry*, 204.

86. Frost, *Setting God's People Free*, para 1.2.

87. Commission on Evangelism, *Towards the Conversion of England*, 61.

88. Wignall, "Kenosis and Total Ministry," 4.

and by bringing to bear the primary direction of Jesus' ministry—"to those who are not" (1 Cor 1:28) and to the notice of a primarily consumer-based society.[89]

## MARKET PLACE MINISTRIES

This movement of ministry has been taken by a whole range of initiatives, often under this term or the phrase "faith at work." David Miller has researched many of these, which have developed since the 1980s.[90] He summarizes this kind of approach as seeking to express faith at work through one or more of four distinct areas—evangelism, ethics, enrichment, and experience. He goes on to highlight the fact that many fail to integrate these four areas together. Miller's particular emphasis centers around such an integration.

## THE SEVEN MOUNTAIN PROPHECY

Yet another approach has been developed by Jonny Enlow.[91] He highlights seven culture-shaping influences over each society, including media, government, education, economy, family, religion, and celebration. He suggests that often Christians lack vision and have a misguided view of the end times, and therefore fail to commit themselves to influence adequately these seven areas. He sees such involvement as a primary task for every believer.

Returning to the dichotomy between representational ordained ministry and the ministry of the baptized, it becomes clear that ministry, in the fullest sense, is being replaced by simply asking lay people to increase their contributions to leading church worship. Such a role of ministry may well be needed as a stop-gap measure, but at the same time it is bypassing the significance of lay vocation, total ministry, marketplace ministry, and theological reflection within every influential area of society itself.

## 7.6 THEOLOCRACY

Another issue, already referred to, that the church needs to address has been pointed up in the contemporary secular economics debate. Economic

89. Wignall, "Praying for the City," 1.

90. Miller, God at Work.

91. Enlow, Seven Mountain Prophecy.

students from Manchester University have articulated how classical neo-liberal economics has been dominated by an econocracy[92] that gives little opportunity for grassroots viewpoints to be expressed or taken into account. It could be argued that the church actually stands in a similar position with regard to theology. Theological thinking and teaching—following the mastery/mystery approach to authority—can be seen to lie in the hands of a "theolocracy" that emanates from senior denominational church leaders, theological college staff—predominantly clerical—and certain erudite clergy. There are some eminent lay theologians, but they still operate from within the same paradigm. The main body of the church, its membership, are seen simply as consumers and recipients of this teaching. It is not expected that they might be capable of thinking or reflecting theologically in their places of work, life, and family. They are left out of the equation as being unskilled and unqualified. Such a situation means that the potential contributions of the ministry of the baptized are not encouraged, or given the opportunity to be expressed. It also discourages and hampers lay people from engaging theologically in their place of work and societal life. All too often they assume that they are not capable or knowledgeable enough to make any contribution. It discourages then to think that they might have a vocation to minister in every context. Such a theolocracy emasculates the true potential of the people of God and constrains it from being expressed.

There have been movements to counteract this domination, such as the Worker Priest movement in Paris, South Bank theology, industrial and urban mission projects in the second half of the last century, and the mission in the world of work today, but little impact is being made to the core of theological thinking which remains in the hands of a senior church leadership theolocracy.

Possibly the most contemporary illustration of this disjunction arose in the Anglican debate (July 2017 synod) over human sexuality. At the end of the debate on the House of Bishops' theological position paper on same-sex marriage, the synod, particularly the House of Laity, failed to take note of the paper. Maybe the end of this story is yet to be written, but it can still be argued that a theolocracy arising out of the House of Bishops sought to lay down a particular norm, but were rebutted by the House of Laity, who refused to acknowledge their recommendations.

92. Earle et al., *Econocracy*.

## 7.7 THE CONTEXTUAL/COUNTERCULTURAL BALANCE

Following this historical journey of the Christian faith and its development in the life of the church, we have identified key eras where contextual changes have illustrated the growing development of the church. That faith grew from its Jewish roots through Hellenistic philosophy, Middle Ages national customs and cultures, Enlightenment thinking, and ultimately through to our postmodern, postmillennial era. In each era it adapted itself to the predominant culture as it sought to survive.

Arriving at our postmillennial period, we have noticed that it is now struggling to come to terms with this ever-emerging context. Its hierarchical, cerebral, institutional model struggles to adapt itself to a networking, innovative, creative, mechanistic society and the fresh questions that emerge daily. It has struggled to grasp how a prophet might reflect on the unlimited list of technological possibilities/choices: it is struggling so much with the context that it hasn't adequately engaged with its countercultural role; it finds it difficult to put itself in the shoes of Jesus; it is so overwhelmed by the complexity of life, it can't grasp how the simplicity of the Christian faith can challenge the outworkings of those complexities; it can't discern how an experience of the Other, of a creator, whom every human can call Abba—Daddy—can offer an alternative to the mechanistic, substance-, and economic-oriented tune, to which we are all drawn to dance. By becoming so drawn into contextualizing our faith—being "of the world"—in order to survive, we have taken less account of the other part of Jesus' statement, that we are not "of the world"; we stand in danger of emulating the German Confessing church in the 1930s, endorsing Hitler, or the Dutch Reform Church attitudes toward apartheid in the 1950–60s; we have forgotten the examples of countless recent Christian prophets such as William Booth, Dietrich Bonhoeffer, Martin Luther King, Trevor Huddleston, Janani Luwum, and Mother Theresa; we have failed to remember the witness of the West Indian Christian lady from Liverpool who, when asked on the national news what she thought of the boys who had just murdered her young son, replied "I forgive them"; we have temporarily lost sight of a clear countercultural perspective.

One of the basic tenets of the Christian faith is that the church which Jesus and his spirit enabled to emerge, "is the great reality in comparison with which nations and empires and civilizations are passing phenomena."[93] Far too often we get this the wrong way around. We assume faith/church is only a contributing part of a greater, public, whole society. But the opposite

---

93. Newbigin, *Gospel in a Pluralist Society*, 221.

is true. The faith/church, in their reflection of the one true creator and redeemer, are the norm to which everything else is to be compared:

> True contextualization accords to the gospel its rightful primacy, its power to penetrate every culture, and to speak within each culture, in its own speech and symbol, the word which is both yes and no, both judgment and grace . . . when the word is not a disembodied word but comes from the community which embodies the true story, God's story in a style of life which communicates both the grace and judgment.[94]

This seminal presupposition highlights the fact that contextualization, crucial to a living faith, sits within a larger whole: the overall mission of God, the centrality and the purposes of the Trinity. The consequences of such a belief will always be that "It is bound to challenge, in the name of our Lord, all the powers, ideologies, myths, assumptions and worldviews, which do not acknowledge him as God."[95] As if that was not enough, Lesslie Newbigin adds a rider—"if that involves conflict, so be it—Jesus has already set us an example in that respect."[96]

So, despite the fact that the Christian faith is deeply drawn into a contextualizing process with the era, that the structures of the church are engulfed in the survival of their institutions, that individual faith is being squeezed out by overwhelming political and economic secularization, the faith/church have to remain undaunted by these circumstances and stand firm in what they are—the people of God. Today the faith/church need to remind themselves that their future existence will depend on their contribution to the uncertain, unknown, and unimaginable future. Holding on to that empirical truth will enable the gospel, the church, and the kingdom to grow rather than to shrivel up. How that could develop becomes the subject of part 3.

94. Newbigin, *Gospel in a Pluralist Society*, 152.
95. Newbigin, *Gospel in a Pluralist Society*, 221.
96. Newbigin, *Gospel in a Pluralist Society*, 221.

# PART 3

## From Here to Eternity

## INTRODUCTION

The River Thames has passed through the Woolwich Flood Barrier, and is now open to the Kent/Essex sandbanks, the Channel's churning currents, and the incessant stream of ships that pass both ways and demand their right of way. Similarly, following the Old Testament story, the children of Israel have survived the ordeal of the Negev, and are poised in Jordan. They are ready to cross the river and claim the promised land, which is occupied by unknown, unquantifiable forces. Only Jericho is in view, and that they hope to take—with a wing and a prayer—with assistance from the red light district. What an auspicious way to begin! Similarly, as we face the century's third decade, the faith/church are drawn into not only crisis but also opportunity. The currents are undoubtedly forceful but the engine propelling the boat is surprisingly strong. There is every possibility that the crossing can be made, despite the fragility of the boat.

In a similar vein, returning to *Blade Runner 2049*, Agent K, a replicant programmed with some degree of human memory, is calibrated to exterminate the last remaining true human rebels, living at the extremities of existence outside the corporate control of the system. Through the hint of human memory within him, K is challenged by their rejection of the system's framework, as they exist in the shanty cities of the wasteland perimeter: rebelling against the elite who control the system through their replicant slaves. In the end, K takes refuge with the rebels as the system is determined to eliminate him for going off message. Deep down, the film is about contrasting developments of humanity and the resultant dystopia—not unlike *The Hunger Games*. The medium of film has often offered future scenarios as, or more effectively than, those articulated by academics.

There is an element of similarity between the above scenarios and the engagement of the faith/church as it faces a cultural paradigm shift of similar proportions to the Renaissance/Enlightenment shift of the past. The size and the significance of the shift is difficult to quantify whilst in the midst of it, but there can be no doubt that the third decade will endorse and clarify what already overwhelms present society.

Primarily we have moved on from universal reason—the primacy of the scientific mind and the centrality of the human individual brought to us through the Renaissance/Enlightenment. We have moved on from a welfare capitalism that acknowledged the needs of all as a significant objective, into a success- and achievement-oriented world of problem-solving optimism, with no limits to human confidence and autonomy, where the mountaintop is illustrated by the winner taking all, and where the valley is inhabited by rough-sleeping nonachievers.

We have entered a postmodern world where everything is relative, depending on where we stand and how we participate; where a plurality of cultures envelop our global family; where complexity arises from the interdependence of so many surrounding factors; where globalism is opposed by local interests and individual objectives; where over-optimistic expectations of the future are challenged by the pessimism of disjunction; where competing interests compound decision-making for each successive generation.

Secondly, we face technocentric development set on an exponential curve that has no end point, giving rise to a whole set of fresh issues and questions that have no easy resolutions, and expectations that can't be delivered for the benefit of all.

Thirdly, we are surrounded by the inadequacy of the anthropocentric, humanist mindset as it seeks to come to terms with an increasingly technocentric ethos. At the same time, we see capitalism as we know it dissolving into a data-centric, surveillance capitalism where the global holders of tech development overwhelm governmental democracy.

It is in this melting pot of change, this paradigm shift of experience, this lack of universal ethical moral values, this complexity/interconnectedness of what it means to be real/human, that the faith/church is having to rediscover its belief, its direction, its empowerment. It is within this materialistic, success-oriented, mechanistic, machine-centered Western society that the faith/church has to reimagine the centrality of the creator Other, holding values of love, personal relationships, and a purpose for the whole of humanity. It is within the third decade that faith and church will need to be released from their pre-Enlightenment dependence on hierarchy and the absolute, together with the Enlightenment's enthusiasm for analytical polarizing debate. They will need to engage instead with the complexity of life and with a more emergent, conjunctive approach; networked through individual believers in an upward direction. Part 3, and chapter 11 in particular, is a contribution to that debate.

In his recent book, Harari[1] argues that there are signs of a dystopic scenario emerging before us. Technocentric expansion increasingly overwhelms us, together with unexpected outcomes, uncontrollable bots/grey goo, and the digital dictatorships of those who own, analyze, and control data. This last issue appears to point us unwaveringly toward gross inequality and ever-increasing uncertainty. This future-scape continues to struggle with the human/machine divide and suffers from there being no developed ethical guide[2] for scientists and engineers as to what is benevolent and

1. Harari, *Twenty-one Lessons.*
2. House of Lords Report, *AI in the UK,* 7.

what is malevolent—reflecting Stephen Hawking's 2014 letter of concern. A technocentric viewpoint also appears to make philosophical assumptions that humanity can simply be reduced down to material individual existence, that culture no longer requires transcendent points of reference, where humanity assumes that empirical existence can dispense with an underlying quest for meaning, where an intrinsic search for good can be sidelined by progress and remorseless uncertainty/instability,[3] where the wholeness of the individual might include a soul, with emotions and relationships, as part of the human psyche.

As we have seen, the Enlightenment, despite its unacknowledged debt to the revolutionary thinking of Jesus and St. Paul, both marginalized and overwhelmed the faith/church, forcing it into a defensive, private belief. Likewise, relativist postmodernism made life uncomfortable for a faith/church seeking to hold its own in a secular age. Now, however, a new opportunity arises. As the third decade approaches, bringing with it more uncertainty, fresh issues and questions concerning human progress come to the fore. Within this scenario the faith/church has a fresh opportunity to reexpress itself, not through a reiteration of the past formulae, but rather as a response to the ever-developing context. First it has to put its own house in order, but at the same time it has to seize the opportunity to be counter-cultural as well as contextualizing.

Having looked at the excitement of the digital present in part 1, and with awareness of historic systemic weakness in church structure—part 2—part 3 will look at the opportunities and choices facing the faith/church today. After taking seriously the four issues that have weakened both faith and church in the past, three choices will be laid out for those who seek to enter the third decade with a fresh and challenging framework. Some of these choices may involve walking away from what has been held dear, so as to risk claiming the uncertainty of a prophetic future. The currents of the sea will undoubtedly be strong but a vision of the beyond is that which empowers the engine of the rebel craft.

The five following chapters will act as a springboard to jump out of the constraining issues of the past, and into a choice between three options from which to engage tomorrow. Addressing the posthumanist and technocentered landscape, needs—following Dee Hock—to begin with purpose and principles rather than existing structures. This, in itself, would institute a paradigm shift. Chapter 8 addresses purpose and principles, whilst chapters 9 and 10 move on to structures—both administration and ministry. Chapter 11 looks forward to practice in terms of a prophetic, countercultural stance,

---

3. Berger, *Desecularization of the World*, 13.

and chapter 12 illustrates some of the unresolved issues/questions that face both society and the church.

Behind all of part 3 lie the four embedded issues and three practical options that faith/church should engage with and choose. The first of the three options is illustrated by the skirmish at Rourke's Drift: resorting to a laager mentality, an orthodox temper, a dependence on a traditional sense of authority—Fowler's stage three. The second option is to hold together a hybrid fusion of both traditional and progressive, cerebral and intuitional, narrative and experience, survival and growth, all of these attitudes, in one diverse body—stages three and four. The third option is an emergent conjunctive organism: engaging with its environment, inspired and empowered through its relationship with the Holy Spirit, dependent on the ministry of all believers, rising from the ground upwards with new forms of leadership—stage five. The hope expressed in part 3 is that the temptation of option 1 will be rejected—due to its cul-de-sac nature—that the attractiveness of option 2, the mixed economy, will be recognized as being only a stepping stone, a staging post, and that the hard graft challenge of option 3 will become the"model target, from which contextual/countercultural engagement and mission can be pursued with society at large.

# Chapter 8

## Power and Vulnerability

Power raises a clear issue for the Christian faith/church today. It has been established that faith and church have been close associates with ruling powers from the time of the fourth century up until the Enlightenment. Since that time they have sought to assimilate their beliefs with philosophical and societal leaders. It can also be established that such a stance is at odds with the position that Jesus took in relation to the state and religious leaders of his day. From birth to death Jesus' life was a ministry of authority that stemmed from vulnerability and suffering, that deeply challenged the mindset of these established authority figureheads. These two very different approaches lead us to consider whether the present medium (outside identity) of the church is effectively reflecting the message (inner identity) of the gospel of Jesus.

The previous chapters have inferred that there is a real need for a paradigm shift if the present-day witness of faith is to truly reflect the Jesus narrative. The centrality of power and authority is so intricately embedded within the mindset of the church, that it is extraordinarily difficult to envisage how it could change. Such power is concentrated in status and respect, national tradition, relationships with local and state government structures, tax and charity relief, not to mention investments, inherited wealth, historic buildings, and the church's influence within society's morals, ethics and norms. Maybe before going any further in the pursuance of such radical change it would be important to delve into the derivation of the word "power."

## 8.1 POWER

Power is the ability to influence or outrightly control the behavior of others. Power relates to the interdependence between two entities and between those two entities and their environment. It concerns how institutions and interpersonal relationships are held together to achieve an end. As Nietzsche is reputed to have said "domination over other humans." It can take the form of prerogative power where those who hold it make or break the rules.

This reference to prerogative power gives rise to a discussion concerning other different forms of power. Power can be negative, involving coercion and the threat of force, or positive, egalitarian, and consensual, in the form of soft power. Its dynamic can be downward, as in hierarchical institutions, or upward as in colonies of bees and ants; it can be disabling, led by destructive patterns of communication, or it can be an enabling influence, using social skills; power can be achieved through a person bringing about outcomes themselves, or through social influence upon others to bring about change and improved outcomes; it can also be resource based—whoever has access to resources can exert power. So the concept of power covers a multitude of ways through which outcomes or change can be effected in relationships and in organizations.

---

### FORMS OF POWER

In terms of power within relationships, French and Raven identified six sources of power. Their description of power, still currently accepted today, includes *legitimate* (through role or authority), *reward* (ability to hand out reward), *coercive* (sanctions and punishment), *expert* (being an expert), *referent* (someone looked up to as a role model, e.g., sports or rock star), and *informational* (knowing things).[1]

---

Bringing the Christian faith and the church into this equation raises interesting reflections. After its early growth the faith grew through the church establishing itself as a hierarchical structure, with a view to maintaining unity, orthodoxy, and control. The first generational New Testament church gained its authority from those who had benefited from referent power, emanating from the inspirational impact of Jesus upon them and the life-changing experience of Pentecost. However, from the second century the ensuing generations of faith began to develop an alternative source of authority, unity, and theology. This ecclesiastical authority, rather than being referent, drew its power from its legitimacy as the apostolic succession,

---

1. French and Raven, "Bases of Social Power."

which in turn morphed into the Ignatian threefold order. This was supplemented in the fourth century by the church being legitimized by the Roman state. As the canon of the Bible was established, that too became a source of legitimation behind the already-established church hierarchy. At times during ensuing centuries, power was also exerted through offering rewards (of heaven) through coercion, as illustrated by the Crusades, and through the expert role of theologians and episcopal administrators. As a result, the referent power of the life and witness of Christ, and the Pentecostal personal encounter, diminished and were overwhelmed by these alternative forms. As the church expanded into Western Europe the church's power centered around the pope, his bishops, and the legitimation of the national authorities. This legislative power could be categorized as prerogative power, which led on to the practical application of such power and authority through the bishops of each diocese. This downward power, often with negative coercion, was required to establish and maintain an organization alongside the power of nation-states. Beside the people of power lay the authority of the Bible. But, because it was only in one language—Latin—it could only be read by the orders of ministry, thereby endorsing their legislative power.

This tradition of leadership and power, aligned with the state, was maintained right up until the Reformation when the reforming churches called on the Bible as a specific additional legitimizing authority for personal faith. Today, although there is a greater variety of church leadership through the rise of denominations/community churches, there remains the same inherited tradition of power within those frameworks. Church leadership today continues to depend on a balance between church tradition and the Bible to legitimize the authority it seeks to assert. The predominant approach however, rather than being referent, continues to be hierarchical and downward in its dynamic, mitigated to some extent by the synodical/conciliar system.

The prerogative leadership style of today is also influenced by the added elements of stress and survival mode behavior. The increasing pressures put upon leadership by structure, finance, buildings, membership, demography, and ethics is more likely to lead towards legislative, sometimes coercive, power, and downward, negative, disabling approaches to power. An example of this is illustrated by the Oxford Thesaurus's decision to use the term "bully" as a synonym for bishop. The more pressure put upon leadership by the need to sustain an establishment under difficult circumstances, the more likely it is that the leadership will revert to more direct, controlling measures. This is compounded in the apostolic tradition where the bishop has virtually autonomous powers in their diocese, constrained only by the House of Bishops or the synods over particular issues. When bishops/church leaders have no line manager to report to, when the pressure mounts up, the temptation to be the final authority can lead to a very autocratic style, hence the term "Princely Prelate." It is not surprising therefore that the terms "bully," "coercion," and "disabling," come to mind when describing many forms of church leadership. The added difficulty to this is that ministers are quite likely, consciously or subconsciously, to allow their leader's example to trickle down into their own church ministry. Another example of this is the way church hierarchy, titles, status, and practices have been handed down to African countries, epitomized by the use of the term "My Lord Bishop" in countries where peerages do not exist.

So the default position for church structures is that power is wielded in a hierarchical, top-down, controlling, coercive way, particularly in times of stress and change. Such power is downward in nature, endorsing the prerogative of ministers, who have the best access to resources and traditional authority. Undoubtedly, in recent years, there has been a move toward more collaborative and enabling styles of leadership, styles that use soft power and enable others to effect change, rather than doing it all directly. However, certain elements have conspired against this trend. First, although a collaborative approach may be exercised at the local level, it may not always be honored and endorsed by more senior levels of leadership. These have been known to ride roughshod over an enabling approach. Secondly, although this approach gained credence in the late twentieth century, it has struggled to maintain its influence, due to the increasing pressure on church survival. As those pressures increase, more direct forms of leadership and power reassert themselves. Thirdly, collaborative, enabling, upward power has never really been owned by those ordained and appointed into traditional, authoritative leadership—with the interesting exception of the Episcopalian Diocese of North Michigan, USA. Prerogative power remains the default position in the structures of the church. Down through the ages there have undoubtedly been sodal offshoots that rejected such hierarchical power—nonconformists such as St. Francis—but over time they have been reabsorbed back into a hierarchical approach.

One of the reasons that this legitimizing hierarchical approach to power has continued down through the centuries has been because up until now it has been the most effective way to run an established institution with considerable assets, wealth, buildings, and personnel. The more the church built its future on substance, the more it had to rely on prerogative power to exert control over those assets. As the New Testament church, centering around relationships and referent power, gave way to the fourth-century church, built more around substance, so too apostolic, charismatic leadership gave way to the legitimizing authority of orthodoxy and control.

## 8.2 VULNERABILITY

However, there are other ways of exerting power and influence and effecting outcomes in both organizations and human lives. Jesus Christ, Gandhi, Martin Luther King, and Nelson Mandela in his prison years have all become the source of referent power to their followers. As has been said, in the decades following the resurrection of Jesus and Pentecost, the emerging church flourished on the authority of this referent power. Coming from a direction which one would least expect, this referent power reflected the vulnerability of Jesus, rather than such prerogative power exerted by religious and state leaders of the day. Vulnerability has been described as being exposed to the possibility of being harmed; being easily attacked/hurt physically, emotionally or mentally by others; being liable to be overwhelmed by stronger forces. It appears paradoxical that such referent vulnerability could also be the starting point of influence and change. There is ample evidence, instanced by Jesus Christ, that that indeed can happen.

Jesus was born into vulnerability. His very life depended on a kind pub owner, and a refugee escape from the sword of a violent dictator. He faced the question of power and vulnerability head-on when tempted in the desert to accept material possessions, fame, and influence. His rejection of these avenues left him with very little room to maneuver. It left him with his family carpentry business, no training for his ministry, and no guidance or mentoring assistance. He chose the latter and stepped out into history on his own. But his vulnerability brought with it certain attributes that came from his lineage. He had a sense of *courage*, instilled in him from the heavenly endorsement at his baptism. He had a *compassion* for all humanity around him, which never left him, even on his walk to Golgotha. As he *connected* with people all around him, he exhibited authenticity, the authenticity of his father's endorsement and empowerment throughout his ministry. Finally he accepted and embraced his *vulnerability*, despite the uncertainty and threat as to where it might lead.[2] Through all of this he exuded a compelling nature, initiating a referent power, that has been influencing people's lives ever since, that has inspired faith, belief, and dedication, that led not only to his martyrdom but also to that of his followers.

### FRANCES YOUNG

Frances Young has described a similar sense of vulnerability, experienced through her close relationship with her son, Arthur. Learning from his vulnerability, in a world where he couldn't fully engage and participate, led her to an

2. Brown, "Power of Vulnerability."

inner-city church in which many felt equally vulnerable. Despite her professional academic position and qualifications, a shared sense of vulnerability developed the deepest of relationships between her and that local community. As she shared her vulnerability things began to happen. "I certainly gave myself to them but I also received, immeasurably received. Preaching there was a different experience from preaching anywhere else, not because I used different material, but because the relationship was different."[3] As she admitted her own vulnerability, inadequacy, and need she became open to receive reciprocally. Just as Jesus accepted vulnerability as he lived with those around him, she too was inspired to acknowledge her vulnerability out of which a deeper understanding of the faith emerged, benefiting that whole church community, of which she was a part.

## MOONSHOT

A similar experience occurred in my own ministry on the Milton Court Estate in New Cross, London. Sybil Phoenix ran the Moonshot Club, whose members were predominantly young West Indian men. A single white person in the club would feel very threatened at that time of racial rioting. At chucking-out time, the tables were turned as I walked up with all these youngsters, leaving the club and going up to the tube station. That slip road was lined with what appeared to be every policeman—all white—in Lewisham borough, standing there to escort those club members off their territory. Out of those shared experiences of vulnerability, on both sides, relationships were built and faith shared.

Jesus clearly exerted power, but it was a power through vulnerability rather than through his prerogative of being the Son of God. His power emanated from his relationship with people, rather than through the owning of material substance, the claiming of human celebrity, or the leverage of power that those positions usually afforded. He finished his life without any assets or credentials—other than a criminal record—and yet his spirit has lived on, inspiring referent power of a very different kind. Part of his life was dedicated to training a team, the result of which was a community that has been central to the faith ever since. Despite his vulnerability he was still able to refer and inspire a vision of the future: a kingdom with dynamic values and powers, a mission that would bring hope to all other vulnerable people. Ever since his time people have become aware of Jesus' transformational vulnerability.

3. Young, *Face to Face*, 99.

The vulnerability of Jesus is therefore so significant that we need to look at some of the points/attributes/indicators/positions/values that such vulnerability exhibits.

## 8.2.1 Choices

The church is surely called to turn from a traditional use of power to the example of vulnerability as seen in the life and ministry of Jesus. Jesus exhibited vulnerability in such a way that leads us towards a different understanding of power—power through vulnerability. Jesus was indeed a very powerful person, but his power stemmed from very particular sources. It was expressed in a very specific lifestyle. It was consummated in what some might see as a counterproductive endpoint. We need to look carefully, therefore, at the sources, the lifestyle, and the end point of Jesus' human existence. Having already referred to the humble circumstances of his birth, we can begin at the starting point of his ministry—his temptation in the Negev.

In today's developed world, the month of August carries with it a particular significance for young people. For many of them it is a month when significant lifestyle choices are made. These choices arise out of receiving exam results of one sort or another. Whatever grades they achieve point then toward choices they can make, and other choices they can no longer aspire to. The exams are not just a matter of pass or fail, they become a guide to all, and to the direction of future travel. In the light of what we have achieved we can choose what we want to do.

The temptation of Jesus in the desert was a similar time of *lifestyle choice* for him. Possible avenues of choice were put to him that would determine what he could do with his life. The choice of material *possessions*, substance, and ownership were put to him as resources he could tap into. All these he clearly rejected. The choice of power through *domination*, control, and manipulation, well within his capability, was a second option that he rejected. A third suggestion was made. He could aspire to the A-list, fame, and *celebrity status* that, then and now, opens the door to popularity, reputation, success, and stardom. That too, with his extraordinary superman powers, was well within his grasp. But again, he forewent the chance to follow that road. All the attractive opportunities that we dreamt of having in our teenage August choices flashed through the mind of Jesus in the desert. All the attractive opportunities we wished we had were offered to Jesus and he rejected them on the spot.

Those choices made by Jesus were particularly significant. They decided his direction of travel, and they determined what he would not do; in consequence he was made to feel far more vulnerable to the forces of life that would surround him from then on. It determined that his life achievement would consist not so much around what he did do but rather that it would be shaped by what others would do to him and how he reacted to those actions. He discounted material substance, power over others, and stardom, and went instead for a chance to be a servant of others. The primary result of that August experience would be that, for all of his life, he would become vulnerable to the thoughts, emotions, and actions of others. From that vulnerability he would inevitably be led towards his lifetime achievement award—criminal conviction and death. So the choices he made in the desert pointed him to the heart of his life ministry, towards the kernel of truth that still lies at the center of the Christian faith. Vulnerability becomes integral to the message Jesus seeks to refer to all who decide to follow his advice.

## 8.2.2 Servanthood

Imagine the scene over the last few years, of Real Madrid winning the European Cup. The celebrations afterwards always start with the team photo, holding the Cup itself aloft. Who will hold the Cup? There would never be any doubt that it would be the team captain and Cristiano Ronaldo, who would hold each side of the Cup. It was those two high-profile places that Zebedee's two sons, James and John, aspired to when Team Jesus came through victorious. However, Jesus' response was quite unequivocal—"hold on mate, you've got it all wrong. The places you should aspire to at the photo call are at each end of the back row."

After James and John had come to Jesus asking for preferential places at the last banquet[4] Jesus realized that the other disciples were none too pleased with this preemptive strike by the Zebedee sons, to obtain leadership on Team Jesus. So Jesus called his team together to explain the situation. Jesus knew how Roman and Jewish cultural models dominated their thinking. Rome's success was all built around the emperor as general of the Roman army, which both created and sustained that vast empire. To the disciples that was *the* ultimate model for all administrations. Power takes people to the top and maintains their position there. Power was, therefore, behind James and John's dreams, and that was what so annoyed the rest of the disciples. But Jesus, remembering the choice he made during his temptations by the devil, replied,

---

4. Mark 10:35–45.

Hold on a minute, you've got it all wrong, you haven't really understood what I am on about. I am not trying to follow the example of the Roman Emperor, or the leaders of the previous Jewish revolt—the Maccabean Uprising, 167–160 BC. I am not trying to replace Rome with a Jewish administration following the same model of power and control. I reject the whole concept of power that keeps the might of Rome in place.[5]

Jesus then goes on to teach about his own alternative—that of service and sacrifice. Jesus seeks to instill into his team the idea that the first shall be last and the last shall be first. The primary purpose for his and their lives is to serve others as servant, and even as slave. If that eventually leads on to sacrifice and death, then so-be it. That servant attitude, with all the vulnerability that it brings, and with all the negation of prerogative power that it infers, lies at the center of the Jesus movement—the mission of God.

This was a real bombshell for his team to hear. It was so different from the norms they were used to. At that point we get no indication of their reaction to his revolutionary approach. No doubt it took time for it to sink in. It probably wasn't until after his self-giving death, and the consequent proof of success in his resurrection, that they had a chance to understand the import of what he was saying. The resurrection showed to them that Jesus' approach could be effective, that they could therefore take him at his word, that they could seek to live that approach out in their own lives. Certainly, Stephen got the message and followed it through to the end.

## 8.2.3 The Mind of Christ

Evidence that such a radical approach to power and authority, illustrated by Jesus, had been taken on board by his team, comes from the letters of Paul. As far as we know Paul had no direct encounter with Jesus until he met Christ on the road to Syria. But that roadside experience clearly conveyed to him this central element of Jesus' life and witness. This comes through clearly in his letter to the Philippian church.[6] In it he describes where Jesus came from, what he did, and where he moves on to.

Paul begins with the nature of God. He points out how Jesus illustrated God's nature by everything he did. He then culminates this with a vision of God's eventual total affirmation of Jesus in his ascension. Paul is highlighting to the Philippian church both the responsibilities as well as the joys of life in Christ. He writes here of "the mind of Christ." C. D. F. Moule suggests

5. See Wright, *Spiritual and Religious*, 58–60.

6. Phil 2:5–11.

that this passage resembles the letter "V." It talks about a descent followed by an ascent, humiliation followed by exaltation. Paul sees the heart of Jesus' ministry as one of emptying himself of his divinity (v. 7) by taking on the role of servant or slave as one of humbling himself to the point of death— death embracing humility (v. 8), as one of being rewarded by his father with exaltation (v. 9), as one of going from the heights of divinity to the depths of despair, followed by a return to the heights again to the father's presence.[7]

So the genuineness of Jesus' sense of vulnerability is based on his experience of emptiness and despair. As Paul Wignall points out, the humility Jesus experiences at that point "is not the price we pay for glory in the future—the humility is the glory."[8] In other words it is not that life in Christ will involve vulnerability and humility in the here and now only, but it is, that life in Christ—being accepted into the father's presence—will be forever deeply embedded in humility, making us conscious that humility has a power above and beyond our present reality. Vulnerability therefore lies at the heart of the kingdom, both here and now as well as in the future. Being prepared to be humbled, to accept servanthood and obedience, is intrinsic to receiving Christ's offer of forgiveness; it is an outflowing of the scandal of the cross. The irrelevance of worldly power in the face of this dwelling in vulnerability, is therefore not a second step of commitment, it is embedded in the very kernel of the gospel message itself.

The propelling force that inspires this vulnerability comes from verse 6, which describes the reasoning behind Jesus' descent into vulnerability. Jesus took the step of becoming vulnerable because he was committed to *referring* the very nature of God. Because he was in the form of God, it was incumbent upon him to empty himself, to become fully human. Biblical interpretation centers around whether this phrase could mean, "*although* Jesus was in the form of God"—concessive—or if it could mean "*because* Jesus was in the form of God"—causative. If one accepts that both readings have truth, then one can conclude that Jesus was reflecting the very nature of God by exhibiting vulnerability, the antithesis of human power. So Paul is saying that if the mind of Christ saw vulnerability as the very nature of God, then we should see vulnerability as being at the heart of our life in Christ. So the poetic reflection of Paul in this advice to the Philippian church ought to form the bedrock of church life if that church life is to refer the nature of God to our contemporary, power-conscious society.

7. Moule, "Manhood of Jesus," 95–110.

8. Wignall, "Kenosis and Total Ministry," 17.

## 8.2.4 A Marginalized Minority

Paul offered further evidence of this radical approach to power, and the wielders of power, in his first letter to the church in Corinth: "God chose the lowly things of this world and the despised things and the things that are not, to nullify the things that are" (1 Cor 1:28). The best visual illustration of Paul's statement is surely the life and ministry of Jesus. Rather than associating with leaders and the powerful in Jewish society, he chose to identify with "those who are not" the marginalized, the outcast. Jesus typified this approach by the way he engaged with those around him, "Jesus demonstrated God's grace toward, and inclusion of, people of all backgrounds . . . he consistently makes the outsider the hero of his parables and the recipients of God's multifaceted grace."[9] When it comes to the great banquet feast, "Jesus constantly invites in 'sinners,' outcasts, the marginalized, and the ne'er do wells,"[10] and invites us to be similarly generous and self-emptying towards the vulnerable.

Jewish society put great emphasis on purity, and so those who were considered impure were forced to the periphery. These outcasts consisted of lepers, beggars, those with chronic medical conditions, such as the woman with the hemorrhage, those quislings who associated with Roman authorities, such as Zacchaeus, and the faceless and nameless slaves. By consorting with the outcast, Jesus contradicted everything Jewish society valued. He gave these people time, took them seriously, went to their houses, and touched and healed them. He spoke to Samaritans. He knew that his actions would inexorably lead to confrontation with Jewish authorities, and, ultimately, conviction. He knew this would make him open to the charge of blasphemy, that this might lead to execution on a refuse tip outside the city walls. This association with "those who are not" was a conscious choice by Jesus to follow a particular path that illustrated the nature of his father. In effect Jesus was committing himself to change the world from the bottom up by having principles that would empower the weak, by offering an alternative to the world's practices.

In today's world, using the language of Cassells and Alberts and Hayes, he was exhibiting projective identity and disruptive innovation. His choice was an example of Charles Handy's point A/point B, or the S-curve of technological innovation. As an alternative to the religious power structure of the Jews and the political military might of the Roman Empire, he offered a countercultural stance of identification with "those who are not", he

---

9. Rohr, *Divine Dance*, 88–89.

10. Rohr, *Divine Dance*, 17.

expressed this identification through his gifts of ministry such as generosity, hospitality, mutuality, and friendship. He was not prepared to be compromised to the power structures of the day; he offered instead an alternative based on vulnerability. He knew that if he did follow this line it would lead him into confrontation and conflict with the powerful, but he continued to do so, knowing that he would be reflecting his father's nature.

Such actions and examples from Jesus raise serious questions for today's church. By attempting to adjust itself contextually to changing society, with its posthumanist survival of the fittest framework, its climbing the ladder mentality, its achievement of identity through power, its winner-takes-all market, the church stands in danger of legitimizing that culture. It appears to take no notice of the projective alternative that Jesus expressed to the power-centered society of his day. By attempting to contextualize superficially, and yet at the same time failing to exert countercultural influence on society in areas that really matter, the church is bringing its message into disrepute. It is downplaying the grace of vulnerability as it seeks to assimilate itself into the altar of power.

Frances Young, alternatively, highlights the value of vulnerability which she learned from her relationship with her disabled son, Arthur. She writes about "sharing the 'soul' of the marginalized . . . receiving from those who are in worldly terms 'below,' but in other respects often 'above.'"[11]

Indeed, it might well be appropriate to reconsider the central theme of liberation theology from the last century and reapply it into the context of inequality expected in the third decade. We could discover that by entering into solidarity with those who suffer, we would engage God's grace with our changing social structures.

## 8.1.1 The Jubilee

In committing himself to "those who are not", Jesus was not initiating a new stance, but rather bringing up to date a feature of God's nature—articulated in the history of Israel from the time of the exodus onwards. From Egypt the cries of pain and oppression reached his heart, and the exodus was enacted. The experience of redemption was very real to that generation of sojourners in the desert. As the tribes settled in Palestine a new society began to be formed, as illustrated in the book of Leviticus.

Although it was recognized early on in the settled societal structure, that "There will always be poor people in the land,"[12] God made it clear,

11. Young, *Face to Face*, 219.

12. Deut 15:11.

through the sabbatical years leading up to the year of Jubilee that endemic poverty was not part of his plan, that extremes of poverty and wealth were not acceptable for a people made in his image and expected to reflect his nature. The principle of jubilee was therefore articulated[13] to ensure that whilst it was acknowledged poverty would be present, structures were to be established to ensure it would not become endemic.

The Jubilee, every forty-nine to fifty years as described in Leviticus chapter 25, was to address extreme forms of poverty that had developed by intervention into two specific areas of societal life and structure—the family and the land. Poverty came about when families, for one reason or another, became so poor that they had to sell their land, and even themselves, into slavery in order to survive. The jubilee principle ensured that their freedom and their land would be returned to them, so that they could make a fresh start. As Chris Wright has put it,

> The primary purpose of the jubilee was to preserve the socio-economic fabric of multiple-household land tenure and the comparative equality and independent viability of the smallest family-plus-land units . . . intended for the survival and welfare of the families of Israel.[14]

The theological assumptions behind the jubilee were the significance of each human individual within an extended family/household, and the idea that the land was God's land—bestowed on each family as stewards of God's land, rather than as being owners in their own right. So even if a family had fallen on hard times, at the jubilee their impoverishment would be addressed by the return of their freedom and land so they could start afresh. Such a principle indicated to Israel that God expected a "broadly equitable distribution of the resources of the earth, especially land, as a curb on the tendency to accumulation with its inevitable oppression and alienation."[15]

Such a principle presents a real challenge to present-day society. Just as Jesus challenges the concept of purity and outcastness that was put forward by the religious leadership of his day, so too the principle behind the Jubilee offers a considerable challenge to the increasing accumulation of wealth by those who control technological development and to those who simply seek to ameliorate that trend by the introduction of a UBW. Although the rural economy of an early, subsistence-based agricultural economy is far distant from the Western capitalist society of today, there

---

13. Lev 25:8–10.

14. Wright, *Mission of God*, 295.

15. Wright, *Mission of God*, 296.

remains a basic understanding of humanity that surely relates each to both. Just as the family unit in early Israel was there to "focus on the identity, status, responsibility and security of the individual Israelite,"[16] so too surely today's declaration of human rights mirrors those same concerns: just as "the jubilee aimed to restore dignity and participation to families through maintaining or restoring their economic viability,"[17] so too those criticizing surveillance capitalism and the lack of human dignity/aspiration behind the concept of UBW have a great deal in common; just as the prophets attacked the elite, wealthy society surrounding the later kings of Israel and Judah, so too today's followers of Christ have a countercultural role in challenging the inadequacies of worshipping "economic growth" and the "elite ownership of technological development," at the expense of the marginalization of those who suffer from the spiraling inequalities resulting from today's capitalist market economy.[18]

## 8.2.6 Prophetic Social Justice

As we have seen, Jesus' commitment to "those who are not" reiterated the underlying Jubilee principle that God is not happy with endemic poverty, where those who suffer or struggle, for one reason or another, are used by those with greater status, affluence, or power. Similarly, Jesus followed in the same footsteps of the prophets such as Jeremiah, Hosea, and Amos, who challenged the behavior of the elite royal courts of their day and the excessive lifestyles of the wealthy. Such prophets attacked the weakness of nominal religious responses to such behavior; they prophesied in a way that pointed out Yahweh's vision of what might be as against the reality of the day—what is. Jeremiah has a pivotal role in reestablishing the purposefulness of God amongst his people. He confirms[19] that God will establish a new covenant with his people, writing his law in their hearts and personally committing himself to them. Jeremiah then makes clear another particular attribute of God's nature.[20] When comparing the life of King Josiah with that of his son Shallum, Jeremiah states that whereas Shallum "builds his palace by unrighteousness and his upper rooms by injustice," Josiah by contrast, "defended the cause of the poor and needy." Jeremiah then commends Josiah by indicating "Is not that what it means to know me" (Jer 23:16)?

16. Wright, *Mission of God*, 297.
17. Wright, *Mission of God*, 297.
18. Schluter and Ashcroft, *Jubilee Manifesto*, ch. 9.
19. Jer 31:31–34.
20. Jer 22:13–16.

From this, José Miranda[21] has pointed out that the very fact of knowing God involves justice for humanity. It isn't possible to know the true nature of God without realizing that he is totally committed to eradicate injustice. It isn't a matter of a two-step process that begins with knowing God and which then leads on to loving others. It is rather a single step of knowing God and being committed to justice all at the same time. You can't have one without the other. Knowing God means doing justice for all.

Similarly, Amos said the same about worshipping God and doing justice, "I hate, I despise your feasts; I cannot stand your assemblies . . . away with the noise of your songs . . . But let justice roll on like a river, righteousness like a never-failing stream."[22] Hosea followed: "For I desire mercy, not sacrifice, and acknowledgement of God rather than burnt offerings."[23] Justice clearly has to feature centrally in celebration and community if God's followers are to reflect God's true nature in their worship and to those around them. This is further endorsed by Jeremiah's words to those living in exile, who kept dreaming of returning to Jerusalem, to their old way of life. Jeremiah insisted instead that the Lord was calling them to settle, and get involved in the foreign society in which they had been placed: "build homes . . . plant gardens . . . take wives . . . Seek the prosperity of the city to which I have carried you into exile. Pray to the Lord for it, because if it prospers, you too will prosper."[24] Jeremiah was illustrating that God had a vision of his people being committed to contribute towards the lives of their captors. Despite the fact that their captors were their enemies, who had destroyed their beloved city Jerusalem, and dragged them into exile as prisoners of war. God called upon his people to pray for the livelihood of these oppressors. Jeremiah was prophesying that the faith of the exiles should express itself by offering a projective Yahweh-centered alternative to a nation that served other gods—a situation surely not unlike our own substance-oriented society.

## 8.2.7 Sheep and Goats

The emphasis put on commitment to the poor, weak, and outcast by Jesus, is illustrated by his reflection on what it means to become one of his followers. On the one hand, he declares to Nicodemus, "For God so loved the world that he gave his one and only son, that whoever believes in him shall

21. Miranda, *Marx and the Bible*, 44.

22. Amos 5:21–24.

23. Hos 6:6.

24. Jer 29:5–7.

not perish but have eternal life."[25] However, that kernel description of the gospel, the heart of the purpose of Jesus, is made more complex by a second definition regarding the salvation Christ came to bring. This was illustrated by Jesus himself in the parable of the sheep and the goats.[26] The king, or judge, describes those who will be welcomed into heavenly glory as those who fed, welcomed, clothed, cared for, and visited those in need. "Whatever you did for one of the least of these brothers of mine, you did it for me" (Matt 25:40). So the message Jesus Christ has left with us is that through him alone lies the path of salvation, and that such discipleship will be identified by total "at oneness" with the marginalized. As Orlando Costas has put it, to come to know salvation in Christ, to become part of his new order, is "not so much a prize won as a responsibility given."[27]

If today's church is to take seriously the image, purpose, and message of Jesus Christ, it will need to remodel its identity around that purpose and message. The church will therefore be both a place where believers meet, and also a place rooted in the needs of people suffering. Jürgen Moltmann reflected on these two strands:

> Whoever does this for the least of these"; and "As the father has sent me so I send you." He concluded "What is the true Church? The true Church is where Christ is present, in the mission of the believers and the suffering of the 'least of these.'

"His community is therefore the brotherhood of the *believers* and the poor, the lovers and the imprisoned, the hopers and the sick. The apostolate *says what* the church is, the 'least of these' *says where* the Church belongs. Only if the Church realizes in itself this double brotherhood of Christ does it really live in the presence of the crucified and exalted Christ."[28]

Further to both Costas's and Moltmann's illustrations of who the church is and where the church belongs comes in Jesus Christ's definition to his disciples of the church's identity. Christ passed on to them the sense of identity and discipleship that he himself received from his father. He indicated that if they were to rejoice in any kind of identity at all, it ought to be one that reflected himself and the relationship he had with his father. "By this" he bequeaths to his disciples, "all men will know that you are my disciples, if you love one another."[29] Surely herein lies the identity of the church:

---

25. John 3:16.

26. Matt 25:31–46.

27. Costas, *Church and its Mission*, 249–50.

28. Dumas, quoted in Moltmann, *Open Church*, 105; italics original.

29. John 13:35.

not in owning property, not in claiming status, not in dominating others, not in claiming that everyone else is going in the wrong direction, but rather in illustrating God's love for humanity through claiming his referent power, by loving each other. Just as Jesus loved his disciples right up to the point of the ultimate sacrifice, so we his disciples, his church of today, should love one another and all humanity as a representation of that core truth, that core witness of faith. By claiming this referent power, above all the other identification marks assumed by the church, we will be proclaiming the identity Jesus Christ bestows on us.

The image, message, purpose, and referent power of Jesus Christ therefore give ample guidance to those who see themselves as the body of Christ today. Not only should such people acknowledge him as the way, the truth, and the life, but we should also be imbued with his teaching, and his power. We receive from him the bread of life, we are cared for by him as the shepherd of our flock, we are inspired by him, as the light of the world, we are empowered by him amongst the suffering and marginalized within our global society. The mission of God and the purpose of Jesus Christ merge together in the new order and its ministry to the whole of humanity: encapsulated in the image of being there amongst those in need and having empathy with rejected nonachievers in our society. As St. John's first letter put it: referring to God's sending of his son so that we could receive his forgiveness, he says "Since God so loved us, we also ought to love one another. No one has ever seen God; but if we love one another, God lives in us, and his love is made complete in us."[30] Surely these words of John are illustrating that if the church is to be the church it should center around the vulnerable, the referent power of the incarnation, in contrast to the legitimating, prerogative, and often coercive power associated with so many human institutions and organizations today.

## 8.3 THE CROSS, SUFFERING, AND VICTORY

The final illustration of the way prerogative power and genuine vulnerability are polar opposites comes in the last days of Jesus' life. Over the course of three years Jesus had challenged the very heart of Jewish and Roman authority. To the Jewish leadership he offered a radical redefinition of what it meant to be holy and acceptable in the eyes of God. To the Roman authorities he was seen as a potential threat to the power of Caesar and Caesar's imperatorial demand for divine recognition/worship. Such challenges resulted in the combined weight of these two superpowers being thrown

30. 1 John 4:11–12.

at Jesus in the form of mock trials, conviction, and a criminal's death. He was subjected "to the grim reality of this world . . . to some of the worst evil human beings are capable of inflicting on one another, and to the deepest darkness of the human spirit."[31] The outward result was that Jesus was buried under the weight of the powers that opposed him, to such an extent that even he appeared to lose contact with his father—"My God, My God, why have you forsaken me" (Matt 27:46)?—but inwardly the very nature of his vulnerability was vindicated when he could exclaim, "It is finished . . . Into your hands I commend my spirit" (Luke 23:46). He had discovered that "in the utter absence of God was the presence of God."[32] Out of the vulnerability and weakness that Jesus exhibited on the cross came the victory and superiority of that weakness, as his resurrection revealed. Vulnerability had defused power: love had overcome hatred.[33]

Jesus' death also highlighted the centrality of suffering. Inevitably vulnerability and suffering can often be found together. Jesus forewarned us of this potential inevitability when teaching his disciples at an open meeting. "If anyone would come after me, he must deny himself, and take up his cross and follow me."[34] Part of the commitment he asks from his potential followers is that they will be called to follow him to the cross and beyond. They may not have fully understood what this meant at the time, but we today can be in no doubt whatsoever. And countless Christians before us have taken him at his word—up to death itself. The point Jesus was making surely, was not that his followers should *accept* suffering, but rather that they should *choose* suffering. By choosing vulnerability Jesus was fully aware that he was also choosing the inevitable suffering that would follow. Jesus knew this in his bones, as he realized that, to achieve his father's purposes, he would ultimately have to pay the price with his own life. It was his suffering and death on the cross that led to his ultimate victory. For him victory could not be achieved without suffering. On the Palestinian hillside, Jesus was forewarning us that taking the path of vulnerability meant that suffering would become synonymous with that choice.

A suffering commitment to the marginalized can only be motivated by mirroring and reflecting the true love of our suffering servantlike God. As Rohr puts it, "When you choose to love, you will eventually suffer."[35] Or put it the other way around, "Some kind of suffering is always the price and

31. Young, *Face to Face*, 77, 79.

32. Young, *Face to Face*, 77.

33. Wright, *Spiritual and Religious*, 65–66.

34. Matt 16:24.

35. Rohr, *Divine Dance*, 176.

proof of love."[36] Similarly Young articulates the same lesson she learned with her son, Arthur. Despite his disabilities, "I found myself able to give thanks even for Arthur . . . it was no longer a case of simply accepting Arthur but of rejoicing in Arthur."[37] Such an image of the church is difficult to imagine for many who have grown up in a static, hierarchical, power- and substance-oriented church. A vulnerable church, situated at the margins of society, is the antithesis of the present norm. But surely we are being called towards vulnerability: towards a paradigm shift in our understanding of the word "church", towards a church that is more of a prequel to the kingdom rather than an establishment in its own right. It may well be difficult to piece such a transformation together in our minds. Nevertheless, we could imagine it as we reimagine the infinite one, the immanent one, and the intimate one combining together to illustrate that God empathizes with suffering just as much as by fulfilling himself through the caretaking of his creation. For the church to become the church, it has to take into its bloodstream that only through absorbing the purpose and principles arising from suffering and vulnerability can it rediscover the true concept of Christian witness.

---

### MUSLIM VULNERABILITY

An interesting illustration of suffering, that went on to inspire reconciliation, comes from an incident in Khartoum Cathedral. On a Saturday morning the Dean, Sylvester Thomas, was violently attacked, so much so that it appeared as though he was about to be murdered. He was saved by a Muslim police officer who threw his body over Sylvester to protect him, preventing his attackers from finishing off what they intended. In the aftermath, Sylvester recovered from his wounds and went on to forgive his attackers. Following that, Sylvester and the Muslim policeman spoke together about reconciliation in Khartoum, followed by Sylvester speaking in Kadugli—center of the Nuba Mountains war zone—and receiving a cross of nails from Coventry Cathedral as a sign of that ministry of reconciliation.

---

John Taylor puts a different slant on this issue of suffering when talking about problems and solutions.[38] He describes today's technological world as one made up of problems that need solutions. We expect that for every problem technology will be able to provide a solution. We expect therefore that suffering can be overcome in similar fashion, one way or another. However, Jesus surely infers that suffering could become a way of life, an

36. Rohr, *Divine Dance*, 161.
37. Young, *Face to Face*, 85.
38. Taylor, *Go-between God*, 143–44.

experience we will have to get used to, part-and-parcel of a fallen world. It will ultimately be overcome by following the way of the cross, by our discovery that suffering "can be transcended through the grace of God."[39] It will be overcome in our own minds as we take the future into account; as we draw the final victory into our present imagination. Jesus, the ultimate victor, is asking us to live in suffering, knowing that it has already been paid for. It is because of having this attitude that we will go to the ends of the earth to stand beside the outcast and the marginalized. We will do this, with a "humble, cross-centered confidence,"[40] simply because it is the Jesus way.

## 8.4 REDEFINITION-REIMAGINING

Concluding this investigation into the word "power," we can see that both Christian faith and church are called to reject the primary definition given by today's Western society. We should instead, as Jesus illustrated, be owning the fact that, for the Christian, power is sourced from the referent power of Jesus Christ and his spirit, and is defined through vulnerability and suffering. These same two attributes oil the machinery of the new engine, and that new engine empowers the mission of God. These two attributes are redefining our primary objective.[41] In the place of a power that lords it over people, we will be proclaiming, through our lives, a referent power that serves people, even if it leads to ostracism and death. This understanding of power, referred to us by Jesus, forms the basis of our worldview—a worldview that is radically different and counterculturally challenging to the worldview assumed by posthumanist, surveillance capitalist presuppositions. But more of that in the final chapter.

39. Young, *Face to Face*, 144.
40. Wright, *Spiritual and Religious*, 144.
41. Wright, *Spiritual and Religious*, 60.

# Chapter 9

## Hierarchy, Hybrid, and Emergence

The basic ingredients of French dressing are two parts oil to one part of vinegar. The two ingredients have different viscosities. They don't mix well. If you shake them up they combine together, but if you allow the mixture to stand for a period, they separate again. They are like chalk and cheese. It can be argued that the same applies to the Christian faith/church and contemporary society. They can be seen to mix together, but there are two significant underlining differences that produce a tendency for them to separate again. First, as we have seen, the prerogative, power-centered, substance-oriented nature of society doesn't blend well with the vulnerable-centered narrative of Jesus Christ. Secondly, we now need to acknowledge that the church's hierarchical, central authority model looks increasingly out of place in our ever-evolving, networking, information society.

Whereas the intrinsic structure of the church remains top-down, centralized, and hierarchical in nature, today's western, technologically based, digital-age society has moved inexorably toward a more networking, decentralized, bottom-up, power-to-the-edge model. So not only is the top-down, hierarchical, power-centered, coercive approach at odds with the ministry of Jesus, but it is also at odds with the emerging networking mindset of the society within which it exists.

In part 1 we identified how the latter part of the last century signaled a change from hierarchy to network from absolute to relative, from simplicity to complexity, from anthropocentricity to technocentricity. In part 2 we noticed how both faith and church did their best to keep up with and relate to the evolving and changing face of Western civilization, from the

Roman Empire onwards. Since the Enlightenment, the faith/church has at least sought to keep in touch as it followed on in the wake of discovery and reasoning. Now the church is challenged to engage with the constant flux of this postmillennial third decade: a context of exponential change creating an ever-changing brave new world, a core of bottom-up, decentralized, innovative, algorithmic, technological development, a potentially all-encompassing paradigm shift even from the pre-millennial period. Not only does this paradigm shift in context affect institutional, governmental, and global aspects of our society, but it also impacts human and environmental relationships at both individual and community levels.

The question facing the faith/church of today is how to respond to this contextual challenge. We have suggested in chapter 7 that the church is already struggling with its pre-Enlightenment roots (stage 3 in Fowler's analysis). We have acknowledged its engagement with both Enlightenment reasoning (stage 4) and postmodern relativism[1] (stage 5). This is all illustrated in the mixed economy response that seeks to hold inherited, traditional faith/church, together with accommodating fresh expressions, contemporary worship, and communication trends. At the same time this mixed economy, whilst still being dragged down by the difficulty of archaic overheads, is also facing the complex questions/issues arising from the culture clash between traditional views and a wide range of pluralist responses to contemporary ethical and moral dilemmas.

But now an even newer postmillennial dawn is breaking: a world of superintelligence, where anthropocentricity is being overtaken by techno-centricity, a world where those who have, could potentially gobble up the limited resources available to humankind, where privately owned data control overwhelms governmental democracy, where a concern for prudence, temperance, and basic human coherence can so easily be undermined by localized micro-communities and extreme pressure groups, where a helter-skelter world of fear and uncertainty discovers that competition for limited resources can degenerate into a dystopic polarization between those who have and those who have not, punctuated by weaponry and warfare as illustrated by Watson and Freeman's "Futurevision-Scenarios for a World in 2040."

So what now? How is the faith/church going to catch up and engage with this postmillennial ethos? How can it move on from its primary instinct to survive, and gain confidence to believe it can grow and flourish in such a world of continuous flux? How does it come to terms with the influences of this new environment? How does it frame appropriate questions

---

1. Cundy, *Tomorrow is Another Country*.

to ask both of itself, and of contemporary society, equally bemused by this paradigm shift? How does it discern and debate its options and go on to create transforming strategies? To use a building analogy, how does the faith/ church, with pre-Enlightenment, Christendom stage 3 foundations, with an existing five-bedroom suburban house built on the Enlightenment (stage 4) debate, either build an extension or pull it all down so as to rebuild a Grand Designs creation in the relativist postmillennial building boom context of today (stage 5)? Putting it theologically: What form should the mission of God take as we move into postmillennial's third decade?

Having looked at the elements and influences of our millennial context in part 1, part 2—following into chapter 8—looked at the development of faith/church through the centuries, together with the questions/issues that remain unanswered or unresolved as the millennium approached. Chapters 9 and 10 will now seek to identify the three possible options that arise as the faith/church seeks to address the present disjunction between the church of today and the brave new world envisaged tomorrow. Following on from those three options and the challenges they bring, chapter 11 will then look at how the faith/church can contribute counterculturally to our present humanitarian flux, to the tension emerging between the temperance and hope of a Sun Tzu fusion on the one hand, and the fear of a dystopian future—an off-the-grid, marginalized, local dissident group, threatening a fragile global equilibrium with a nuclear torpedo carried in the sidecar of its motorbike—on the other.

## 9.1 CHANGE AND CHOICE

Although somewhat dated, the 1967 film *Zulu* still remains a cult classic. Starring Michael Caine and Stanley Baker, it depicts the skirmish at Rourke's Drift in South Africa, where a handful of British soldiers faced a huge army of Zulu warriors, determined to exterminate the colonial forces. Stanley Baker stands out as the commanding officer, ordering the wagons to create a laager, and fight to the bitter end. Despite the odds he is determined to hold his ground. The similarities between that image of a laager mentality and the attitude of many traditional (stage 3) orthodox churches is not difficult to imagine, with dwindling clergy numbers and elderly congregations with a maintenance mentality all desperately caught up in KTLO—Keeping the Lights On.

A second image is of a transformed cathedral interior, totally filled with the sound of a Christian rock band pounding out through massive speakers to an excited crowd of believing teenagers, dancing and chanting till the early hours of the morning—with even a bishop pogoing around on the fringes. Here was an illustration of contemporary witness, epitomized by younger people wanting to identify with a new perspective on Christian worship. Behind this contemporary expression were undoubtedly youthful churches engaged in a search for a relevant faith—stage 4 progressive churches.

Then thirdly, and more quietly, in the background of our experiences, arises the example of churches deeply involved in their local community through housing the homeless, establishing after-school clubs, providing space for addiction sufferers, and debt counselling. This third church exemplar appears to have taken over the whole church building, which has to be hastily readapted when Sunday worship takes place. The organization is dependent on volunteers and alternative funding. A clergy person appears from time to time as an iconic figure in the background. Here the atmosphere is both earthed in reality, and yet inspired by hope arising from an imagined future (stage 5 "conjunctive"). Every now and again the volunteers slip off to a celebration conference involving similar dedicated activists, where thoughts and experiences are shared and fresh inspiration gained (stage 6).

## 9.2 CROSSING THE BRIDGE

These three cameos describe, somewhat inadequately, three possible choices facing the church of today. The first choice emphasizes survival within a safe bubble, a *laager mentality*, a rump committed to KTLO; maintaining an equilibrium that gives peace to those within but struggles to engage with those outside (stage 3).

The second choice is to go for a *mixed economy*—the hybrid. Maintenance mode/inherited church is honored, but fresh expressions/emerging church—a more relevant approach—is permitted. These two approaches run in tandem, "two structures—one organization" in the John Kotter model. But although progressive thinking is acknowledged and even endorsed, the mixed-economy, top-down model still revolves around an Enlightenment agenda. Only sometimes does it begin to engage with postmodern/contemporary issues in a conjunctive way.

Then there is choice three—the emergent church, *an emergent organism*. This choice is very different in nature: it emerges from the living personal, experiential faith of its membership; it exists deep within a local community; it is inspired by the example of Christ's relationship with those around him; it has a distinct bottom-up dynamic and referent power bubbles up at the edges; it is vulnerable to external forces all around; it is unafraid to engage with postmodern and postmillennial issues/questions, and is prepared to hold divergent views in tension; it exudes confidence despite being surrounded by complexity; its longevity and sustainability are not assured; its uniformity to a Christian norm is debatable (stage 5, conjunction).

But there is one key element of dynamic that separates choices one and two from choice three—it involves crossing a bridge. Out of the three options, the third option is earthed in a very different dynamic. Whereas the first two accept the underlying framework of a pre-Enlightenment, Christendom-molded church context, and exist within it, the third option emerges out of a very different framework much more conducive to contemporary networking society.

For the church to transition to the third option, there lies a paradigm shift in itself. It incorporates the radical change from anthropocentricty to Christocentricity, from power to vulnerability, from downward, prerogative control to upward, referent initiative and diversity. Similarly, but from a different tangent, the Anabaptist network newsletter has thought-provokingly identified seven significant ecclesiological shifts: from center to the margins, from majority to minority; from settlers to sojourners; from privilege to plurality; from control to witness; from maintenance to mission; and from institution to movement.[2] All of this is based on a fresh fiduciary framework, to use Polanyi's term, not so much constrained by the Christendom maintenance model/the empirical, objectivist Enlightenment project/ the relativist postmodern understanding/or a postmillennial, mechanistic, technocentric framework but rather on a transcendent referent/value-oriented model centered around the life, witness, and work of Jesus, and a fresh experience of the Pentecost event. This is exemplified through vulnerability from the margins, and the nonreciprocal gift Christ offered to humanity— from incarnation to resurrection through the gift of life made possible as a result of Christ's death. Such a Christocentric framework would not only be discovered, articulated, and contextually relevant to our third decade, but would also input counterculturally to that same context. In the past, contextualization has been sought at the expense of a clear, prophetic, countercultural role. But here, in this conjunctive model, the contextual and the countercultural run side by side—just as the river and the canal made up a complex transport network from one side of the country to the other.

Such a possible jump from anthropo/technocentricity to theo/Christocentricity would take us back to the concepts of institutional change illustrated in part 1. Cassels, Alberts and Hayes, and Handy and Hock all

2. Anabaptist Network Newsletter, February 2004.

have their own description of this dramatic point in institutional life where a traditional framework is supplanted by a new idea. Cassels refers to the legislative being overtaken by the projective. Alberts and Hayes refer to sustaining innovation being sidelined by disruptive innovation, and perhaps most clearly of all, Charles Handy talks of a point A/B, when a second sigmoid curve grows out of and transforms the first. From a more practical point of view, Dee Hock describes the paradigm shift from the controlling authority of Bank of America, to the free-standing collaboration and trust expressed by the Visa International Board.

In reality, making such dramatic paradigm shifts can involve enormous upheaval.

---

### A FORK IN THE ROAD

In his memoir, *A Fork in the Road*, the well-known Afrikaaner novelist André Brink reminds us of the dilemma faced by the PW Botha/FW de Klerk apartheid-sponsoring South African Government—legitimized by Dutch Reformed Church Calvinist biblical theology—when challenged by the oppressed black majority of the country. In no way did the institution want to change, despite world condemnation of its policies. Brink then likened this dilemma to the Sorbonne student riots of 1968 in Paris—which he vividly described from personal experience—who were pressing the de Gaulle Government to respond to their demands. Both institutions used their special security/riot police to maintain their positions. Ultimately, through the charismatic leadership of Nelson Mandela, the apartheid regime was forced to concede, but in Paris the de Gaulle government rejected any such dramatic shift in government policy.

More contemporary examples include the Street Protest Movement against the National Islamic Front-sponsored Bashir regime in Sudan—inspired by medical and other professionals, such as Professor Asma El Sony and others in early 2019—and the Climate Change Movement highlighted by Greta Thunburg and her message to the United Nations in September 2019. Although the street protests in Khartoum have appeared to achieve a radical turnaround in Sudan, the Climate Change Movement has yet to achieve the significant policy change from world governments that they propose.

These examples all illustrate the massive task involved if an established institution is called to make a voluntary paradigm shift in policy or structure. In turn they highlight the size of the challenge facing institutional and authoritarian church leaderships if they are to relinquish power in favor of vulnerability, release downward control and foster upward initiative and diversity, and relinquish their authority in order to rekindle the presence of the spirit in each and every believer.

In reality the main body of the church is well past Handy's point A. The plateau is over and the curve is descending. Point B has been reached, with some fresh expressions and mega-churches seeking to initiate a second curve at this point. But the inauguration of a second curve, Handy suggests, will be hindered by a culture of bitterness, recrimination, division, and pessimism. At this point the magnitude of change required to overcome resistance, initiate legislation, and overwhelm the status quo is phenomenal. A refutation of the past will need to occur. A rejection, even a confession, or acknowledgment of past inadequacies, needs to take place. That point may be sudden/radical, but it needs to happen if a second sigmoid curve is to take root.

So, for the faith/church of today, there would need to be a significant walking away from a Christendom mindset, from a control-oriented orthodox theology, from Enlightenment confrontation, from the power, status, substance, wealth, and property of its history. All of this would be extraordinarily difficult, both in the mind and in practice. Walking away from established church structures, episcopal/leader jurisdiction, and diocesan/area order; from those sustaining KTLO; from historic buildings and the status of being the church—all of this would be a tsunami in itself.

To make such a change would not only require a walking away, but it would also require an outline articulation of a new alternative—option three. It would require a recentering on Jesus' message, lifestyle, dedication, and gift; a Christocentric approach to the Bible; a fresh grasp of the Holy Spirit's inspiring and empowering presence, in each and every believer—power to the edge. It would also express a view that, although some form of structure will be needed if anarchy is to be avoided, such structure should not be sought too quickly or too firmly. Past history, including church history, affirms that often revolution is followed by a reestablishment of the old structures under different names. It will also surely be a structure centered around referent servanthood rather than prerogative power; innovation and creativity rather than rigid regulation; holding diverse views in tension rather than polarizing debate. All in all, such a future, although it needs to be imagined, will not need to be drawn too tightly toward an unchangeable blueprint; it should be envisaged as a skeleton rather than as a body; as a framework of construction rather than as a building in its entirety. In Fowler's framework such a transition will lead clearly from stage 3/4 to stage 5.

## 9.3 THE RUMP

The visual description of the Boer tactic of laagering its wagon trains—copied by the British Army—in the face of enemy forces, is a telling one. As we have seen, such churches have been faced by a tsunami of threats, with few expectations of survival for the long term. At the same time, technological capability, innovation, and change have raised a string of questions with no apparent easy answers. Inherited churches that have been established by pre-Enlightenment orthodox traditional boundaries and cerebral, narrative, judgmental backgrounds, are genuinely struggling with what they face.

When struck by these overwhelming challenges, the mainstream structure of the church can easily revert to the process of lockdown—well articulated by the work of Cassels and others. This identification of legitimizing identity, sustaining innovation, and the maintenance of the primary sigmoid curve when point B approaches are all reflected in the church's default position when faced with rapid social change. So it comes as no surprise that Fowler's description of a stage 3 mentality can easily dominate church responses to exponential change, resulting in a desire to laager and KTLO.

---

**KTLO**

"Keeping the Lights On," in IT terminology, refers to the basic level of energy required to keep a computer functioning on powered-up mode. In this instance it would refer to keeping the existing church organization functioning as in the past. A computer in KTLO mode would be in more of a static position as compared to the more operative mode enabling innovation, imagination, and the development of new products.

---

The emphasis of this response will be on institutional maintenance/survival rather than growth/mission; illustrated by the search for improved management capabilities and maintaining high clergy numbers in order to perpetuate existing practices. Evidence suggests that the laager/lockdown approach will center around suburban churches, with the deep rural and inner cities being sacrificed when resources are depleted. This response will also reflect how churches with a strong traditional and/or biblical authority—will outlast more liberal approaches. Even so these traditional approaches, based on more cerebral, narrative, centralized, historic foundations, will increasingly struggle with the more decentralized, innovative, creative, experiential, and intuitive landscape of our technocentric culture. At the moment the laager is holding, the lockdown is comparatively effective. However, the future prognosis for this rump, remains on the knife edge of uncertainty.

## 9.4 THE HYBRID

As the information age gained traction, and networking emerged as an alternative model of organizational shape, large traditional institutions became aware that their tried-and-tested hierarchical structures were struggling to compete with the new emergent business model. As a result, many organizations reenvisioned themselves. They reordered themselves so that their life force could more easily arise at the perimeters and work upwards rather than the other way around. Ebay, which sells and resells commodities, began with customer needs rather than with central control. Amazon began with reader preferences and then created an appropriate structure to supply those needs cheaply, with the customer list becoming more crucial than central management.

Fearing the thought of being left behind in the marketplace, large traditional organizations therefore began to ask themselves how they could compete with more lightweight competitors. Their top-heavy organization was too slow to respond to market changes/fresh innovation/new products and expectations; their central control was not making the best use of workforce skill and creativity in an information-rich culture. In many cases the reaction was to develop *hybrid structures*, reducing the overhead hierarchical influence and increasing networking capability. Niall Ferguson[3] highlighted this concept with his description of Sienna society in the Middle Ages, where the city worked through a liaison between the tower/city rulers/administrators, and the marketplace/network of city traders. He pointed out that, historically, hierarchy and networking have had a cyclical relationship. Before the printing press hierarchy reigned supreme, the Gutenberg invention began a networking process that revolutionized Western Europe. Likewise, the internet has repeated the cycle, with hierarchies struggling to compete with networking internet information.

### 9.4.1 Variation on a Theme

Different forms of hybrid structure are now well established, with many large companies benefiting from groundwork achieved by Dee Hock at Visa, and many others. From the other end, many consumer-oriented networks

---

3. Ferguson, *Square and the Tower.*

such as Facebook, Uber, Airbnb, Alcoholics Anonymous, and BBH NZ backpackers have all needed to develop their central structures to cope with consumer demand. The dilemma, caused by increased consumer activity, was experienced by Facebook when huge numbers of toxic posts required them to increase their central organization simply to be able to respond quickly to delete unacceptable posts in the light of public outcry.

One example of a thought-out hybrid approach was put forward by John Kotter in an attempt to hold together a traditional, hierarchical system, with freedom to encourage fresh innovation at the perimeter. This approach was taken up by some church denominations, in their attempt to meld traditional, inherited structure with new forms of worship, mission, and ministry.

---

### XLR8-ACCELERATE

John Kotter's "two structures-one organization"[4] approach, was adapted to develop a dual operating system, with the hierarchical order providing policy and management, together with an agile, innovative ministry network, at the local church level. With the leadership authority providing unity, stability, and organizational structure, the networking system would be free to encourage innovation, creativity, individuality, with fluency at the local level.

The advantage of such a system would be to maintain the best attributes of the past structure whilst at the same time release fluid, flexible, and issue-centered initiatives at the local and congregational levels. The disadvantage would be that it would not be easy to operate in practice. The two-structures approach requires a great deal of patience, discussion, and cohesion between the two elements. Total belief and commitment to the concept would be required on both sides, with the center being prepared to relinquish some authority to those operating the networks at the ground level. The possibility of discord arising between the two would always be an issue.

---

Kotter's approach comes with the already-quoted concept from Ferguson. Instead of contrasting hierarchies and networks as binary opposites, Ferguson contends that it is perfectly possible for the two approaches to work together in tension, as in Sienna. These hybrid approaches would make transition from straight hierarchy towards a more networked organization considerably easier.

---

### PIONEER MINISTRY

---

4. Kotter, *Accelerate*, 6.

This ministry, seen clearly in Anglican spheres, is an element within Kotter's "two structures–one organization" hybrid, hierarchy/network model. Following a recommendation in the 2004 Mission Shaped Church Report, an alternative form of minister, with appropriate training, was initiated. Instead of having to work from established structures, rules and traditional patterns, these pioneer ministers were encouraged to be agents of change, innovators with an entrepreneurial style, not bound by existing parishes/congregations, free to step out towards people untouched by the Christian message, free to establish new contextual worshiping communities. They were to engage where people were, rather than seeking to draw people into an existing traditional church community:

> Pioneers are people called by God who are the first to see and creatively respond to the Holy Spirit's initiative with those outside the Church; gathering others around them as they seek to establish a new contextual Christian community.[5]

Such a concept is seen to be following the example of Jesus, the pioneer. The four references to "pioneer" in the New Testament all relate to Jesus, epitomized by breaking new ground with people who would often not be associated with organized religion. Within the established denominations, pioneer ministry is not set primarily within an existing framework. It operates out of the fresh expressions network as a kind of alternative operating system. But it still remains within the overall traditional structure. Part of the overall fresh expressions movement, it acts as an alternative operating system within an existing denominational organization, deployed by those structures as either fresh start pioneers or church-based pioneers to stretch the boundaries of ministry beyond existing patterns. Some begin with a blank canvas, initiating engagement in areas where the church's influence is minimal. Others might work from an existing church base, "developing a mixed economy, expanding the growth and reach of the Church."[6] But overall these ministers are expected to "spend a greater proportion of their time engaged in community leadership roles, intentional outreach, and using social media, more than other stipendiary ministers."[7]

This alternative form of ordained ministry is encouraging action at the periphery of the church's influence: it is expected to be innovative and unshackled from the weight of the structured organization; it follows the concept of disruptive innovation, looking for new ways of being the church. The pioneer ministry website uses the example of the Fosbury Flop, a completely different way of high-jumping, created by Dick Fosbury around 1968, which revolutionized the event. That

---

5. Male, "Pioneer Ministry/Fresh Expressions," 2–3.

6. Male, "Pioneer Ministry/Fresh Expressions," 4.

7. Male, "Pioneer Ministry/Fresh Expressions," 4.

innovation was not without pains and difficulties for its initiator, but ultimately it has become the norm in high-jumping. Pioneer ministry is seen in this light.

A further illustration of a hybrid system comes from the British Education Authorities, entitled distributive leadership.

## DISTRIBUTED LEADERSHIP

This was developed initially in the education sector, where head teachers were faced with complex school environments. *Leadership* became shared by a number of people, with different elements in the task being led in different ways; with shared, democratic, and collaborative styles all being developed as appropriate.

As this kind of networking leadership faces the complex *situation*, it is broken down into its constituent elements, such as history, culture, physical attributes, and purpose/policy. How the shared leadership approaches these varied and complex elements within the organization is then seen in their relationship with their pupils—the *followers*. The outworking between leadership, situation, and followers, within a moving timeframe, is called *practice*.

These three examples of hybrid approaches do lead on to the aspect of fear. Within traditional organizational management circles there lies a deep uncertainty and disquiet as to whether real leadership is possible if central control is relinquished, if there is no playmaker in action. "How can you have leadership if there is no one there centrally to make decisions? Without central decision-making there would be chaos." This kind of uncertainty and fear is encountered in many traditional hierarchical structures, prompting the suggestion that new forms of horizontal, networking, innovative leadership will often lie beyond the imagination of traditionally trained managers, who only foresee chaos emerging from such an approach. Probably those who are growing up in this new digital age will become the seedbed of fresher, networked infrastructural management. But the overwhelming feeling of fear, when central control and decision-making is to be relinquished in favor of shared horizontal activity, is not something to be underestimated.

This hybrid approach, with its fears arising, its difficulties of implementation, its challenge to existing central authority, is one that has been endorsed by some church denominations. Entitled a "mixed economy" by Archbishop Rowan Williams, it seeks to take seriously both the authoritarian structures of the past, together with the innovative freshness of youthful faith.[8]

---

8. Moynagh, *Church for Every Context*, 432.

Behind the whole hybrid approach lies what Fowler has described as the tension between his stages 3/4 and 5, between those who want to maintain the past equilibrium and those who wish to ask difficult questions/ pursue radical changes. Again, it is an illustration of legitimized identity being threatened by projective identity/disruptive innovation/seeking radical change. In between this stand-off lies Cassels's "resistive identity" that seeks to divert the disruptive new ideas into a cul-de-sac or ghetto where they can be contained sufficiently for the status quo to carry on with near normality. A mixed economy/hybrid system could be seen to encourage such resistive identity. Such resistance can leave churches in stage 3 and 4 in a kind of limbo, unable to address future challenges effectively. The risk from strong resistive identity is that it would, in effect, reject points A and B on Handy's first sigmoid curve, reducing the possibility of a second projective initiative being established, thereby ensuring instead plateau and decline. Whether this hybrid approach continues to develop remains uncertain but the temptation for the hierarchical framework to laager will remain.

## 9.4.2 Windmills of the Mind

Further reflections on this uncharted territory between Fowler's stages 3 and 4 come from a variety of sources. The thought of changing from a top-down, centralized approach to a bottom-up, networked, and decentralized one, from the center to the margins, from pre-Enlightenment engagement towards a Postmodern context raises deep-seated questions/fears. Faced with technological futures/novel changes/hybrid adaptations, some would fall back on the more traditional patterns of cerebral, narrative, ordered, dwelling elements of their Christian upbringing. Alternatively, others would be more likely to be attracted to a more seeking, experiential, innovative, and diverse approach that is attracted to, and challenged by, change and development.

So, the tension within hybrid approaches mirror the tensions within the human body. Some feel at home in their narrative selves, thinking, analyzing, and judging their way through life, undergirded by an ordered structure. Others are happier being uplifted and inspired by their present experiences: attracted to innovation, challenged to engage with fresh discoveries, influenced by the constant perceptions of networkers around them, unconstrained by rules and regulations set by higher authorities, the somewheres happier dwelling in the known, but with anywheres attracted to explore with others the new presenting horizons.

### 9.4.3 Tipping Point

Whilst a mixed economy, influenced by personal preferences, allows all to find a place within one system, it covers over the tension that still resides below the surface. The overwhelming framework, within which the system is situated, remains one of a hierarchical, top-down, controlling authority. A rich variety of innovative expressions and pioneer ministries may be permitted and even praised, but in the end they all exist within the remit of the traditional authority. Nothing really changes unless the momentum of change rises high enough to respond to Handy's point A/B sufficiently to instigate a second sigmoid curve of innovation, where a new future for the organization can emerge from its chrysalis and fly. Within present church life there is little evidence of point A/B being acknowledged. In card-playing terms, despite the fact that tricks have been won by more radical approaches, the ace of trumps is still held by the original bidder.

## 9.5 THE EMERGENT

The third option facing the Christian faith/church rejects the backward-looking view, understands a gradual, evolutionary, intermediate, hybrid breathing space, but is inspired by a more radical scenario: a bottom-up, emergent approach inspired by a changing environment and empowered by the Holy Spirit, with a fresh relational understanding of the Trinity.

Up until the last fifty years, Western society has taken for granted that large organizations were centered around top-down hierarchical structures. What the last fifty years has shown is that large complex structures do not have to be top-down. They can exist, develop, and mature as bottom-up organizations. What the research into the habits of slimemould, our understanding of the human brain, and the colonies of ants and bees has illustrated is that large, complex structures, engaging with their environment, can be built from the bottom up without recourse to a traditional, top-down playmaker/leader. Higher levels of sophistication can emerge from lower, simpler levels, and the overall result can exceed the sum of the original parts. Mold can grow and develop, using the benefits of its environment, coalescing together when it is appropriate and dispersing when it is not, without the benefits of central leadership. Ants and bees can produce highly complex colonies to achieve their continued existence without resource to a functional orchestrator.

What is being suggested is that such an emergent concept within complex organizations could well be applied to the growth of the Christian faith as an alternative to the traditional, central, top-down-ordered hierarchy that has its roots in the church of the second century. Such a suggestion is based on the way Jesus himself ministered, the way the Holy Spirit inspired and empowered every believer from Pentecost onwards, the relational nature of the Trinity that already reflects networking communications.

If we can accept such a radical proposition as a third option, based on the ministry style of Jesus and the Spirit's presence in every believer, we need then to ask what the nature and structure of such an emergent movement/organization might be?

## 9.5.1 Theistic Emergentism

Although the whole concept of an emergent church will be described as a bottom-up approach in the following pages, this concept has to be set in an overall "top-down, downward-powered" fiduciary framework. The starting point for faith emanates from a God who reveals himself voluntarily to humankind, a given from which we all benefit, an other who cannot be imagined, defined, or contained within human experience. Religious thinkers have reflected on this in terms of how such a higher order can impact on a lower order of humanity. They describe it as "emergentism," the way a creator God relates to and engages with the universe. Various interpretations have been made, including those who step on from emergentist anthropology towards *theistic emergence*—God's self-revelation through the human capacity to know God, that "the ability to know God is understood to be an emergent property of the created world, infused with God's creative spirit."[9] Put in another way "our capacity to receive and accept a divine presence in the world is based on understanding God's revelation as emergent,"[10] and as Rohr has put it, "It is only God in us that understands the things of God."[11]

The relevance of this term "emergence" for today's church, therefore, not only relates to how lower-order networks can impact on a higher level of organization (emergent anthropology) but it also relates to the way a creator God gradually reveals himself to his own created order (theistic emergence) through his own emergent creative spirit—in Christian terms, his Holy Spirit. It illustrates the ability of God's creative spirit engaging with collaborative members of a networking society directly, without the medium of a rigid, hierarchical structure that claims to hold the key to learning about God. Or, as Stephen Pickard has put it, "Collaboration is encoded into the

---

9. Manning, "Mere Summing Up?," 54.

10. Manning, "Mere Summing Up?," 54.

11. Rohr, *Divine Dance*, 123.

way God creates and acts . . . these theological roots lead to collaborative life founded in creation and oriented towards redemptive existence."[12] Having referred to this primary top-down framework we now need to return to the bottom-up concept of emergence.

## 9.5.2 Bottom Up—Upward Power

The incarnation of Jesus sets the scene, illustrating God's nature, in allowing his son to be born into the most inauspicious circumstances. In today's world, refugee status with no identity papers illustrates total powerlessness over events and life circumstances. That was the scenario into which Jesus was born.

That starting point was continued as Jesus began to establish his ministry in Galilee, and then in Jerusalem. He set his followers a clear example of being prepared to work from the bottom upwards; from the margins inwards. Having rejected the temptations to go for human power, and status in society, he put that into practice through his rejection of doing business with the powers that be; preferring instead those whom society had sidelined. Jesus was ensuring that his place lay amongst ordinary people, whom he knew to be capable of spreading his teaching when he was gone. If there was any power in his person, and within his followers, it was going to be upward power. Just as he was the servant of his father, he was to be the servant of his disciples. He then expected them to be the servants of others. Bottom-up growth was central to his life approach.

This open, bottom-up approach continued with the inauguration of the church at Pentecost. No preference was given. All received the blessing and gift of the Holy Spirit. That principle continued throughout New Testament times. The faith was a horizontal movement that spread out in every direction, by word of mouth. It may have been initiated by a vertical gift from above, but it spread like wildfire from person to person. Just as slimemould, ants, and bees all use pheromones for communication, so too the Holy Spirit operated in similar fashion, from the very beginning. It is the spirit that networks at ground level: making the upward power of transformation available to all; available even to influence later structural community life. As every believer senses the spirit's presence, they can learn/adapt/change to become the living church.

As with emergence, it is from a simple level of belief that more complex levels of community and lifestyle, behavior and witness can emerge; it is from that primary source that structures can be developed, to convey the

12. Pickard, *Theological Foundations*, 6.

faith around the world, and down through the centuries. In effect, the Christian faith is an upward power, horizontally disbursed; a transformational experience, given as God reveals himself as creator and savior. Examples of this can be seen all around, but maybe the example of Hugh Brown, a convicted member of the Ulster Volunteer Force in Northern Ireland, can serve as an illustration of someone who caused havoc to other people's lives before being transformed into a person whose chaplaincy ministry has benefited so many lives in Kobe Prison, Japan.

---

### HUGH BROWN

In the 1970s Hugh Brown joined the UVF in West Belfast, at age 15. After considerable action he was arrested, convicted, and imprisoned for six years in the Maze prison. Near the end of his sentence he came to a personal faith in Jesus Christ, while watching the film *Ben-Hur*. After being able to extricate himself from the UVF, he trained as a missionary, and for the last thirty years, has dedicated himself to ministry amongst prisoners in a Kobe jail often populated by considerable numbers of Yakuza, the Japanese mafia. In Japan, a chaplain's relationship with prisoners is severely restricted, particularly after a prisoner's release. Brown recounts one particular experience which illustrates the continuing power of the Holy Spirit to transform lives. Despite these chaplain restrictions, Brown became convinced that God had revealed to him that when God starts a good work in a person's life he "will carry it on to completion until the day of Christ Jesus" (Phil 1:6). At one point after that, Brown counselled a particular prisoner, who was later released. Some time after his release the prisoner made contact with Brown and explained that he too was living as an evangelist, preaching on a text that he had found most helpful in prison, John 8:36: "If the son sets you free, you will be free indeed." Hugh Brown, saw this as a vindication of the ministry of planting the seed and leaving the Holy Spirit to continue working in the lives of those touched by that same spirit.

---

An emergent church is one based on a Christ-centered view of the Bible, and an expectation that the Holy Spirit can inspire/empower each and every believer, out of which Christian community can be established; that Christian witness can spread worldwide, and church life can impact society at every level of life; that an emergent church can be open and adaptable, horizontally free-flowing, and with the potential to network/build appropriate structures that serve both believers and a local community.

## 9.5.3 Decentralized and Networked

Christ's church is in principle a decentralized organization. It begins, not from top-down leadership, but from the individual's reception of the Holy Spirit's presence—from the margins inwards. If it had a structure at all during New Testament times it was predominantly networked, rather than controlled vertically.

In Western society the last fifty years has witnessed organizations turning away from centralized systems toward more decentralized ones; benefiting from the innovation and networking communication of the digital age. And whereas the former structures revolved around command and control, the latter flourish from fresh information and innovation, where new life emerges from the bottom up, from its periphery. It is epitomized by the phrase "power from the edge."

Possibly the most vivid example of this, already quoted, is that of Shenzhen in China, and its "New Shanzhai." Growth—from 30,000 to 12 million inhabitants in forty years—is attributed not to top-down centralized orchestration, but rather to open-source/open-sourced hyper-speed innovation, where development is not planned in detail by hierarchical business companies, but emanates from a bottom-up innovative spirit where creators build on each other's work, co-opt, repurpose, and remix in a decentralized way. The result is becoming less an urban area producing technological hardware, and more an emergent city that is challenging Silicon Valley as the primary global center for scientific and technological innovation, where the big conglomerates are drawn towards the benefits arising from the emergent potential of an inspired and creative workforce.

---

### CENTRALIZED HIERARCHY OR DECENTRALIZED NETWORKS

A *centralized system* is typified by the spider that grows an enormous web. However, if you cut the head off, it all dies. On the other hand, the starfish illustrates the alternative, if you cut off a part of it you get two starfish.[13] Centralized systems are based on an ontology of order that is both structured, mechanistic and substantial: their structures have a clear controlling leader in charge, a specific place where decisions are made, clear rules that are set and enforced, coercive command, and control ethos, clear boundaries, and a track record of efficiency and functionality.

*Decentralized* organizations—which have increased in our information age— center around innovation, horizontal communication, self-organization, flux, and change, with different forms of leadership, little hierarchy, no central HQ,

---

13. Brafman and Beckstrom, *Starfish and the Spider*, 34.

leadership endorsed by the community, and done by example, consensus, and collaboration rather than by control. Power and influence tend to be distributed around the community rather than in one person or one place. Coercion is a foreign concept disturbance is good, leadership often happens on the edge.[14] All of these attributes tend toward a more relational approach even if the content of the organization is still of a substantial nature.

Spanish invasions of South America show how Aztec and Inca societies, with their centralized organizations, were each subdued and destroyed in two years, whereas a century later, the decentralized/more relational organization of the Apaches in Mexico thwarted the Spanish for two centuries.[15] Such a duel between the centralized Spanish army and the decentralized Apache tribe was a forerunner of many later battles in the twentieth century between, for instance, the established centralized powers of the record labels, including MGM, and the decentralized pirate music sources of Napster and those that followed. Quite possibly the music labels won to begin with, but Napster spawned so many others which led all the way through to Spotify today.[16] These music battles are an illustration of the way decentralized organizations have taken on centralized organizations and overtaken them.

Instead of knowledge, information, and strategy being formed and authorized by the center, the decentralized nature of internet culture ensures that knowledge, innovation, and activity can all arise from anywhere. It can be discussed widely around the whole body of the organization, hence giving upward power to the edge (P2E). So networks distribute knowledge far more responsively, speedily, and effectively than more traditional centralized control. Such knowledge is also conveyed voluntarily, without the coercion associated with command and control.

## CORE ELEMENTS

Brafman and Beckstrom suggest the following five elements that, if working together, can enable a decentralized organization to take off successfully.[17] It starts with small *circles*, groups of people who have common interests. They have norms rather than rules, which members abide by amongst themselves. Such circles/units, like those of Alcoholics Anonymous (AA) are the base of a decentralized system. Networks need a *catalyst*—an element or compound that initiates a reaction without fusing into that reaction; some person or group who

---

14. See Horle, *Article in Transmission.*

15. Brafman and Beckstrom, *Starfish and the Spider*, 16–21.

16. Brafman and Beckstrom, *Starfish and the Spider*, 22–27.

17. Brafman and Beckstrom, *Starfish and the Spider*, 87.

facilitates thinking, action, growth, and unity, and yet fades into the background as the concept takes off. Although Maria and Mary Poppins are very similar roles—in two popular musicals—Maria marries and stays with the family von Trapp, whereas Mary Poppins disappears after her work is done. Mary is seen to be more of a catalyst than Maria.[18] Networks need a *purpose* for existing. AA has a purpose, which is foundational. The anti-slavery movement had its purpose. For decentralization to take off it needs a strong, clear purpose around which its members gather. As well as purpose it helps to have *a preexisting network*, into which to slot itself. The anti-slavery movement took off because it benefited from the Quaker network. AA took benefit from the Oxford Group as a starting platform. In today's world the internet/digital communication energize, empower, and network these emerging groups. Finally, such networks benefit initially by having a *champion*. Whereas the catalyst is often the visionary thinker who works behind the scenes to energize others, the champion is up front and personal, the charismatic front person, the salesperson with media savvy. A good champion can always help to take an emerging network to the next level with determination, persistence, and bravado.

Three other examples—as well as Dee Hock's Visa International—can illustrate further how creative, free-flowing, decentralized systems work.

## VIRAL CHANGE

Leandro Herrero and his work on viral change has developed a way of effecting radical change within an institution through identifying the elements that block change and those that unlock change, and then by establishing a method that works through the latter to enable change to take place.

Traditional change management depends on top-down, rational analysis, sets of proposals, and using existing power structures to implement them, which often makes it difficult and expensive to break away from existing norms. Viral change, on the other hand, rather than starting with a top-down strategy for change, begins instead with people's behavior and some key values which can affect the culture of an organization. These in turn can lead to implementing a radically different strategy. It starts from where people are, accepting certain core values, harnessing the power of teamwork, and everyone's capacity to innovate, often resisting the temptation to choose what appears to be the easiest solution.

Such a process depends on a few well-connected, facilitating people, and networks that enable new mindsets, attitudes, and behavior to become the influences behind change within an organization. Rather than being top-down,

18. Brafman and Beckstrom, *Starfish and the Spider*, 93.

> static, mechanistic, hierarchical, linear, and process-driven, it is instead more like a multi-centered, interrelated organism; peer to peer, nonlinear, value-, and behavior-driven. Viral change is a creative, virulent, decentralized, relational, social movement for change.

The second example of transforming hierarchical structures into alternative management models for voluntary groups is the model of agility and collaborative leadership.

### AGILITY AND COLLABORATIVE LEADERSHIP

Developed in the 1990s out of software IT solutions, it highlights how the abilities of teams and groups in an organization can respond quickly and flexibly to new challenges in both policy and strategy. The principles have been described by the think tank Demos as "fast decision making, flexible resource allocation: an ability to identify emerging trends, appropriate risk taking, flexible policy making; a balance between short term responsiveness and long term management of uncertainty; an ability to shape the external environment to maximize opportunities and minimize risks, and, a shared values base."[19]

Agility goes on to identify four key steps that can be taken and achieved: moving from organizations to networks (webmaking), hierarchies to collaborative enterprises (teammaking), management of structures to the leadership of human teams (peoplemaking), and an assumption that we react to circumstances, to an assertion that humans create outcomes through a responsive engagement with environment and circumstances (luckmaking). Each of these illustrate the core steps that can be taken for a centralized organization to transform itself into a more decentralized one.[20]

A third way to illustrate and implement decentralized ways of working is by using co-operative enquiry.

> Peter Reason—following Paolo Freire and Peter Senge's generative learning—explains cooperative enquiry as research *with* people rather than *on* people. The research goes through four stages: exploring the activities/issues together; becoming co-subjects more than co-researchers; immersing and engaging in both action and experience; then coming together to discuss what was learned through all forms of knowing—propositional, presentational, and experiential. Learning and change do not emanate from a top-down expert in teaching mode,

19. Wignall, *Collaborative Ministry Review*, 25.
20. Wignall, *Collaborative Ministry Review*, 25.

but rather from a shared networking of people, the juxtaposition of ideas, and experience—resulting in growing knowledge/shared decision-making.

Adding to Brafman and Beckstrom's five core elements that are central to emergent start-ups is another key ingredient—*feedback*. Feedback is essential for growth and self-regulation.[21] Just as you tear your finger away from a hot boiling kettle for fear of being burned, through the actions of your brain, nerves, and muscles, so too lessons need to be learned and communicated all the way around a decentralized organization. "All de-centralized systems rely extensively on feedback, for both growth and self-regulation."[22] Success is then amplified and failure is not repeated. In a decentralized one it goes each and every way—just as the pheromones network the ant colony.

The above examples illustrate that change from centralized, industrial-age, top-down, dominating organizations toward a decentralized, power-to-the-edge, innovative, participatory, relational, information-age organization is perfectly possible if the will is there. They illustrate that there is no one correct method to follow: that each organization needs to recognize its needs for change, search for principles that will draw all together, expect that time, patience, and collaboration will be required, value every member on the journey, cross-fertilize, and give feedback where appropriate. Far from thinking that the established centralized, coercive organizations are destined to irredeemably collapse, these illustrations offer hope that, through emergence and change, even the most hierarchical organization can mutate when the need for change is acknowledged and owned from the top.

One final core element to the development of a decentralized approach relates to the topics of participation and leadership within emergent organizations. For years biologists who were studying the behavior of slimemould, were convinced it was motivated and ordered by a pacemaker. They were sure there had to be a pacemaker/leader even if they couldn't find any evidence that there was one. There appeared to be a natural, in-built assumption that there had to be a pacemaker, a leader, a central chain of command, a static sense of top-down order.

> Emergence and our present networking society show that this isn't necessarily so. It is possible to innovate, grow, and, "solve problems by drawing on masses of relatively stupid elements rather than a single intelligent executive branch."[23] It is possible that "agents residing on one scale can start producing behavior

21. Johnson, *Emergence*, 132–38.
22. Johnson, *Emergence*, 133.
23. Johnson, *Emergence*, 18.

that lies one scale above them: ants produce colonies, urbanites produce neighborhoods, simple pattern-recognition software learns how to recommend new books.[24]

This replacement, therefore, of centralized leadership by a participatory, networking, emergent dynamic brings a real challenge for such centralized institutions, opening up extraordinary possibilities, wider horizons, deeper resources, and potential giftings. This could be particularly relevant for today's church. It could also relate to the Holy Spirit working in every believer's life, opening up the possibility of far greater participation by the membership in church life/leadership.

However, this concept of organizations emerging from bottom-up initiative rather than from top-down leadership has to be set within the practical lessons being learned by the development movement in terms of the giving and receiving of aid. As has been referred to earlier, in the late twentieth century, bottom-up participation was seen as the panacea for all development approaches. In practice however it was found to raise as many questions as it answered. Criticisms around the time of the millennium argued that bottom-up participation didn't deliver the claims of the theory, and in the process also produced side effects that were counterproductive.

Today, as the debate continues, there are signs that these criticisms can be addressed, and that bottom-up participatory approaches can be effective. The debate has led to constructive engagement, whereby local partnership can work effectively between those who contribute financially, and those who receive. But it has to be done on the basis of full accountability, transparency, honesty, and trust.

---

### TRUTH CENTERED TRANSFORMATION

In 2003, Disciple National Alliance established Truth Centered Transformation in South East Asia, with the twin aims of churches being strengthened, and people being set free from all forms of poverty. Centered around local churches, it interlinked the growth of understanding, of belief, of practical action, and the reduction of poverty. The movement was initiated through one volunteer and a training module targeting ten churches, which quickly exploded at the grassroots level into 160 churches. Out of those churches, 16 more trainers were selected as the concept was owned and spread. Further training modules were then developed, and the number of trainers doubled. Within a year, 300 churches were involved. With the trained participants activating what they had learned, the movement caught fire and mushroomed to the bewilderment and amazement of the central parent organization.

---

24. Johnson, *Emergence*, 18.

The western initiators feared the explosion of interest, worried that they would not have the resources to maintain this growth, and were concerned that chaos would result. However, with the only input being the training modules, and help with the training of trainers, resources emerged from the villagers themselves. The most noticeable effect was that food production increased, poverty was reduced, and sharing of surplus produce—in the Macedonian tradition—became a reality. Such increased food production was quickly followed by stable homes, latrines, wells, and vegetable gardens. It was the villages and villagers themselves, and their growing understanding of faith and discipleship, that became the primary resources for growth.

The heart of the movement, and the training models provided, are centered around seven core principles. These principles inspire holistic discipleship, and are illustrated by participants declaring, "I do this. I am this. Isn't this what a Christian does?" The seven core principles include a primary dependence on God, a nurturing of truth, a rejection of lies, a mobilizing of local resources, a sense of building God's kingdom, a sharing and partnership with other churches, and finally, a focus on the most vulnerable.

This movement, which merged into a larger organization—Reconciled World—in 2013, is now tied into other movements involved in holistic ministry such as microfinance, ending genocide, response to HIV/AIDS (India), Food for the Hungry (South Asia), and working with autistic children. It has now spread out from Southeast Asia to Africa. In all these spheres the emphasis continues to be one of developing Christian discipleship, expecting resources to be homegrown, and being committed to respond to the vulnerable.

## 9.5.4 Relational—The Trinity

An empirical quality of an emergent organization is that it is relational, with a horizontal dynamic rather than a vertical one. Every member or part of such an organization participates with each other through a network of horizontal relationships. Through those relationships, innovation is created, change is initiated, and output is registered. Relationship, lying at the heart of an emergent organization, becomes the basis upon which more complex levels of organization/ability are built. The upward, networking nature of those relationships takes the place of the downward, coercive control of a hierarchical structure. An emergent organization therefore, through its relational nature, exhibits entirely different characteristics to that of a hierarchical one.

As we have seen, in their description of an emergent organization, Brafman and Bergstrom have identified five key elements. The first one of which is circles of people centered round a common interest. Those circles of people, acting as a catalyst, network together, identify purpose, and coalesce to become an emergent body. Relationships within those circles are the glue that hold them together.

Now if we can imagine an emergent church, two interlinked elements are added to the equation. The first concerns the very nature of church. It has been argued that the nature of western civilization has been built around the first of Aristotle's ten key attributes of life, that of "substance".

---

### SUBSTANCE

Richard Rohr[25] has argued that *substance* has had a profound effect on the evolution of western thought and the culture within which we live, affecting the heart of our understanding of existence. Markets, hierarchies, networks, technological developments, laws of ownership, national boundaries, personal achievement, fame, success, and even much of the church's tradition all rest on substance and materialism as the basis for all measurements, achievement, and identity.

---

What is now becoming more clearly apparent is that centering a society on the basis of substance and demoting the significance of relationships has inherent weakness for the whole concept of human identity. Rohr goes on to point out that *relationship* was another of Aristotle's qualities, and that its significance is now becoming more important. Rohr proposes that relationship lies at the heart of a Christian position. Substance may build up wealth, power, empire, fame, and reputation, but without an understanding of relationships between people and possessions, between people and the environment, within those having a spiritual perception, a world based primarily on substance can prove to be quite fragile. Alternative to a substance-based world, is that advocated by the Cursillos movement.

---

### CURSILLOS

Following the end of the Spanish Civil War, a movement to encourage young people to pilgrimage to St. James in Compostela, Spain arose in response to the bitterness of Spanish society at that time. Leadership training for these pilgrimages began to take the form of Cursillos, developed by Eduardo Bonnin. Although initially a Roman Catholic movement, it later spread to other denominations worldwide.

Based on a three-day event, led by laity and clergy together, Cursillos aims at remedying "ignorance of faith, the superficiality of ritualism and the apathy of

---

25. Rohr, *Divine Dance*, 44.

nonfaith commitment in daily life,"[26] centering around the key elements of Christian experience—grace, faith, and action.

Group workshops, prayer, and quiet reflection fill out the three days in preparation for the fourth day—returning to daily living. Deepening one's personal relationship with God amongst fellow believers within a local community lies at the heart of these events. There is also an opportunity to discover personal gifts and explore how to use them to build up the church in the world on the fourth day.

Unencumbered by responsibilities for church structures, these events center around people meeting, sharing, learning, and being inspired together by God's mission in the world.

The second element, integral to understanding the nature of the church, is put forward by Richard Rohr, together with Stephen Pickard. They both link relationship with the overall nature of the Trinity. Rohr sees the Trinity in terms of mutual, integral, and interwoven relations between the three. Rather than God being a static, imperial, supreme monarch, he sees the combination of the father as creator, the immanence of the son, and the transforming nature of the Holy Spirit, all exuding as a single flow into which we can all be incorporated. Rather than a hierarchical, pyramidical approach to faith, he sees it more in a circular or spiral form into which we are all centrifugally drawn.

Referring to Andrei Rublev's icon "The Trinity," he comments, "If we take the depiction of God in the Trinity seriously, we have to say 'In the beginning was the Relationship.'"[27] He refers to the "symbiotic nature of the Trinity,"[28] illustrating the different roles of them as the infinite one, the immanent one, and the intimate one,[29] or as the mystery of the father, the crucifixion of the son, and the anonymity of the Holy Spirit, or as the father, the source of the flow, the son as God alongside us, and the Holy Spirit as God within us.[30]

Rohr poignantly highlights that the energy in the relationship can often be in the spaces between the three, as well as from the three themselves. Take a child, he says, who, in the middle of the night, creeps into their parent's bed, and lies between them—"they literally rest in the space, the relationship between you."[31] The energy of this trinitarian relationship is always

26. British Anglican Cursillo Council, "What is Cursillo?," 1.

27. Rohr, *Divine Dance*, 30.

28. Rohr, *Divine Dance*, 152.

29. Rohr, *Divine Dance*, 90.

30. Rohr, *Divine Dance*, 100.

31. Rohr, *Divine Dance*, 92.

outward, looking towards creation, towards humanity, towards us. We are invited to "join hands with Christ, and the Spirit flows through us, between us, and our feet move in the loving embrace of the Father."[32] Although Rohr doesn't necessarily talk about the ministry of the church, in fact his whole approach is pointing towards an explosion of that ministry in a holistic way as every baptized person enters, engages, and participates in the flow that emanates from the circle of the Trinity.

So instead of a church assimilated into a substance-oriented, hierarchical western culture, Rohr suggests that the church should reflect the nature of the Trinity: one that is held together in relationship, one that thrives in the spaces between those three persons. His understanding of the Trinity in this way fits seamlessly into the concept of an emergent church founded upon relationships between its members and empowered/inspired by the nature of the relationships within the Trinity. Such a church would, once again, take on a very different shape to our present top-down, power-oriented, substance-oriented body.

## 9.5.5 Relational—Churches

One potential outworking from an emergent church concerns relationships between the existing denominations and the rich variety of community churches. At present, the authoritative hierarchical model is not only followed by the established church, but also by many other churches, in some variation or other—the predominant dynamic being a top-down form of leadership, with each denomination/grouping being separate from each other.

If, however, a more emergent model was to be adopted, not only would there be a more horizontal dynamic *within* each denomination/group, but also a more horizontal relationship *between* denominations/groups. Top-down authoritarian structures would begin to give way to growing inter-denominational relationships and sharing; existing ecumenism could be reenergized; traditional, often intransigent theological positions could be softened through shared experiences at a local community level; and individual personal experience and the circumstances of shared community witness could begin to inform theological debate from the innovative bottom.

As greater emphasis was laid on horizontal networking, earthed in each local community, and as that experience was juxtaposed with biblical source material, then the significance/influence of top-down denominations/groups and their outward identities would diminish in favor of living, vibrant, emergent organisms living out Christian engagement as life. The

32. Rohr, *Divine Dance*, 64.

same would become true with regard to the worldwide church. Instead of worldwide connections being denominationally based, international connections would more likely develop, revolving around shared contexts, issues, experiences, and biblical/theological insights.

## 9.5.6 Local Community Environment

Kester Brewin, in his challenging book on the emergent church, helpfully highlights the main characteristics of emergent systems.[33] First on the list is that emergence is built on *open systems*. Quoting the example of slimemould, he illustrates that emergence arises out of the environment. When food is there, the mold congregates; when it is consumed, the mold disappears. Emergence arises out of existing circumstances; it then expands through cross-fertilization, using the benefits of pheromones, exuded by the organisms of the organization, be it mold, ants or bees. Brewin goes on to list that emergent systems are also *adaptable*, adjusting themselves contextually to the environment in which they exist. Mold, ants, and bees scour the country to find food. Emergent systems also *learn and distribute knowledge* from within their existing body, networking that information in order that the body may grow and develop. Colonies of bees and ants can emerge out of nothing and become highly complex entities that survive for years. And, as will be referred to later, within such colonies a model of *servant leadership* is expressed that doesn't rely on a central playmaker. Every participant exists to serve the whole, without the need to depend on a higher-level leadership role. Brewin points out, in relation to their environment/context, that the mold/swarm survive and grow, often *at the edge of chaos*. Their existence is dependent on working together in order to find food; without that resource and that connectivity they will perish.

It follows then that an emergent church will need to exhibit similar characteristics. Primarily it will need to be earthed within some form of environment or local community; be adaptable to differing communities and differing social contexts by learning from them and growing within them; and be available to respond to local needs, offering a servant mentality, available for the benefit of the whole. It would be a group of people being church together, not necessarily tied to a building, but rather reflecting the Holy Spirit as the reign of God. It would be an outward-looking, servant-oriented group, living out the referent power of Christ in their lives as the mission of God. It would reflect the nature of God in its worship—in every aspect of life, rather than just in Sunday church, giving honor to the father, expressing humility

33. Brewin, *Signs of Emergence*, 97.

towards the son, and rejoicing in the spirit. And, just as in some biological examples, it would reflect the mystery of an eternal body, which cannot be seen, pinpointed, or articulated in physical form, and yet which exhibits a power and authority far greater than any of its individual members.

This emergent church, witnessing to and worshipping a vulnerable Christ, would later need to search for an appropriate organizational structure with which to enable the movement of faith to be sustained by ongoing generations. The very nature of an emergent organization is that, out of the simplest of organisms, higher levels and more complex structures are achievable. But such structure has to arise from the bottom up, rather than being imposed from above, and should never be seen to be an essentially permanent endpoint, a sign of having arrived.

The good news is that the postmillennial church doesn't have to start from scratch. Such expressions of emergent church are already present and growing—such as the Cursillos movement and the Truth Centered Transformation organization. Many are very different simply because they have arisen out of a variety of environments and circumstances.

---

### CHURCH AND COMMUNITY MOBILIZATION—UMOJA

Tearfund, through the primary inspiration of Francis Njoroge, Peter Gitau, and Gladys Waithega in East Africa, have established "Umoja"—the spirit of people working together—a church and community mobilization approach incorporating a participatory evaluation process now being encouraged in a number of East African Anglican dioceses.[34] It is an emergent concept, originating out of a local community facilitated by Francis, aimed at bringing forward socio-economic development fitted to cultural values, community economics, and the natural environment. It is aimed at a partnership between the church and community, helping communities to realize their own strengths and resources, and act for themselves following the International Development seed scale theory of social change. It expects communities to use their own resources and help people break free of a dependency mindset. It takes time, requires a competent facilitator, and can be unsettling to existing leadership, but it expects to overcome dependency and loss of confidence within the community.[35] It also offers a set of guidelines not dissimilar to Brafman and Beckstrom's "five legs."[36]

Umoja is now being rolled out in other continents, including in the UK under the title of Church and Community Mobilization (Tearfund).

---

34. Njoroge et al., *Umoja Co-ordinator's Guide*.

35. Njoroge et al., *Umoja, Co-ordinators Guide*, 8.

36. Brafman and Beckstrom, *Starfish and the Spider*, 87.

Such an East African roll-out can be a benefit in itself for all. There is no fixed blueprint to follow; blueprints are anathema to the very concept of emergence. But these examples do inspire and offer hope for those wanting to journey within their own environment. Not only has Tearfund rolled out Church and Community Mobilization (and its blog "Churches Changing Nations) in this country, but the Church Urban Fund has also developed a similar approach in their Asset-Based Community Development, particularly in urban areas.

---

### ASSET-BASED COMMUNITY DEVELOPMENT (ABCD)

The Anglican Church Urban Fund cites the example of Hodge Hill Church in Birmingham, raising three key principles. First, rather than pointing out the inadequacies in a particular area, ABCD seeks instead to discover and celebrate the gifts and capacities of local people. Secondly, it aims to build strong sustainable communities from inside out rather than through "top-down" regeneration projects, or from "outside in"—external agencies delivery services: beginning with neighbors interacting, local networks emerging, and by discovering how change can actually result. Thirdly, it is all "relation driven," connecting people and gifts, discovering "webs of connections" already present, and freeing up "the God that liberates and activates the gifts within each person, and weaves connections between people."[37]

They see such an approach as a helpful, practical framework for translating belief into meaningful Christian presence and activity in a local community: reiterating the point Sam Wells highlighted, of being with people rather than doing things for people.

---

These examples come from existing churches seeking to engage afresh with the community within which they exist.

Another aspect of an emergent church is raised by Kevin Brewin. It concerns what he describes as "dirt" and "boundaries."[38] In Jesus' day the Jewish faith was centered around the temple in Jerusalem and in the religious leadership that surrounded it, together with the local synagogues. That leadership consisted of priests, Pharisees, Sadducees, scribes, and rabbis. The center point of their activity was to perpetuate the purity of the faith and the purity of the lives of its adherents. The faith and its followers were therefore circumscribed by laws, boundaries, and regulations which prescribed the highest possible levels of human purity. Now, one of the most dramatic features of Jesus' ministry was to flout these laws and break down those barriers.

37. See Church Urban Fund, *Tackling Poverty in England*.

38. Brewin, *Signs of Emergence*, 166.

By associating with Samaritans, lepers, beggars, and those with chronic illnesses, Jesus was getting involved with the dirt, which the religious leaders were doing their best to avoid. By associating with prostitutes, eating with tax collectors—quislings for the Roman overlords—and drinking with a Samaritan woman, Jesus was breaking down barriers designed specifically by the religious leaders to keep those unclean people out. This led finally to Jesus paying the price for such behavior. In an attempt to maintain purity, the only way out was for him to be sacrificed as a scapegoat outside the city wall.

The essence of an emergent organization is that it is open to every aspect of its environment. It does not exist by defining/maintaining boundaries, but rather by the exact opposite. Boundaries are abhorrent to it. Instead of being boundary-set, an emergent church is more likely to be center-set, with the church having a dynamic of discovery and deepening faith, from no faith at all, towards the center—the focal point of Jesus.

In contrast, churches—described by Fowler as stage 3—are defined more often than not by their boundaries. They are boundary-set, hesitant about those who live and behave outside those boundaries. They insist that any new adherents conform within reason to those same boundaries. Churches in stage 4 are beginning to question those boundaries, and those in stage 5 are beginning to break down those boundaries and associate themselves with the dirt outside. The clear sign of an emergent, conjunctive church is its willingness to live outside those boundaries and dogmatic definition. Further, they accept that those whom they encounter through dialogue, outside the barriers, do not necessarily have to dispense with their former behavior as a prerequisite before joining the church. They can be drawn to Christ through the Spirit on their own terms and in their own time, rather than being challenged to accept a dogmatic proclamation of faith.

### TWO SPARROWS

The Two Sparrows Youth club, on a Wandsworth estate, was aimed at "un-clubbable" youngsters. There was Colin, who went on to compete with Big Daddy and Giant Haystacks on TV-circuit wrestling events; Happy, who had to disappear for a couple of weeks and so left his belongings, including his gun, with Chris the Vic; Big Ron, with a soft heart; Mel the plumber and Les, the road sweeper's daughter; Josie and Pat, the trainee hairdressers; and so many others. The sound system blasted out Fleetwood Mac, whose first gig was in a Wandsworth pub. Indoor football was the main event, ruining, in the process, the church hall for any other usage.

Why did they all keep coming back? Simply because of Linc, a woodworker-turned-youth-leader, and Joyce, his wife, a council cleaner, who offered an open home to everyone, a depth of love, and a faith worth sharing.

Jesus placed very few conditions on those to whom he ministered. He did this on the basis that his love would inspire referent and transformational behavior. An emergent church is likely to relax its boundaries, relying on faith and trust to reflect the transforming love of God.

Examples of such Christian commitment and community are already in evidence around us. A few simple examples illustrate such emergent-church features. They show a commitment to the homeless, addicts, those in debt, refugees, and rejected asylum seekers, as well as teenagers seeking support.

---

### CHURCH ARMY INITIATIVES

The Church Army has acted as a sodal catalytic movement within an established denomination, particularly with regard to evangelism and working at the fringes of church life, moving with the times, and continuing to engage at the edges of society/outside the boundaries.

The Church Army Research Unit has been engaged in analytical work with regard to fresh expressions, producing four key reports which have been of considerable assistance to the modal church. Churches can use this material as they seek to develop their own strategies, aspirations, and deployment approaches.

Working alongside the research being done is an impressive list of Church Army Centers for Mission, together with the deployment of Church Army personnel all around the country. These consist of work on a more emergent basis, stretching in the north, from Bradford, Chester, Scunthorpe, Selby to Sheffield, and in the south, from Greenwich, Thanet, Southampton to Torquay. These centers are involved in a rich variety of projects that emerge out of local need. Many of them are working with young people establishing youth churches, centering in deprived social and economic areas, dealing with addictions and endemic poverty. The vision of the Scunthorpe Centre is "Transforming Communities, Building Church," which typifies the kind of work in which they are all engaged. They use a variety of ways to interact, including a youth club bus, a narrow boat, as well as the more regular schools work/after school clubs.

As well as the Church Army Centers, they have specific projects aimed at the homeless and the plight of vulnerable women, including the Marylebone Project in London, and residential services in Cardiff. Working with homeless, providing shelter, and searching for job opportunities, have been a part of the Church Army for nearly 35 years. More recently this has been extended into the care of vulnerable girls caught up in addiction, petty crime, and prostitution. They offer spirituality (that God loves each person regardless), hospitality (that all are welcomed), empowerment (equipping women to make informed choices), and resettlement (encouraging and supporting women towards independent living).

In all this work there is a contextual relevance for young people: a preparedness to engage with suffering/exclusion from mainstream society; a countercultural challenge to society as a whole, by drawing to its attention those who are "slipping through the net." On the one hand, one can praise the persistence and strength of Wilson Carlisle's original vision. On the other hand, one can be saddened by the church, in general, failing to realize one of its central roles.

Green Pastures was initiated in 1999 by Pete Cunningham, an Assemblies of God pastor in Southport. It has one single simple objective: to encourage/enable partner churches to be able to make housing available for the homeless in their area, within an atmosphere of committed, open-ended, Christian caring.

## GREEN PASTURES

"We can't change the world overnight, but we can change the overnight world."

"Our bottom line is lives transformed."

Working out of Southport and London, Green Pastures has accrued a property portfolio of more than £40 million. At present it draws in investment capital to fund house buying of over £6 million a year and rising. Partner churches/Christian organizations have been recruited around the country and total over 60 at present—with an expected increase in partners of around 15% per year—providing accommodation units for over 1,000 homeless people.

The real heart of this decentralized, growing Christian organism lies in its partner churches and their response to the needs of the residents being housed. Despite the offers of accommodation being unconditional, these partner churches have seen considerable growth of faith, not only within themselves, but also amongst the residents whom they serve. At the annual Partners Conference, the encouragements shared, the rapid growth in the number of housing units becoming available, the extraordinary care and commitment exhibited by faithful church members, illustrate the emergent, networked growth of faith and belief, at the grassroots level, satisfying societal needs, and yet requiring comparatively little central facilitating support.

Work amongst refugees, asylum seekers, and failed asylum seekers has been a feature in many cities in postmillennial times. An example of this comes from Coventry.

**TOGETHER FOR CHANGE-FRESH START, COVENTRY**

Fresh Start was established in the center of Coventry; befriending and providing practical support for refugees, migrant workers, and asylum seekers, and led by a cultural links worker establishing a number of exciting initiatives, experiencing God working in amazing ways. These initiatives have included Saturday morning football sessions where, together with the football, relationships are being built up. Often everyone ends up having lunch together at a nearby church.

Relationships have also been developed through the Companionship project, where volunteers have provided a listening ear to new arrivals and new friendships have been established. A Conversation Café held in the Belgrade Theatre offers the chance for newcomers to develop their language skills, as well as to learn about Coventry's history, British values, and the education system. Hafizur comments that he "really likes coming to the conversation cafés. They have a relaxing atmosphere." Another participant, Abdulla, says "practicing conversation is very important. It is great to speak to lots of different people."

Such a Christian initiative is clearly offering help to the recently arrived to make a fresh start and begin their lives anew in a different country.

Working for structural change is as significant as working for personal transformation, even if it often seems less fashionable.

**JUST SPACE**

With Christian involvement, this organization is encouraging participation in the issue of public engagement in the planning process, particularly when local communities, often in low-income areas, are being pressurized by the interests of developers. Although situated mainly around London, they have also arisen in other cities. This has followed the Open Communities movement, initiated by an interfaith group in the northern suburbs of Chicago who advocated fair and affordable housing through the affirmation of local residents' groups.

## 9.5.7 Leadership and Gift

Another element of an emergent church lies in its form of leadership. Every organization needs some form of leadership, from autocratic to anarchic. Change and revolution may well dispense with one form of leadership only for another form to arise to take its place. Sometimes that leads to improvement, sometimes the opposite. Now early research into emergence suggested that there appeared to be no playmaker/leader orchestrating the organization.

Complex structures of bee and ant colonies were seen to arise without such a traditional leadership role. So an emergent church may arise and at some stage an appropriate leadership role might begin to emerge to achieve sustainability. Such leadership might be less about standing up at the front, offering vision and strategy, and more about enabling the right conditions to be present so that forward movement can continue. Such an approach relates to Brafman and Beckstrom's concept of a catalyst if emergence is to be sustained. As Brewin put it, leaders "are not there to announce change but to resource change."[39] Such a description sounds uncannily like Roland Allen's description of Paul's ministry, paraphrased in contemporary language, "Take the good news to a town; allow the Holy Spirit of Christ to convict; then leave the believers to get on with it—enable it to happen, and then set it free to develop."

Now there are distinct similarities with this approach and the one taken by Jesus. Jesus ministered at the most basic levels of society. He acted there as a catalyst, recognizing the needs of the people there. He activated the power of his father by bringing the good news, and then wandered on to the next place, leaving the message to sink in. As we have seen, undergirding this approach was a servantlike quality. He was there to enable the right conditions whereby people could see the choice and then make their own decisions about it. He explained this role to his disciples, describing himself as their servant, and encouraging them to be servantlike to others. Surely this servant leadership style has great similarities with what seems to be needed in emergent organizations. It is enabling power and achievement to rise upwards out of the lowest level of humanity in order to achieve higher levels of relationship, community, and achievement.

Brewin makes one further point about the ministry/leadership of Jesus exhibited which he connects again with how emergent organizations are established/sustained. Earlier reference was made to market forces, how exchange of commodities in the marketplace demands a form of equilibrium, the law of supply and demand, where a price of exchange could be arrived at that is acceptable to both parties. This marketplace is of course the center of our producer/consumer society and depends upon giving and receiving being reasonably equally balanced.

Now Brewin introduces us to a rather different form of exchange.[40] He refers to a book by Lewis Whyte entitled *Gift*, which is about the relationship between an artist, his work, and the person who buys that work. That exchange may be contractual, with money changing hands, but it is also a gift from the artist to the new owner. The artist gives something of himself to the

---

39. Brewin, *Signs of Emergence*, 115.

40. Brewin, *Signs of Emergence*, 146.

receiver that can never be financially quantifiable: it is a gift of a part of him-self. Brewin goes on to equate this element of transaction to the ministry of Jesus. Whereas society in Jesus' time centered around market exchange, with a reasonable equilibrium between giver and receiver, Jesus himself offered a very different model. Instead of following the model operating around him, Jesus offered instead a free gift—himself—that no one could or need pay for; it was unconditional. Jesus, in offering this gift, rejected the devil's transac-tional model—from the desert encounter—of fame, power, and possessions being provided, in exchange for acknowledging/worshipping the devil's agenda. Alternatively, Jesus' ministry went on to offer to everyone something that they could never, and would never, have need to repay. That nonrecipro-cal gift went all the way to Golgotha: to the cross.

Now an emergent church, therefore, should be one, not only centered on servant-enabling, bottom-up leadership, but also centered on gift rather than reciprocal exchange. Such a church will not have the stability of an equalizing deal: an equilibrium between giver and receiver. The dynamic of Christ's church should be one of disequilibrium, where the balance between the giver and the receiver is not equal. The weight of the gift comes totally from the giver, with no payment expected in return. This model of gift therefore is distinctly countercultural and should be reflected in all relation-ships within and outside the church. It is a servant attitude, illustrated at its highest by giving with no expectation of anything in return. Maybe this can be illustrated by Ann Morisy's description of a "non-anxious presence."[41]

---

### NON-ANXIOUS PRESENCE

Multiple anxieties permeate so many individual lives: job scarcity, external eco-nomic influences, being a stranger in a foreign country, technological innovation, security of living, insecure or disintegrating family relationships that cause stress. Within church communities it might be propping up aging congregations, caring for decaying historic buildings, not knowing where funds might come from to heat the church for Sunday morning. Wherever anxiousness occurs it can con-tribute to a high level of anxiety experienced by so many people/organizations. Morisy points out how our reactions to these pressures can so easily lead to a downward spiral of response where we react fearfully, with the *reptilian*, more primitive side of our brain, where we begin to scapegoat others, herd together with kindred spirits, then hate what we identify as being the primary cause. This downward spiral results in a negative, unattractive, and unwelcoming commu-nity, be it a local community or a church congregation.

---

41. Morisy, *Journeying Out*, 193.

Morisy then goes on to point out how Christians have a real ministry to offer, both within the local community and within their congregation. Referring to Murray Bowen's "The Differentiated Self," Morisy highlights the importance of separating our own personal feelings from the contextual problems we face. As we become at peace in ourselves and in Christ, we can then address the issues before us far more effectively. Having parked our own anxieties—through the gift we have received—we can then offer a nonreciprocal, "nonanxious presence"[42] to the community we are called to serve. We can more easily separate the issues of grievance, and identify their multiple causes. We can act as a "transformer"[43] to those around us by "reducing the voltage"—from 220 to 12 volts—of the issues to manageable proportions. We can bring laughter and humor, enabling us to "soften our eyes" as when we "look upon a new-born baby" so we can bring to a community, wound up with tense worry, a feel for the referent power of Christ.[44]

This "nonanxious presence" can be empowered by drawing on the way Jesus did things—his referent power. Rather than being overwhelmed by an economy of scarce resources we can instead "find ourselves party to an extraordinary cascade of grace,"[45] rather than being shaped by survival strategies, we can instead be buoyed by the hopeful possibilities of the kingdom economy. As we seek to do it like Jesus—as a gift—we can become a beacon of hope and encouragement.

Frances Young describes a similar view that she learned in ministry towards a bereaved couple who had just lost a stillborn child. She recounts how she realized that by reliving her own pain—over her son—she was "too involved" through her own feelings. "Only when (that) self-involvement was purged could I begin to be of use to those who were suffering."[46] This "cascade of grace" that Morisy describes is surely the gift, the referent power, emerging from the ministry of Jesus. And it is that gift/power that needs to become the catalyst, the heart, the environment, of an emergent church.

## 9.6 THE EDGE OF CHAOS

Finally, an emergent church—similar to the situation described by Fowler as stage 5—takes on a very different character to the contained, defensive, pre-Enlightenment position of stage 3 and the reasoned questioning within an Enlightenment framework of stage 4. The safety and security of certainty

42. Morisy, *Journeying Out*, 193.

43. Morisy, *Journeying Out*, 192.

44. Morisy, *Journeying Out*, 193–94.

45. Morisy, *Journeying Out*, 235.

46. Young, *Face to Face*, 238–39.

and the absolute are gone; tradition, order, and dogmatic proclamation no longer automatically provide stability and perpetuity. Boundaries have become porous. There is no blueprint for success. Final authority and leadership no longer reside at the center. Authority will arise from a combination of the referent inspiration of Christ, the Spirit's touch on individual talents, respect gained by the witnessing church community as it seeks to transform secular society, the imitation of Christ, and a clear understanding/vision of the kingdom that is to grow in the here and now.

The emerging church is seeking truth stranger than it used to be: it seeks to achieve that within each environmental situation by holding together the complex questions, by uniting together and focusing on the gift of Christ, by being earthed within the vulnerability and needs of others, by honoring the Spirit-inspired periphery rather than a self-authenticating center, by networking relationships rather than coercing certainty, and by emphasizing the present at the expense of the past and the future.

Fowler and Brewin base their thinking on Jung's concept of conjunction "where complexities of life are held together, where hierarchies have given way to networks of organization."[47] Others describe a similar journey but use different terminology. Dee Hock coins the word "chaordic,"[48] where chaos and order are simultaneously held together by individuals and organizations; not a destination, but a journey; a community engagement; a different dynamic of judgment, behavior capacity, and ingenuity.

An understanding of Fowler's stage-5 concept of a conjunctive approach, and the initial unpacking of Brewin's ideas, have both been moved forward considerably in the last two decades. They include the writings of Marti and Ganiel,[49] K. S. Moody,[50] Gibbs and Bolger,[51] and Mobsby.[52] Driscoll[53] has identified three differing theological approaches within the Emerging Church Movement—Relevants, Reconstructionists, and Revisionists—ranging from the more conservative relevants views of people like Dan Kimball, to the Community Church Movement's reconstructionist emphasis on transformed lives highlighted by Frost and Hirsch, to the more liberal, revisionist, postmodern-oriented emergent thread articulated by Brian McLaren and others. Light was shed on this more liberal position in

47. Brewin, *Signs of Emergence*, 32.

48. Hock, *Birth of the Chaordic Age*, 3.

49. Marti and Ganiel, *Deconstructed Church*.

50. Moody, *Radical Theology and Emerging Christianity*.

51. Gibbs and Bolger, *Emerging Churches*, 44.

52. Mobsby, *Emerging and Fresh Expressions of Church*, 24.

53. Driscoll, "Relevants, Reconstructionists and Revisionists," 89.

a debate/interview between Katharine Moody, Kester Brewin—of the Vaux Community—and Peter Rollins—of the Ikon Community, Belfast—during the 2013 Greenbelt Festival, Cheltenham.[54] Clearly the controversial and wide-ranging debate in this emergent church movement is both thought-provoking and unfinished.

---

### EMERGING CHURCH MOVEMENT—THE REVISIONISTS

The more revisionist approach within ECM would reject Fowler's stage 3, pre-Enlightenment, conservative, traditional, and institutional church—based either on historic hierarchical orders and static creedal statements or fundamental evangelical constructions—as inappropriate to contemporary Western philosophical culture. They see a foolish disconnect between both the inherited church and the very exciting fresh expressions wings of church and the rest of postmodern life. Neither part of this mixed economy, they believe, reach sufficiently into contemporary reality. They suggest, significantly, that this disconnect is not simply a generational and communication problem, but rather one of differing philosophical positions, that neither pre-Enlightenment foundations nor Enlightenment rationality hold water in the multi/video-camera world of Facebook, and machinecentric technology. In essence, the more revisionist wing of the ECM is seeking to unpack what a conjunctive, emerging church might look like in practice as it engages with the questions/issues arising from our relativist postmodernism that inhabits postmillennial Western society.

---

The primary intention of this debate is surely to articulate the mission of God for generation Z: how the present church can engage, both contextually and counterculturally, with the ethos of contemporary culture.

The debate centers around three key areas: first, institutions and movements; secondly, text and practice—historical truths and every-day reality; and thirdly, community and the individual. All of these three are interlinked. Whereas the turn of the millennium indicated that all this debate could be held together by a mixed economy approach and better contextual communication, further thinking since the millennium suggests that it goes much deeper than that. If the Christian faith really wishes to enrich the third decade, the revisionist ECM is suggesting it will need to comprehensively test out/engage its core belief with the philosophical culture and practical realities faced by tomorrow's teenagers. That in turn may require release from traditional baggage surrounding institutional structures and static assumptions/authorities/dogmas. The conjunctive dilemma is centered around how far to move contextually without losing the opportunity to speak out counterculturally.

---

54. Moody, *Radical Theology and Emerging Christianity*, Introduction.

As we have seen, the authority that lies behind pre-Enlightenment think-ing rests either with the hierarchical institution and/or with specific biblical interpretations/authoritarian assumptions. Today, postmodern, relativist, technocentered reality severely questions both these presuppositions/authori-ties. Millennials/Generation Z are skeptical about institutions, believing their future lies in disengaging with—or at least reinventing—the institutions that have thus far defined our culture. Hierarchies are giving way to networks. Central authority is being undermined by power to the edge; one single, de-finitive, referee's-eye view is being enhanced by two line judges and a VAR using five strategically placed video cameras. A set-piece, repetitive formula is no longer adequate in a continuous flow of fresh, complex questions.

A key point that the emerging church has identified from Generation Z is that if institutions, as such, now have a limited shelf life, faith in the future will be more likely to be communicated by small, locally based communities of faith. Such Christian communities will no longer accept the authority and advice of expert professional theologians/biblical expositors, but rather their faith, practice, and witness will arise from individuals within those communities of faith as they engage theologically with the reality of life within their social environment—not unlike the situation ethics concept.

Outworkings of these ideas indicate that a) faith is more likely to be identified through building communities of faith, outside church walls, being committed to social justice as equally as social action, and through living socially, politically and environmentally just lives, b) that any form of institutionalization of such Christian communities will be resisted, leading to short life expectancy, the death of the group, and resurrection in new for-mations as the discourse continues; c) that, in such self-determining, self-regulating communities, there will be serious tension between the collective identity of the believing, witnessing community and the individualism of each gift-contributing member, and d) that, with the playing-down of the significance of the historically handed-down text in favor of the witnessing community's practice of faith, the fact that the text preceded the practice is often conveniently sidelined.

Moody goes on to describe the practical outworkings of this with reference to the Ikon and Vaux communities established by Rollins and Brewin, who decided to reject any move towards an institutional communi-ty. They "shot it (Vaux) dead" leaving "a community of curators" to continue to "explore what to reuse and recycle, how they might build up something new, how something else might be possible . . . an exploration into the twin orbits of technology and theology."[55] These emerging church communities

---

55. Moody, *Radical Theology and Emerging Christianity*, 23.

appeared to switch from a "congregational model that requires the identification of local communities as 'emerging Churches' per se, to a notion of an emerging Church discursive milieu with which a variety of individuals and community agents are engaged."[56]

This example leaves us with an opportunity to assess practical outworkings of emergent church together with the theological thinking out of which it has developed. The three key areas already mentioned provide the structure for that assessment.

Central to the whole emergent church concept is the difference between institution and movement. Institution appears tainted by historic, hierarchical order/authority, and is given little respect by the emergent movement. The first-generation movement of faith is respected but consequent generations of institutionalized faith are frowned on. Leonardo Boff's experience-filled Latin American words—that a movement will never be sustained unless it becomes an institution—are not listened to. The need for some form of community norms/structure, other than being self-determining and self-legislating, appears to be played down. Recognition that the Christian faith is a multicultural, global network that brings out different emphases is not really taken into account. However, such an approach that appears to fly away completely from any form of institutionalization is open to the criticism of throwing out the baby with the bathwater.

The second area of debate, using a different colloquialism, comes under the question "Which came first—the chicken or the egg?" There is considerable debate around *text* and *practice*. In the past, text dominated, with practice merely being viewed as an application of the text with preconceived, handed-down understandings of the text overwhelming contemporary questions of cultural circumstances/practical behavior. Instead of centering the discursive milieu around the text, emerging church debate is more likely to center around practice within the community. This is done at the expense of remembering that it was the text of the Christ narrative that came before Christian community. This emerging church viewpoint is in contrast to Brewin's earlier book where he highlights the centrality of the *gift* that Christ unconditionally offers to everyone.[57] The prime text is surely the unique gift of Jesus Christ, together with the outpoured gift of the Spirit at Pentecost. Surely the empirical Christ narrative, emanating from the biblical text and the church's understanding of that text, needs to hold a significant position when it comes to debating how, in practice, the church should be in the world but not of the world.

---

56. Moody, *Radical Theology and Emerging Christianity*, 16.

57. Brewin, *Signs of Emergence*, 146–54.

By so accommodating to the postmodern emphasis on the here and now, and by playing down the concept of a historical narrative text, the emerging church runs the risk of taking little account of the ways in which God has intervened and related to his people in the past. Further, by emphasizing the contemporary activity of God building the present kingdom, it is in danger of paying scant homage to the eschatological kingdom—the full reign of God—to which the mission of God today is directed.

The third area concerns the tension between collective identity and individualism. With resistance to any form of institutionalization and the severing of links with the historic church institutions—from which the faith has been handed down—great emphasis is placed on each gifted individual, their contributions, and the pluralistic context of their lives. This approach however could well be seen to exhibit the same shortcomings as situation ethics. It is difficult to imagine how such communities could be sustained without some form of structure, leadership, and authority linking it back in some moderating way to the church/faith framework.

There is a fourth area of critique that should not be glossed over. It is certainly important to pay close attention to the present reality, to the cultural mindset of the postmodern technocentric generations enabling the Christian faith to be expressed in ways that are easily accessible. However, it should not be done at the expense of forgetting that the Christian faith will always have a countercultural difference with all forms of human culture, simply because it is not of this world in certain important ways. The Christian message is never going to fit easily into a secular, postmillennial view of society.

In conclusion, it has to be acknowledged that more theological discussion is needed over inherited church, fresh expressions, a mixed economy, and the differing approaches to emerging church—illustrated in the ECM. All these differing expressions highlight the tension between pre-Enlightenment, Enlightenment, and postmodern cultures, which presents a serious challenge to the minds/lifestyle of the postmillennial, third-decade generation. As they ponder these different approaches, they will hopefully discover some form of conjunction between institution and experience: between the historically handed down text/structure and the existential encounter with postmodern technocentric reality; between community connectedness and individual realization. That tension/conjunction ought to be an expression of what Taylor described as "the integration of the intuitive and the rational,"[58] the experiential and the cerebral. It could also chime in with Sun Tzu's view of chaos, as being both crisis and opportunity.

---

58. Taylor, *Go-between God*, 221.

# Chapter 10

## Holistic Ministry

### 10.1 STATE OF PLAY

From the very beginning ministry and mission have been central to the expansion of the Christian faith. The first and second generations of faith were epitomized by this ministry of mission being fulfilled by the ministry of the baptized. The Holy Spirit's presence in their lives ordained them to declare and spread the good news. By the third generation of faith, ministry and leadership developed, centered around a threefold order established by Ignatius. Ever since then the Roman Catholic Church, followed by the Anglican Church and others—using different terminology—have followed that tradition, leading more to maintenance than mission. This leadership approach claims its authority from traditional and biblical sources, from a Levitical order all the way through to St. Peter in the New Testament, with responsibility for ministry and theological development lying with an ordained or ministerial class, authorized and legitimized either by church tradition or by particular biblical emphases.

From the third generation of faith onward, the dominance of leadership and authority by the "orders," over and above the "ministry of the baptized," led to an institutionalizing of the work of the Holy Spirit.[1] Ministry, and access to the authority of the Holy Spirit's presence, was controlled and distributed by the orders of the church, with the church's membership becoming subservient to them. At the same time, the first- and

1. Taylor, *Go-between God*, 208.

second-generational emphasis on apostles and evangelists gave way to the third and subsequent generations emphasizing the roles of pastors/teachers, often with an eye on orthodoxy and maintenance. The growth of this dichotomy has continued to be the norm, despite sodal breakouts against it.

Reviewing the mission and ministry of the church, people such as Roland Allen highlighted this disjunction between the New Testament pattern—illustrated by Paul—and that threefold tradition established by Ignatius. As we have seen, that debate has continued over the past fifty years. However, it took a South Australian visiting Oxford at the turn of the millennium to bring to light the key sticking point. Stephen Pickard clearly identified a duality of approach, as an Anglican, between "representational ministry," of the orders, and "other ecclesial ministries"—the ministry of the baptized.[2] He insisted that there would always be dominance/control over ministry by the former—with insignificance attributed to the latter—unless that duality was resolved and a unity of ministerial expression achieved.

However, since his clear articulation of that disjunction, little further progress appears to have been made. Even recent Anglican papers on ministry[3] referred to this dichotomy—talking of the "river and the canal" running side by side, but hardly ever meeting—but offered little toward a solution to the dilemma. The question has to be asked, therefore, as to why this duality has not been addressed, and how it might be addressed now. These questions are made even more poignant by the practical point that such a professional class/structure is becoming increasingly difficult to recruit, train, and maintain. So how could a holistic approach to ministry be arrived at? How could the immense potentiality of the ministry of the baptized, the priesthood of all believers, be released? Or as John Taylor so eloquently phrased it, "the upward pull of unrealized potential."[4]

## 10.2 CONSTRAINTS AND POSSIBILITIES

The intransigence of finding a resolution to the present dualistic view of Christian ministry can no doubt be attributed to the difficulty of identifying an adequate solution. The duality is so deeply engrained in the life of so many church denominations no one appears to want to disturb it. The fact that it was clearly articulated by Stephen Pickard in 2009, and yet since that time theological minds have studiously avoided responding to the challenge—with the exception of Cocksworth and Brown's reference to reciprocal

2. Pickard, *Theological Foundations*, 53.

3. Frost, *Setting God's People Free*.

4. Taylor, *Go-between God*, 31.

ministries[5]—suggests that there is no stomach for pursuing the debate. The implications of this stalemate stretch to the very core of church structure.

## 10.2.1 The Core Disjunction

This intransigence goes to the very core of the church structure. Ministry/leadership of the church is deeply embedded and anchored in a hierarchical, authoritative, power-oriented structure. We have seen that this dynamic has been established and strengthened with the turn of every century since Constantine. On the other hand, the ministry of Jesus and the annunciation of the church at Pentecost indicate that the Christian faith arises out of a free gift to all, encompassed by vulnerability, networked by every believer from the bottom upwards, through the Holy Spirit specifically bestowing power to the edge within an emergent body. This deep-seated disjunction is surely the cause of centuries worth of circumvention and prevarication, despite efforts, such as those of the Anabaptists, to resolve the duality.

However, there are signs that a reconsideration of this duality is both possible and immanent. The first is that elements of this present techno-centric society have considerable affinity with New Testament society: that the questionings between the Judeo-Christian faith and the Greco-Roman society have considerable similarity with the questionings of a traditional stage 4 church mindset in our emerging technocentric future, that humanist charges of hypocrisy surrounding the church's dependence on status/power at every stage of its development are beginning to be acknowledged. An example of this came with the recent visit of the pope to Eire.

---

**POPE AND EIRE**

In 2018, Pope Francis visited Eire. Public opinion clearly voiced the chant of hypocrisy for the church's failures in the light of child abuse. The pope's response was to publicly accept both the failure and the hypocrisy, recognizing that confession and repentance were the only way forward. Time will tell whether his sincerity will be sufficient to implement satisfactory penitence, actual remedies, and real change within the Vatican Curia and throughout the worldwide catholic hierarchy. Everybody is watching.

---

The second sign is that existing church structures of ministry, in their present form, are becoming highly precarious: the physical nature of the traditional historic church structure appears insurmountable as days go by.

---

5. Cocksworth and Brown, *Being a Priest Today*, 19.

This tsunami of threats has already been articulated. In effect the present structure of most established denominations is probably unsustainable in the long term. Wishful thinking of the laager mentality will only delay the eventual outcome. The survival of the faith may not be in doubt, but existing church structures/status in their present form have a far-less-certain future. As Ann Morisy has put it, "The wine has run out and the party seems to be drawing to a close."[6]

So what are the options for resolving this impasse? What is needed if the faith is to become a genuine contributor to life, in this postmillennial period?

## 10.2.2 Possibilities—Acknowledge/Repent

To juxtapose the ministry of Jesus and the Pentecost experience with the Constantinian church highlights a dramatic change. It has been suggested that, during this period, the essence of what Jesus and his spirit stood for evaporated in an attempt to contextualize/establish permanence within the Greco-Roman world. Acknowledgment of what was lost in that transition— from vulnerability to power; from relationship to substance; from gift to control; from bottom-up to top-down—has to become the starting point of an emergent church. Such a step needs to acknowledge that this traditional structure, apparently thought to be essential in the fourth century, has in actual fact become an obstacle—a millstone around its neck—a hindrance to expressing the Jesus narrative in today's world.

Brewin has helpfully suggested[7] that a period of waiting and silence needs to accompany such acknowledgment. He describes it as dropping from the foothill upon which we stand down into a valley of uncertainty where we can be equipped to rise again to higher peaks: on the road to the ultimate not-yet peak of Everest proportions—the reign of God. He refers to Elijah, who, after the victory over Jezebel's prophets of Baal on Mount Carmel, runs into the silence of the Negev, where the still small voice of God redirects him toward Elisha, who is to take God's purposes to even higher peaks with the Everest of Jesus' incarnation still a long way off.

Acknowledgment of deviation, penitence for its continuation down through the centuries, and confession for the part we continue to play in that much earlier deviation are surely all part of the foundation of an emergent church. Gone is the apparent certainty of a stage 3 mindset. Present are the questions of stage 4 uncertainty. But surrounding an emergent church is

---

6. Morisy, *Journeying Out*, 230.
7. Brewin, *Signs of Emergence*, 44–45.

the belief that there is a way forward today that will spring from the Spirit's presence in every believer, together with Christ's gift offered to everyone.

Centered around that acknowledgment, penitence, and expectation is the belief that the usurpation of power, taken by the hierarchy of the church, can be reordered by a fresh take on the ministry of Jesus/the personal empowerment of the spirit/the relational nature of the Trinity. It is not that church leadership should "fall victim to the illusion of primitivism, to the dream of a recaptured pristine purity, as though nineteen centuries of Church history had not transpired."[8] It is rather that rigid/cerebral structures could give way to a reimagined focus on mission-oriented ministry, that a return to the first-generational emphasis on mission as compared to the subsequent generational absorption with maintenance could offer a release from the tsunami of threats threatening to overwhelm traditional church life and structures, that structures, boundaries, and definitions of orthodoxy could be reinvigorated by a truth stranger than it used to be.

So after the silence and the waiting, what would be the next step? Surely an emergent church, whilst rejoicing in the radical nature of faith in Christ, will need to walk away from the security/structures of hierarchical power. Being prepared to walk away from the safety of the known, into the uncertain valley of faith, without a real factual blueprint to follow, is surely the calling of those with faith who approach the third decade.

## 10.2.3 Possibilities—Walk Away

Walking away, inspired by "projective identity" at Handy's point B, will be both fearful and exciting. It will involve being prepared to give up the bird in the hand in expectation of a bird in the bush, giving up what is safe, known, and protective in the expectation that emergent innovation, power from the edge, promised by the risen Christ, and made possible by the Pentecost event, will lift up the church to higher foothills on the journey towards the not-yet reality of Everest. It is to allow God's activity of the past and the expectation of an eternal future to inspire the present. It is allowing the what is to become transformed by a vision of what could be—the ministry of the prophet. It is to allow the outer identity of the church to be reinfused by its inner message. It is to await an extraordinary cascade of grace.

In practical terms, this point B could well be traumatic. Thinking over all that the church has accumulated over the past centuries, both seen and unseen, there is a great deal at stake. For so many, the church has been identified by its inherited wealth, its ownership of buildings, its status in

8. Peachey, "New Ethical Possibility," 32.

governmental and societal influence. All of this would be questioned, if the church was to embark upon a second sigmoid curve based on vulnerability, decentralization, relationship, and the primacy of the nonreciprocal gift. Hierarchy would give way to networking: centralized authority/control to diversity/power to the edge; substance to relationship; order to innovation; certainty to open questions, status to insignificance; boundaries to dirt; calculated transactions to unreturnable gifts.

So what would this mean in terms of the ministry and mission of the church? How would it affect the backbone of the church, the class of professional ministers, the administrators of its substantial organization, the controllers of cerebral theological influence? Let us look at this in terms of a holistic ministry, a servant-episcope/leadership, an alternative center point.

## 10.3 HOLISTIC MINISTRY

Based on Christ's words to his disciples, "As the father has sent me, I am sending you,"[9] the ministry of the whole church is to proclaim the mission of God that "baptism into the death and resurrection of Jesus Christ is the foundation of all Christian ministry. Through baptism each follower of Christ is called into that ministry and the Holy Spirit gives the necessary gifts to carry that out."[10] This reiteration of biblical principle states that all Christian ministry derives from the empowerment of baptism, coming from the assertion in Galatians 3:27–29 that our baptism in Christ clothes us and makes us all, on a totally equal basis, heirs of Christ. Acts 1:4–8 assures us that our baptism will empower us, through the blessing of the Holy Spirit, with the ability to express and witness to the very nature of Christ and his kingdom. In 2017, another Anglican Synod Report endorsed this, stating that, "Baptism is the mark of our incorporation into the life of the Church, and the commissioning to participate in God's mission in the world."[11]

However, despite this clear articulation of biblical tradition, the reality in church practice remains somewhat different. Back in the 1980s, Bosch contended that "for almost nineteen centuries, ministry has been understood, almost exclusively, in terms of the service of ordained ministry"[12] with the ordained minister holding a "dominant and undisputed position in Church life."[13] Although changes have indeed taken place since then, many

---

9. John 20:21.

10. Lambeth Conference, *Official Report on the Conference*, 182.

11. Frost, *Setting God's People Free*, 1.

12. Bosch, *Transforming Mission*, 467.

13. Bosch, *Transforming Mission*, 468.

would argue that the old dynamic still remains in place. And although it is easiest to discern in Anglican practice, it is not too difficult to identify this professional leadership role, under different legitimizing authority, in many other denominations/community churches.

## 10.3.1 Unresolved Issues

As we have seen, this dualistic approach to ministry, with the representational ministries and the other ecclesial ministries identified separately, perpetuates a disjunctive and implosive dynamic. In 2002, Cocksworth and Brown highlighted the relational nature between the two when they wrote, "The presbyter needs the people to be a presbyter. The people need the presbyter to be the people of God."[14] They recognized that this reciprocity was intrinsic to a holistic ministry of the church. However, Pickard reflects on this line in 2009, indicating that "the nature and dynamic of the reciprocity that might obtain is uncharted. The integration is incomplete."[15]

Pickard helpfully goes on to articulate this unresolved dilemma in which the church continues to find itself.[16] He notes that, although the relational nature of ministry is uncontested, resolution of these two elements is unsettled. He traces the continuing separation to the way the subject is approached, which is to

> focus on the nature of representative ministry and ordained ministry—and then show how its embedded-ness in the ministry of the whole people of God is generative of more respectful and interdependent relations between the ministries. The focus is thus on one node in the complex of ministries—ordained— and the wider ministries fall out of view. Inevitably this approach betrays the failure to press the (relational) trinitarian dynamic of the ministries as far as it should be.[17]

He concludes that "it remains fundamentally unclear why and how . . . to use the words of JAT Robinson nearly five decades earlier . . . the ministries of the people of God generate an ongoing mutual expression of each other, let alone 'bringing each other to be.'"[18]

---

14. Cocksworth and Brown, *Being a Priest Today*, 19.

15. Pickard, *Theological Foundations*, 120.

16. Pickard, *Theological Foundations*, 120–21.

17. Pickard, *Theological Foundations*, 121.

18. Pickard, *Theological Foundations*, 121.

What is even more revealing in this dilemma is that within this Anglican debate[19] there is little effort to articulate how this reciprocal nature is to be achieved—appearing to be unaware of Pickard's research, and the intransigent issue of the need for a holistic outworking of ministry, that he highlights. Similarly, within the community church movement, the authority of ministers/elders appears to remain unchallenged, with the ministry of the baptized membership remaining subservient to that senior biblically authenticated leadership.

One possible approach to resolving this issue might be that, instead of starting at the node of the ordained/authorized ministry, it might be more appropriate to start with the ministry of the baptized—where the ministry of the church began. The starting point for ministry should surely be inspired by the original order, placing considerable pressure on the ordained/authorized ministry to justify their present role. A large part of this present role is function; maintaining/propping up the institution/structure of established denominations. The ordained/authorized role is then further infected by accepting that they proscribe/limit the possibility of the baptized ministering fully and effectively.

There is a real urgency that this disjunction should be addressed/resolved, even as the future of the professional, ordained/authorized minister is increasingly under pressure. So what are the alternatives if the debate is to be initiated from a holistic starting point?

## 10.3.2 Relational Alternatives

An interesting biblical illustration has been brought to mind by David Rhymer. He points out that[20] there is a marked difference in approach between Ezra and Jeremiah. When it came to rebuilding Jerusalem after the exile, Ezra stood up on a platform and commanded that the law be read out. He then sent a body of Levites/scribes to explain to the people what the law actually meant.[21] Teaching was therefore left in the hands of a few trained professionals who told the people what to think. However, Jeremiah indicated through his prophetic declaration of God's new covenant[22] that this covenant was going to be directly between God and his people, that there would be a direct relationship between the two sides: "a situation in

19. Frost, *Setting God's People Free*; Scott et al., *Report of the Lay Ministries Working Group*.

20. Rhymer, "Jeremiah 31:31–34," 294–96.

21. Rhymer, "Jeremiah 31:31–34," 294–96.

22. Rhymer, "Jeremiah 31:31–34," 294–96.

which the Torah . . . is directly responsible to, and understandable by, the least of them to the greatest . . . no teachers, no preachers, no pulpits, just unmediated access to the word of God."[23] Following Jeremiah rather than Ezra, in this instance, offers a signpost to those who stress the development of the ministry of the baptized today. Clearly Ezra illustrated the roots of a threefold order pattern, but Jeremiah certainly indicated that God's word was perfectly capable of being understood by his people directly.

Following Jeremiah's approach has interesting links with the world of computers and the internet. Up until now the ordained role has had more in common with Ezra's approach to explaining the word of God to the people. In recent years that has moved somewhat; from direct teaching more toward an enabling or collaborative approach. However, even in this approach, it has been the ordained who control/share ministry amongst the laity. Now the computer world has introduced us to the concept of *curation,* which has similarities with Jeremiah's approach.

---

**CURATION**

Curation is, in IT terminology, the processing, annotation, and integration of data, collected from various sources and made available to wider audiences. It can add value to the material, and also process the high volume/complexity of the raw data.

---

Instead of ministers teaching and leading, curation would be more a way in which ministers curate the appropriate data/resources/training tools and then make them available for the local church to use, similar to the way in which Jeremiah declared God's new covenant to the people, making that covenant available for everyone to download for themselves within their own relationship with God. With curation, the emphasis would be on each believer availing themselves of God's purposes, with the ordained being there to assist them in their quest. To use the language of social media, the role of the ordained would be less of one publishing the good news, and more of one platforming the good news, so others could draw down the information for themselves, with the ordained becoming more of a conduit rather that a distributor.

---

**PLATFORMS**

Platform-based business models create added value by facilitating exchanges between interested parties. Such platforms draw together, and harness into networks,

---

23. Rhymer, "Jeremiah 31:31–34," 294–96.

users who have mutual interests so that amongst themselves resources can be accessed, innovation can be encouraged, and development fostered without a central role being required. The platform therefore provides participators themselves with the opportunities for growth and emergence without reference to a central control.

Such a platform-based model could be expressed both by central resources and by clergy themselves. This could lead to a decisive change, from central resources being distributed by ministers towards a centripetal dynamic whereby the ministry of the baptized draw down what they need to equip themselves for their witness and ministry in their community—power to the edge.

This curational/platform-based model fits well with the debate as to whether the ordained should fulfill a *functional* role as compared to an *iconic* role. At present many of the ordained/authorized leaders fulfill a functional management, task-oriented role within the structures of the church whether they like it or not. Indeed, without it many church organizations would collapse immediately. Although such a role is not necessarily what ordination/authorization is all about; it becomes the minister default position. If, on the other hand, the ordained/authorized were seen more as iconic figures, living out Christ's gift to humanity, pointing toward the message of faith within the local community, operating mutually with the baptized rather than in a dominant role, then that *iconic* role would fit in closely to the model of *curation* and *platforming*. They would be an asset to the local ministry, rather than its fulcrum. In turn, such a change of role would bring to a head the whole issue of continuing to perpetuate overweight organizational/denominational structures.

If the clergy withdrew from a central functional role, it would certainly put in doubt the ability to maintain the present level of structural organization; but, at the same time, it would primarily open up the possibility for the ministry of the baptized to grow into their true calling—baptism as ordination for ministry.

With the fulcrum of ministry to humanity resting on the ministry of the baptized, on lay vocation, the ministry of the church would be turned on its head. From every point in society, a Christian voice, a Christian witness, could emerge reflectively. It could transform theological reflection. Rather than being a top-down, cerebral process, performed by the theolocracy— church leaders, elders, and theological college staff—it could instead stem from everyday encounters and experience by the baptized in every area of life. And not only would there be internal theological reflection at that point but also critical, outward-facing contributions to society. However, the cost of such a move, from the practicality of the functional ministerial role to the inspirational iconic calling of the ministerial vows, would, as has been stated, necessitate serious forms of organizational review.

To give such weight to the ministry of the baptized—with the ordained/ authorized primarily offering iconic, curational, platforming roles—would raise questions concerning leadership, authority, rules, and boundaries. The norm of central control would be challenged by the diversity of innovation at the periphery; unity, instead of being imposed from above, would become the responsibility of every participant; personal satisfaction and self-discipline would need to be restrained, if anarchy was to be avoided; from the security of a rigid format, diversity would continuously threaten leadership, stability, and long-term sustainability; and authority would be stranger than it used to be.

Churches open to such a centripetal dynamic—with innovative energy arising out of the faith of every believer—would lead to questioning the norm of what it means to be church—the suburban stage 3 model. Instead of being drawn to a central, authoritative declaration of truth, believers committed to witness within their community would have the confidence of seeing themselves as the true identity and manifestation of the church.

With the ministry of the baptized being attracted to this reimagined identity, with its missionary opportunities toward those around them, they will be drawn to respond to Jeremiah's call to put aside the temptation to return to Jerusalem and to, alternatively, commit themselves to pray for the city in which they found themselves in exile. They would be encouraged to forsake the security of an ordered, controlled, safe, stage 3 environment and affirm God's plans to "give you hope and a future"[24]—in a contextual stage 5 community of faith—grappling with the question, "What does it mean to claim God's covenant, empowered by the gift of Jesus Christ/his spirit's presence, amongst a local community?" Following such a path will not ensure security or longevity, but it does promise hope to the prophetic imagination of those who take the risk.

## COMMUNITY NEEDS—STREET PASTORS

A number of emerging organizations link Christian commitment to contemporary social needs. Church Army, as has been quoted, runs homeless projects in Marylebone, and the Amber Project in Cardiff works with young people who self-harm. Street pastors/street angels, working in many cities/towns around the country, have a very real ministry amongst young people on the street late at night, or in the early hours of the morning. These voluntary organizations, often

24. Jer 29:11.

established and supported prayerfully by city/town center churches, have a real impact on the lives of lonely youngsters.

## REAL DEAL PLUS—ASHINGTON, NORTHUMBRIA

This independent charity has been set up to assist vulnerable people, particularly the homeless, living in poverty/isolation, or those who have struggled with drug and alcohol addiction.

It assists those attempting to develop new skills and qualifications so they can progress on to an independent and productive lifestyle within their community. It has a particular concern for young people. The center does this through a community café, a Teen Bar, Job Clubs, community shop, clothing bank, food bank, and both arts and crafts clubs—all of which are predominantly staffed by volunteers.

The work emanates from the Old Police Station building in Ashington, which has particular significance for the center's founder, Davey Falcus. Davey regularly speaks publicly about his experience since he was arrested in this police station after years of drug-dealing, violence, and gangland warfare in 1980s Newcastle's West End. After a number of prison sentences, he describes how his life was turned around at his child's baptism service in 1995. Through the way the light of his Gran played on the darkness within him, it inspired him to pick up a Bible, praying, "Jesus, if you really are God, you can help me, and I am yours." He then experienced a light coming through the window. This led Davey to an experience of peace, with Jesus saying, "Your sins are forgiven, go and sin no more." Davey now testifies that, at that moment, years of drug and alcohol abuse were broken.[25]

Since that time, Davey Falcus has dedicated his life to "Love in Action–Lives Transformed" through the establishment of Ashington Life Centre, a church in the town where he has now become a pastor, a church ministering to the needs of the community. A highlight of that ministry was when the police officer who had arrested Davey in that same police station met Davey, came to faith, and was baptized in that same building, which is now also a church. Such a story of personal faith and witness illustrates that it is not only Bobby and Jack Charlton who have come out of Ashington to bring happiness to many lives.

25. www.realdealplus.org.uk/page4.html.

## 10.4 THE AUTHORITY OF LEADERSHIP

In our present world of celebrity and fame, certain individuals rise above the rest of us to achieve popularity, status, and even worship. Pop stars, film stars, and football players are recognized globally as people to whom we should referently aspire to follow. However, rot can easily set in. It begins when the person themselves begin to believe all the hype about him or herself. Anyone who believes in the way others see them—on a pinnacle—is in a precarious position. The same is true of most forms of leadership, including within the church.

An unspoken understanding in the church is that ordination/authorization to senior leadership brings with it ultimate authority. Within the church, the pope/bishop/superintendent/apostolic leader has the final word. Around such titles as bishop/leader, expectations run very high— "The bishop/apostolic leader will be able to decide and sort this out." At the same time, these leaders themselves are severely tempted to believe the hype surrounding their role, though these are certainly unachievable expectations. The extent that they believe what is said and expected of them, leads them to a slippery slope.

Alternatively, these leaders may not be taken in by the hype, but are still conscious of what is expected of them. They are acutely aware of these expectations, yet at the same time, are also very conscious of their own personal inability to deliver such expectations. In both these instances, autonomous leadership brings with it serious potential pitfalls.

---

### TERMINOLOGY

It is important, within this discussion, not to be put off by denominational terminology. Whatever term is used— apostolic leader, superintendent, bishop—the issue can relate to many denominations, not just those who actually use that specific term. Apostolic leaders, superintendents, and bishops can all have an episcopal role just as apostolic teams/House of Bishops/area coverings/spheres/dioceses can all equate with each other. The nature of leadership and organizations can be remarkably similar in most church groupings.

---

In the first- and second-generational church, leadership emerged out of Pentecostal power and those who referred back to knowing Christ. By the second century, leadership came to be legitimized/authorized through the Ignatian threefold order claiming apostolic succession. Later the acceptance of a biblical canon of Scripture added a further source of legitimation, going hand in hand with the tradition of apostolic succession. Since the Reformation, leadership in all churches has resorted to authorization from either or both of these two primary sources. However, as we face the paradigm shift of the millennium, the fragility of these legitimating sources becomes more apparent. On the one hand, traditional hierarchical power is being seriously undermined by networking, information-fueled, technological innovation. On the other hand, the absolute nature of the biblical text is continuing to be questioned by the relativist ethos of postmillennial culture.

So, if more networking, emergent church structures are to take root, what alternative forms of legitimating power for leadership should become appropriate? How would such leadership come into being? A first-/second-generational model of referent leadership—leadership derived from the personal experience of knowing Christ through the Holy Spirit, undergirded by a holistic, historical, more objective, biblical dimension—could offer an alternative model. If such a reimagining could be grasped, dependence on legislative, coercive, prerogative power could be foregone in favor of this referent authority based on imitating the vulnerability of Christ, on a church immersed in reflecting Pentecostal empowerment. Transition to such new forms of authorization could surely be the hallmark and equilibrium for an emergent church model.

## 10.4.1 Theory and Practice

The starting point of present-day church leadership began with church authority being legitimized by apostolic succession implemented through the Ignatian threefold order. Since then the Western church has followed that pattern through to the Reformation, when the balance between church tradition and biblical text were reevaluated. Stephen Pickard has researched this journey extensively,[26] delving particularly into the legitimacy of the three-fold order and the practice of episcopal leadership today. The centerpoint of his argument is that there is a disjunction between theory and practice: between the vows undertaken at a bishop's/leader's ordination/authorization, and the ecclesial role she or he is expected to fulfill. And although the disjunction refers to episcopal ordination/leadership, the dilemma can easily refer to all churches, who have a functional order of ministry which sustains its structure/organization.

As has been referred to before, churches with ministerial order induct those ministers in a form of ordination. The spirit of that ordination is that the recipients are inducted into a role of being minister, preacher, pastor, or curer of souls. The difficulty is that, although that understanding of clerical

26. Pickard, *Theological Foundations*, 169.

ministry is fully accepted and understood, in practice it is replaced by the
necessity of having to manage/lead/sustain an overweight structure similar
to that of a CEO or manager in a commercial organization.

The concept of the minister being the iconic image of Christ, has
therefore been submerged into the role of CEO/administrator of the organization: the nature of the servantlike Christ, fulfilled in his relationship
with his disciples, has been supplanted by a coercive, centralized business
model within which all authority rests. The person available to respond to
personal/community needs has been replaced by the theologically trained
professional, who has little time for face-to-face encounter; the calling/
dependence upon God's grace as a means to fulfilling those vows has lost
out to computer literacy and technological competence; the roles of pastor,
teacher, and evangelist have been supplanted by the principles propounded
by contemporary business practice—that improved management can
provide the tools for ecclesial restoration and faith development; that the
*theory* of being called has been supplanted by the *practice* of organizational
management.

## 10.4.2 Roots and Critique

Pickard argues that one of the root causes in this disjunction lies in the
difference between the Ignatian order and the order developed later by
Cyprian in Carthage. For Ignatius, the whole concept centered around the
presbyter bishop being president of the eucharist, a minister amongst his
people, a relationship within a community. Whereas Cyprian developed a
model of the bishop expressing leadership within the context of a diocese,
a geographical area, Ignatius saw the role as one of authoritative teacher,
linking this up with the role of the apostles themselves. Cyprian developed
it into an administrative office, with a considerable jurisdictional role added
to it. Losing sight of the relational aspect of leadership, taking on a more
authoritative and judicial role has, Pickard argues, had a profound effect on
ensuing and contemporary church structures. The bishop and their local
church have been overtaken by the bishop as administrator of a diocese,
an upholder of all the substantial assets, status, and structure acquired over
time. Such a significant change of purpose and direction makes it increasingly uncertain whether the present model reflects the church of Christ.
It questions whether the existing ecclesial structures renders the curing of
souls, the iconic witness to the ministry of Christ, achievable.

Cyprian's jurisdictional approach has been compounded in this age
with a greater emphasis on quality selection and training, and with the

whole culture of performance/appraisal now espoused by ecclesial authorities. Such power in the hands of the bishop/leader has tended to demand effective administration and communication skills more than anything else. Within established denominations this has been further endorsed by encouraging improvements in management capability, and by endorsing the ordained ministry as pivotal for achieving aspirations of growth and expansion. As has been pointed out, the right to rule, behind the Cyprianic model has been transposed into the right to manage in this twenty-first-century business management model. This leaves the ministry of the baptized lying as a distant memory: a second-class option. In the process, "effective pastoral care" and "active prophetic imagination"[27] have been left behind.

The critical point, therefore, may be not those who are actually failing to fulfill their ordination vows but rather the inadequacies of the ecclesial structure itself. However, the only way in which the structure can evolve or be revolutionized lies in the hands of the existing leadership itself. Yet they are "trapped in a steel hard casing of inflexible ecclesiology."[28] Without a radical reappraisal of structure and authority, it is difficult to see how the vulnerable ministry and mission of Jesus can be iconically portrayed by the ministry of the baptized within the setting of the third decade.

## 10.4.3 Wrong Direction

One further point, before we look at positive options, concerns the secularization of western European society. As has been referred to in chapter 6, the development of the Christian faith in Western Europe has been in marked contrast to the global expansion of that same faith in other continents. Instead of the exponential growth exhibited in the latter, within the former a number of social and value surveys[29] have all indicated that religious belief has declined in Western Europe during the post-World War period.

This decline has been attributed to the rise of secularization, and the influence of anthropocentric enlightenment values such as individuality, reason, modern scientific discovery/fact supplanting the pre-Enlightenment, theocentric culture/influence of the church, with its belief-/value-oriented traditions and teachings. However, this initial view has engendered considerable debate, encouraged by the interesting trends revealed by these surveys. Whereas it had been assumed that the Enlightenment project would see religious thought and belief decline in the face of modernization—and

27. Pickard, *Theological Foundations*, 176.

28. Roberts, *Religion, Theology and the Human Sciences*, 179.

29. Social Values Surveys, discussed in Davie, "Europe," 68–71.

even become extinct—the surveys indicated that this scenario was not as conclusive as hitherto thought. In fact, from a global viewpoint the opposite was taking place. Religious revival, in the form of the evangelical and Pentecostal movement, swept across most continents, whilst at the same time extreme Islam grew to become a major world influence. The question therefore arose as to whether the secularization of Western Europe was the norm to which all would ultimately follow or whether it was, for certain local reasons, the exception to the global scene.

Sociologists worked on the data of the surveys and pointed up the complexity of the issue. Grace Davie, Peter Berger, and others came to the conclusion that "while many Europeans have ceased to participate in religious institutions, they have not yet abandoned many of their deep seated religious inclinations."[30] This led Davie to suggest it would be more accurate to recognize, "western Europe as an unchurched population rather than simply secular."[31] She came to identify a difference between believing and belonging,[32] "between feelings, experience and the more numinous religious beliefs and those that measure religious orthodoxy, ritual participation and institutional attachment."[33] So the jury is still out on the divergence between the Western European reaction to the Enlightenment and the global expression of faith. There are some who believe that, as modernization overwhelms other continents, that secularization will follow, and yet others who claim we are now entering a postsecular era.

An interesting illustration of the above issue is raised by David Tacey, who suggests that, in this postmodern era, religion is not dead or even dying. Alternatively he postulates that "the search for 'primal spirituality' and 'the return of the religious' continues unabated."[34] What appears to be happening is that, surrounded by spiritual enquiry within society, the church is not engaging with those who are searching; instead it is resorting to a last-ditch stand of increasing management capability in an attempt to maintain institutional stability. The ecclesial body, through its leadership, is seeking therefore to address questions in which few are interested. At the same time, it struggles to engage with the questions that people are actually asking. Ecclesial bodies are so blinded with trying to catch up contextually with business management methods that they fail to grasp their evangelistic role:

30. Davie, "Europe," 68.

31. Davie, "Europe," 68.

32. Davie, *Religion in Britain*.

33. Davie, "Europe," 67.

34. Pickard, *Theological Foundations*; Tacey, *Spirituality Revolution*, ch. 8.

they fail to realize they could offer a prophetic edge to those searching for spirituality amid the uncertainty of exponential technocratic development.

## 10.4.4 A Way Forward—Servant Episcope

During a study leave to visit worldwide Anglican dioceses with developed lay-ministry practices, not only did I encounter such examples in the rugged wilderness areas of New Zealand—where the sheep far outnumber the human settlers— but I also visited a retired bishop, dying of cancer, at the edge of a wilderness, in a wooded cove on the shores of Lake Michigan. In his time, Tom Ray put into practice a *servant episcopacy* in the Diocese of North Michigan, continued by Bishop Jim Kelsey and others. He came up with a list of three essentials for the episcopal role that could easily be equated to other ecclesial forms of authorized senior leadership.

---

### SERVANT EPISCOPE

*Servant-Episcopal Oversight* reflects to the big picture: bringing a dynamic catholicity where the local is fed by the whole and the whole is reflected in the local, where the local is brought in touch with other locals, giving each congregation a wider perspective. Drawing the weak to the attention of the apparently strong can lead to a two-way process of spiritual and physical growth, giving each congregation a wider perspective, enabling the individual worshiping group to become more conscious of its global family. Iconic *oversight* doesn't have to come from a functional hierarchy. It could flow through a variety of levels in the church's ministry.

*Education for Faith* lies at the heart of Christian maturity. Testing God's revelation within the context of each culture is the responsibility of each generation, of each geographical ethnic area. Discerning inappropriate answers and fighting doctrinal fragmentation has always been part and parcel of church and kingdom life. A *servant-episcopal educational* role needs to be present in all church life, encouraging and inspiring lay people to theologize for themselves in their own life and place of work.

*Servant-episcopal oversight,* expressed in Tom Ray's phrase "witness to the world," has and remains a crucial element in the growth of the kingdom. Bishop Nazir-Ali talks of "the bishop's apostolic and prophetic responsibility for bringing the good news to bear on local, national and international situations."[35] Such oversight has spoken, and can continue to speak, to humanity outside of the church in striking ways. It draws attention to the gospels' engagement with social

---

35. Nazir-Ali, *Shapes of the Church*, 6.

structures, deprivation, working conditions, desecration of the environment, the difficulties of parenting, and the temptations of consumerism. A voice spoken clearly by a respected Christian leader will both speak for others functionally, and at the same time inspire iconically all Christians to engage in this way in their own lives. This latter step would encourage the addressing of what some see as the weakest point of present church life—that of not engaging with society around it. Existing in a predominantly middle-class bubble, the church is often out of touch with what the body of the population is thinking, just as remainers were taken aback by the Brexit vote, unaware of what many were thinking.

Similarly, Stephen Pickard, who was a Bishop in Adelaide, South Australia, identifies a list of attributes appropriate to the leadership of an emergent church which affirms and amplifies the list from Tom Ray. He emphasizes the importance of "face to face relations, a high quality of interpersonal life, and the embedding of episcope in the local Church."[36] He backs this up with a call for smaller dioceses—administrative units—where these attributes can be more easily facilitated and trust built up. He goes on to promote the concept of a *missionary bishop*, following the Celtic example, that episcope should be "generous in its presence, (reflecting) the generosity of the triune God's holy and faithful presence in Jesus and the spirit."[37] He also assumes the gifts of "active prophetic imagination and effective pastoral care"[38] will be an essential ingredient in the episcopal role. Pickard therefore synchronizes, using different phrasing, with Tom Ray's points of oversight, education, and witness in/to the world.

An example of this kind of episcope arose a short time ago in Bradford, Yorkshire, when the local bishop bumped into a dedicated Christian care worker.

### WHEN TOBY MET HELEN

In 2017, a Baptist church charity, Hope Housing in Bradford, was responsible for a fifteen-bed accommodation unit for homeless, destitute migrants, but was fast running out of funding. A chance meeting with the local bishop, followed by him speaking to city council officials, led to a restoration of council funding, including back payments, which enabled the work to continue. Such a chain reaction of events illustrated how a bishop, with his feet firmly in the local community, can make a decisive difference, and can offer a clear, iconic Christian image, side by side with those deeply involved with the marginalized.

36. Pickard, *Theological Foundations*, 184.

37. Pickard, *Theological Foundations*, 184.

38. Pickard, *Theological Foundations*, 176.

However, the charity worker Helen, together with the voice of those sleeping rough, had stories to tell: of release from addiction, of changed lives, of Christ's transforming power today. The voices of "those who are not", became a starting point of Christian witness within a broken society. That Christian charity worker went on to be invited to pass on the message of those voices to European Union Representatives in Brussels. The dialogue that ensued led to changes in how Eastern European migrants are dealt with by local officials. That countercultural contribution did make a difference within the lives of struggling people. It was assisted by a bishop engaging with a church in touch with "those who are not".

A further contribution from David Heywood takes us back to the theme of servanthood. He reminds us of the centrality of Isaiah's prophecy in chapters 40–55, and the role of the suffering servant fulfilled by Jesus alongside his messianic calling. The combination of these two roles surely lies at the heart of the Christian story, with Jesus, during his final meal, washing the dusty feet of his disciples. Heywood points out that a servant is loved and chosen, is filled with the spirit of justice, and endures everything regardless of the cost.[39] Such an image of servanthood brings us back to the calling of ordination, of being committed to a witness for justice within society, regardless of the cost involved in such countercultural activity.

These illustrations of *servant episcopal leadership* activity, though resonating with our understanding of the faith, jar strongly with the reality on the ground. If present at all in the episcopal/ordained role, they would tend to remain in the background, taking second place to the demands of the CEO/superintendent sustaining the ecclesial structure. So, is it possible for the present church leadership to morph into a Christlike model within the present ecclesial order? Could today's top-down leadership authority give way to referent leadership modeled on the iconic nature of Christ, serving, inspiring, and drawing out the ministry of believers? Would the straitjacket of today's CEO-type order be prepared to dissolve itself, in order to enable a servantlike, curer of souls to emerge and minister to the whole body?

**PASTOR PETE**

Servantlike, episcopal leadership is modeled by Pete Cunningham, an Assemblies of God minister in Southport. Inspired by biblical authority and the presence of so many homeless in the town, he founded Green Pastures in 1999, a Christian charity dedicated to raising money to buy and provide houses for the homeless in the area. Today that organization has over 60 partner churches across the country; providing housing for more than 1,000 clients rising year on year.

39. Heywood, *Reimagining Ministry*, 177.

The administration is now done by others; Pete is, in effect, a pastor to the pastors so they in turn can be pastors to their clients. He is an example of an iconic episcope, with his feet firmly rooted amongst "those who are not". As has already been quoted, the motto he started off with was, "We can't change the world overnight, but we can change the overnight world." Pete has offered an example of servant episcope throughout his life. He has inspired so many others to follow that same iconic episcope in their own lives and through their own ministries to the benefit of those who are not.

Undoubtedly there are many other examples of servant episcope, even if they don't bear that title. The concept is not new—one only has to think of St. Francis. The question is, can the present structures recognize "point A/B" and commit themselves to a second sigmoid curve? Could this take place through evolution, or will it require the existing establishment to collapse before the rebuilding process can begin? The fact that very little appears to have changed since Pickard and Brewin raised such issues more than ten years ago might suggest evolution is still not on the agenda.

## 10.5 A NEW REFORMATION

The disjunction between the top-down, authoritarian management style of existing churches and the servantlike, vulnerable ministry of Jesus—combined with the effervescent global explosion of Pentecostal personal transformation—is clear for all to see. As part of the Reformation, Cranmer turned away from the papal tradition, calling for a ministry centered around the importance of personal faith/transformation and the "cure of souls." Maybe another reformation is required where the straightjacketed Western church learns from the vibrantly rejoicing worldwide church, where a new "post-Christendom ecclesiology which is missional in its identity"[40] could develop.

Present church leadership, aware of the tsunami of threats encompassing the shrinking Western church, have concentrated on some revamping of the existing management, and a reiteration of static, traditional, biblical norms. But maybe we are looking in the wrong direction. Surely the foundation of the church's ministry is baptism—an experience of repentance, forgiveness, and renewal. It goes back to the truth that baptism is ordination for ministry. Engaging with this disjunction between traditional ministerial authority and the ministry of the baptized requires us to not just to look at how the authorized, ministerial management should operate, but more

40. Shenk, "New Wineskins for New Wine," 73–79.

toward releasing the baptized to fulfill their primary calling. If this involves the ecclesial structure facing radical reformation, then so be it. Maybe O'Donovan's "outer identity"[41] of church structure has to be reformed by the "inner identity" of the ministry of Jesus, the referral of that ministry into the ministry of the baptized.

It just so happens that both contemporary societal developments and the New Testament evidence combine to hint at the nature of such a Reformation. Certainly, today's networking, bottom-up, innovative, cross-fertilizing society bears a striking resemblance to the dynamic of the early church/Pentecostal explosion. Our view of Jesus' vulnerable ministry, beginning with those who are not, together with the church's empowerment by the Holy Spirit, both endorse that view. If the church is to have a structure appropriate to the ongoing century, then surely it should relinquish the legitimizing prerogative power of hierarchical tradition in favor of a referent witness to the vulnerable Christ and the Pentecostal ministry of the baptized.

Such a reformative approach would be supported by what we are learning about emergence—that from basic levels of humanity, higher and more complex levels of expression and organization can arise. As humans we are excitedly becoming aware of this. But, of course, our Pentecostal God has known it all along. Maybe we are now becoming aware that he might have even more in store for us. The importance for the faith is that the church rediscovers this emergent principle and acknowledges that purpose should mold structures rather than the other way around. In offering to give up that which the church has held onto for so long, tomorrow's church is opening up the possibility of transformational new life. Point A/B needs to be grasped with faith and hope, with confidence and expectation. The safety, security, and dwelling of stage 3 needs to be forsaken for a mutual discovery of new, appropriate, seeking attitudes, as expressed in stage 5.

Grasping this opportunity to reform will expand into the subject of our next chapter. How can the church develop a more prophetic, counter-cultural role to the uncertain, pluralist, technology-driven melting pot that is the third decade?

41. O'Donovan, "What Kind of Community?," 186.

# Chapter 11

## Contextual/Countercultural Balance

There is no difficulty for anyone to imagine the balance hanging over the Royal Courts of Justice in London. The weight on one side is expected to balance the weight on the other. Down through the centuries, as we have seen, the Christian faith has sought to engage with, and relate to, its contemporary setting in both place and time. Because of the nature of its message—which is somewhat different to the views of every society in which it finds itself—the faith/church has followed a path somewhere between adapting its message to suit the contemporary audience, and speaking out prophetically with the core of its gospel. In effect the church has sought to balance its approach between being contextual and being countercultural. One of the issues raised in chapter 6 encourages us to take a deeper look at that balance as our church faces this third postmillennial decade.

Steven Bevans has made an excellent analysis of this balance and offered a range of approaches in the form of different models.[1]

---

**DIFFERENT APPROACHES**

These models range from the anthropological at the one end, to the countercultural at the other. Bevans maps the intervening approaches as being transcendental, praxis, synthetic, and translation. At one end the anthropological model emphasizes human experience, culture, social location, and social change. At the other end of the spectrum the countercultural model emphasizes Scripture, and tradition—the core of the message/movement itself. With the first approach the faith is adapted significantly so that it can be easily absorbed and assimilated into

---

1. Bevans, *Models of Contextual Theology*, 32.

the contemporary setting; with the last approach the faith highlights its unique-ness/radical challenge to the setting in question. The first approach emphasizes the present context, whereas the last is conscious of the story so far and has its sights set clearly on a future endpoint.

The anthropological approach is clearly seen in postmodernism. Today we live in a relativistic world where you can decide whether a foul in football has occurred, depending on which TV camera view you prefer: it all de-pends on where you are standing as to what constitutes the truth. Taylor quotes Joseph Fletcher on situation ethics—a good illustration of this ap-proach—who describes it as "an ethic of decision—of making decisions, rather than looking them up in a manual of prefabricated rules . . . It does not ask *what* is good, but *how* to do good to *whom*; not what *is* love, but how to *do* the most loving thing possible in the situation."[2] This first approach starts with the context and then asks what the most appropriate presenta-tion might be of the point or truth in question. It starts with where people are, beginning with the surrounding culture, and then it seeks to define the message in terms relevant to that setting.

At the other end of the spectrum, the countercultural approach starts with the unique and unchangeable nature of the gospel. It recognizes that "all human beings and all theological expressions only exist in historical and culturally conditioned settings" warning that "context always needs to be treated with a good deal of suspicion."[3] It goes on to stress that "if it is truly revelation it will involve contradiction, and call for conversion, for radical 'metanoia,' a U-turn of the mind."[4]

In extreme forms this approach leads to world-denying positions—that there is nothing good to be found in human culture. Churches such as the Strict Brethren and Strict Baptists have followed that line. However, others have taken a less extreme position—rejecting the demonization of culture, anticultural attitudes, and the dangers of sectarianism. Instead they have emphasized not only their rootedness in Scripture but also the impor-tance of "being relevant to the context, while at the same time remaining faithful to the gospel."[5] They stress the constructive, positive, challenging, and transformational power of the gospel, and view the context as being a fallen/malevolent society.

2. Taylor, *Go-between God*, 164 (italics mine); Fletcher, *Situation Ethics*, 52.

3. Bevans, *Models of Contextual Theology*, 117.

4. Newbigin, *Foolishness to the Greeks*, 5–6.

5. Bevans, *Models of Contextual Theology*, 124.

Bevans insists that there is no one model that is preferred above others, and that "every person involved in doing theology needs to be aware of the range of methodological options available."[6] He goes on to point out that it is

> not contradictory to hold a high value of both gospel and culture, nor is it wrong to take one's theological agenda from various sources: society at large; the current world scene as expressed in both economic and political realms; the biblical data; or the guidance of the Holy Spirit.[7]

However, he does accept that certain models are more appropriate than others in particular circumstances. He goes on, in relation to the countercultural model, to say that, "I believe strongly that in the situation such as that in contemporary Europe, Australia, New Zealand and North America, only a theology that engages the secular context critically, can be one that faithfully presents and lives out the Gospel."[8]

The preceding chapters of this book have sought to do just this—to have a high view of both culture and gospel—and to engage the two in a constructive and critical conversation with each other. This ensuing chapter seeks to indicate how a more countercultural approach could well be appropriate, together with the contextual adaptations that undoubtedly need to be made. It will seek to establish that the millennium itself has ushered in significant technological developments and a range of fresh questions/choices that have no straightforward answers; that an emergent church, with a prophetic voice arising from the baptized at the periphery, could provide constructive engagement with the diverse, networked, ever-changing society within which it exists; that present church structure/authority/leadership will need to be seriously reimagined if such a prophetic stance is to be effective; that the postmillennial/Generation Z, surrounded by postmodern presuppositions and values, will place that milieu within the context of the Bible and the Jesus/Pentecost Church narrative, which distinctively articulates eternal truths—truths which are relevant to every generation, culture, and place.

---

6. Bevans, *Models of Contextual Theology*, 139.

7. Bevans, *Models of Contextual Theology*, 139; Priest, *Doing Theology with the Maasai*, 160.

8. Bevans, *Models of Contextual Theology*, 140.

## 11.1 SIGNIFICANCE OF THE MILLENNIUM

Paradigm shifts within society provide a window of opportunity. Disruption, upheaval, and change produce instability that can be unhelpful while also opening up fresh avenues. Facing change involves risk but can also herald opportunity. We have already established the church is in urgent need of recontextualizing itself if it is to contribute to this present society effectively. At the same time, we are also aware that society itself is uncertain and unstable as it inhales and absorbs all that technological development has and will bring. Society is struggling to choose and implement constructive growth, whist at the same time avoid malevolent outcomes. Indeed, because of these questions/choices that are now arriving in a continuous stream, society itself is having to revisit primary questions such as: What is benevolent? What is malevolent? What is real and what is human? Is our primary context national or global? What is the glue that holds communities together, enabling them to make and implement mutual decisions?

Western society has been used to debating in a pre-/post-Enlightenment context. Only a few years ago, that context changed with the advent of postmodernism. Now even that is under threat from technocratic, machine-centered algorithms, and data controlled by giant organizations and super accountancy firms. National governments have never been so emasculated and marginalized in such a way.

It is within this postmillennial context that the Christian faith and the church have to see and grasp their opportunity to resubmit their proposals. The questions and choices are in no way straightforward, but the postmillennial period of uncertainty provides a window of opportunity for the faith/church to reengage with society with a fresh, post-Christendom, Generation Z initiative not seen since New Testament times. As this chapter moves on into the next, we will identify some of these questions and opportunities.

Before looking at such a countercultural stance toward society, we need to remind ourselves of the uncertainty already existing in today's churches before suggesting confident forward movement together.

## 11.2 EXISTING ISSUES WITHIN THE CHURCH

The top-heavy institutional structures of the church are already struggling with waves flowing from an innovative, networking, information-age context. As well as being engulfed in a tsunami of running costs, building upkeep, minister shortages, demographic/falling membership, and withdrawal from large areas of the country, it is also engulfed in a tide of complex, moral, ethical and gender issues that can't easily be resolved. As well as all of this there is a crisis of order and control. Up until now a semblance of unity and balance has been maintained and a broad church has tenuously held the faith together—just. Now diverse opinions have gained confidence, declared unilateral independence, and rocked the up until now unity of the body.

As previously mentioned, Rowan Williams put forward the concept of a mixed economy with regard to worship styles: two structures-one organization; inherited church and fresh expressions. To a degree this hybrid option has worked within established denominations, keeping diverse expectations fulfilled. But doubt remains as to whether this is a long-term solution, as it doesn't go to the heart of societal change/gospel relevance. It doesn't take seriously enough the bottom-up movement of innovation and diversity. It doesn't acknowledge the need for future generations to discover for themselves a faith relevant to their world.

With regard to these established denominations, they are creaking at the seams. They are just managing by KTLO, but in doing so they are concentrating on survival rather than growth. Such a step in and of itself foretells collapse. In the days of paradigm shift, it will only take one needle in the haystack for the whole pack of cards to fall. There is no way of knowing where/when such a tiny insignificant event will occur. But with the whole edifice shaking for a number of reasons, it could well have a devastating effect.

The area of more inward-looking ethical, moral, and gender issues is one that has already caused considerable shaking and disintegration. Feminism, the ordination of women, headship and leadership, have already destabilized most churches in one way or another. Sexual behavior issues began in the arenas of abortion and practicing homosexuality, but have quickly spread to gay marriage and transgender issues. Again, the divide has arisen between those deeply embedded in contemporary liberal experience, and those who see, in the biblical canon, clear objections to certain contemporary attitudes. Other wider issues, such as euthanasia, genetic modification of crops and genetic engineering in human life, again threaten the unity of the church and may well lead to greater fracturing.

It has already been noted how the Enlightenment had a far greater influence on the faith than the church was prepared to recognize and admit at the time. Postmodernism similarly has insidiously woven its way into the church's life, without being fully recognized: consumerism is rife, particularly in larger churches; believers search around, like shopping, for the church with the best bargains, with little concern for their local communities; churches themselves design their programs in order to attract a certain cultural market; the Anglican parochial system is in tatters because transport enables people to follow consumer desires; postmodern concentration on the here and now, the existential experience, the present need, is high on the agenda, relegating the not yet of the kingdom to the shadows.

The significance of the past, so well articulated by Walter Brueggemann, is relegated to lower levels of interest by the now generation, who place far less weight on what their parents did, let alone what happened in previous centuries. Emphasis on the New Testament message, rather than on the acts of God throughout history—articulated so well in the Old Testament—can again be noticed in sermon topics and Bible study passages.

The relative nature of truth, typified by TV cameras recording a football match, has significantly changed our concept and understanding of truth. Aabsolute truth has long been left behind by many believers, as postmodern attitudes accept that nothing can ever be absolute, no worldview can ever be appropriate. Life is centered more around a best guess approach to truth. Choices on "What is truth?" follow the same spectrum from total relativity to total absolutism. There can be no doubt that postmodernism has led to many churches/individuals having far less confidence in the eternal compared to the general acceptance of the relative.

So, if the church of the third decade is to begin looking outward, to engage with the issues arising from postmillennial society, it has to acknowledge that it will do so from a base that is already unstable, uncertain, and fractured.

## 11.3 A COUNTERCULTURAL APPROACH

So how and where would the Christian faith and church stand if it were to commit itself to a more outward-looking prophetic role through engagement with the excitement/trauma of twenty-first-century living, with all the risks that such a stance would involve? Maybe this approach can be summed up by that famous phrase from Jesus' last conversation with his disciples. He exhorted them to be "in the world" but not "of the world."[9] They were, and we are, to engage with society, encountering that society on its own terms, yet at the same time, doing so through expressing the core elements of the faith, committing to understand where society is at, and yet, at the same time, bringing the critical sharpness of the Christian faith to bear; to risk

9. John 13–16.

being engulfed and swamped by the persuasive/pervasive waves of societal norms and targets, and yet having complete confidence and knowing trust, in the unique inspiration/power of the presence of Jesus Christ, in both individual and community witness.

The heart of such an approach lies in acknowledging the very different presuppositions that lie behind the Christian position on the one hand, and the humanist, posthumanist, postmodern, secularized position on the other. Whereas one centers around the significant Other, a transcendent eternal creator God, the second sees life emanating from providence, chance, a bootstrapping capability. Whereas one articulates a difference between good and evil, the second struggles with such sharp judgmental articulation. Whereas one is intrinsically relational, giving real significance to emotions, feelings such as love and sacrifice and giving, the other is directed by a mechanistic, materialistic, problem-solving and marketplace-transactional mindset. Whereas one centers around vulnerability and identification with the marginalized and the nonachiever, the other centers around a success-oriented, achievement-rewarding society. Whereas one relies on a sense of the past and a vision of the future to live out the present, the other is absorbed simply with present human capability and its potential to improve and keep control of the future.

Having acknowledged such differing starting points, it is perfectly possible for a countercultural approach to affirm so much contemporary culture whilst at the same time reserving the right to express the unique difference of its message and the transforming capability of its followers. This goes back to Taylor's point about the *bisociation* of the prophets. The Christian faith is called to live in and celebrate what is, the here and now, yet at the same time that same faith is able to highlight what could be. Following Amos, Hosea, Jeremiah, and Jesus, the Christian church is called to envision a reign that is very different from the anthropocentric and datacentric horizons of technological development. Instead of seeking to hold on to its Christendom heritage, as a respected part of the affluent status quo, it could alternatively grasp the prophetic nuisance role of challenging complacency surrounding the increase of inequality. Such a position does not emphasize "tremendous faith in the self-sufficiency and moral autonomy of the human individual,"[10] but rather it returns to Jesus' identification with those marginalized by Jewish religious authorities and the Roman Empire. It is not centered around human and computer potentiality, but rather draws from the witness of the Old Testament prophets, the sermon on the mount, and

---

10. Young, *Face to Face*, 218.

Christ's transforming free gift of love, all emanating from a creator to whom every person can relate to as Daddy.

As a consequence of these differing presuppositions and perspectives, urgent, emerging, complex issues, arising from within society, may well spark radically different responses. It is here where the Christian faith has a real contribution to make to the continuing evolution of humanity. It is offering Jesus Christ as the "clue to all of human and indeed cosmic history, and it is against this fact that all human experience or context is to be measured."[11] At the heart of it, this is surely the cornerstone of Christian belief with which to address our posthumanist, technocentric society.

## 11.4 DRIVING FORCE

This reality of Jesus is now to be reflected in the continuing life of the church, the faithful congregation. The witness of Christ's transforming power is to be illustrated in these local expressions of faith, belief, and action. Within this countercultural approach, the local Christian community is the inheritor of the ministry of Jesus, and the focus of the reign of God. So the fulcrum of Christian expression is not so much to be found in the role of the elite, trained, ordained professionals, inculcated into the perpetuation of a "hermeneutic of order."[12] Rather it will emanate from the ministry of the baptized, enveloped in a "hermeneutic of obedience,"[13] inspired by a "hermeneutic of justice,"[14] and empowered by the Holy Spirit's presence. As that body of believers rediscovers the human ministry of Jesus and lives it out in the context of a local community—strengthened through the spirit's continuous guidance—an alternative referent power is offered, born out of real human encounter. It is faith being incarnated again in the ever-changing context by the body of believers themselves. Such an expression of faith, as the basis of "church," is seen as a "contrast community," a community of "resident aliens" in the spirit of 1 Peter, living lives that reflect another city, "where the gospel is lived out fully, over against the surrounding context of materialism, individualism, consumerism, militarism, and quick gratification."[15]

11. Bevans, *Models of Contextual Theology*, 121.

12. Murray, *Biblical Interpretation*, 231.

13. Murray, *Biblical Interpretation*, 186–205.

14. Murray, Biblical Interpretation, 231

15. Bevans, *Models of Contextual Theology*, 122.

## MISSIONAL COMMUNITIES

Missional communities, initiated by Mike Breen at St Thomas's Crookes, Sheffield, have been developing over the last twenty-five years, and are now spread worldwide. Usually emerging out of a parent church body, they consist of small groups of people—such as in Westwood, Coventry and Budbrook/Chase Meadow, Warwick—most often lay-led, committed to reach and serve a particular local community/area as a flexible, locally incarnated expression of church. They exist as a "close knit spiritual family on mission together, small enough to care and large enough to dare."[16] They are normally lightweight and low maintenance in structure and style; maintaining links with their parent body on a low control-high accountability basis, enabling them to put high value on their relational life together.

This movement is based on the principle that every culture and subculture finds community in groups/extended families. Missional communities are tapping into the basic human feature that, where family and community values break down, humanity is hardwired to recreate alternative extended families—of race, faith, ethnicity, and even cultural or class similarities. They center around three principles that Jesus himself fulfilled in his own lifetime: time with God in worship, prayer, and teaching; time with the body of believers, building a vibrant and caring community; and time with those who don't yet know Jesus, similar to Michael Moynagh's model of four relationships, mentioned later.

This movement, centered around the heart of Jesus' message, is based on a lightweight, low-maintenance networking structure, existing on the periphery of church, and held together by a high sense of accountability. Through innovative leadership it has spread and grown out of many established church situations and engaged with local communities untouched by traditional worship centers, including the homeless and former addicts. They see lay-leadership being pivotal in the mission of God as he seeks to redeem contemporary society. Again, this sodal, emergent life form has arisen out of the traditional modal norm. It expresses expansion and growth by engaging with the needs of so many in urban areas; seeking to find a way forward in an exciting, yet uncertain time frame. By building up and reproducing itself continuously, this movement is expanding out of a stable base and toward a more flexible, fluid heartbeat centered around purpose rather than historical structure. Where that ultimately leaves the parent sending body, from where stability has been drawn, remains a question still to be answered.

The power source of such a movement becomes the whole of the baptized, living out their faith in their local community, place of work, school, and engagement with the big issues facing society. It is a faith not left to the expert to

16. Breen and Hoskins, *Clusters*, 36.

articulate in safe, protected surroundings, but a faith emerging, bottom up, from everyday marketplace ministry with people. Kosuke Koyama entitled his book *Water Buffalo Theology*—a theology that arose from below—where developing a theology of the Christian community was determined not by the theolocracy, but "by the everyday realities that Thai farmers experience: water buffalo, peppers, bananas, cockfighting, sticky rice. I begin speaking from where they are—i.e., cockfighting. From talking about the human condition I go on to call God into the real human situation."[17] Although written about a very different context than the one we face today, there is no difficulty acknowledging the principle and transposing the sport of cockfighting to many of the events and encounters we experience in work, pleasure, and consumer living today. The principle of lay vocation—as compared to lay ministry—is surely at the heart of this witness as the contrast community juxtaposes the biblical text with the societal framework, seeking to enable that faith to come alive within the issues and questions of contemporary living. Koyama describes it as rerooting the biblical text, "guarding, watering and nurturing it as it roots itself in the native soil."[18]

Koyama's approach, illustrated by missional communities—and other examples mentioned—has been articulated by Fowler in his description of a conjunctive—stage 5—church witness, engaging with our postmodern postmillennial society. "Postmodernism needs convictional images that mediate hope and courage. We need communities that mold justice, and engage in liberating praxis and understand it as part of the praxis of God."[19]

## 11.5 RELATIONSHIPS—THE IDENTITY OF THE CHURCH

If the church is to be the church in this kind of way, it is important to acknowledge the true nature of the church. To begin with it is essential to see the countercultural church community not as a physical body identified by its order, substance, physical presence, or practices, but rather in terms of its relationships, how it coalesces around the reality of Jesus, how it reflects and mirrors that encounter, in obedience to it. It is in and through the relationships that revolve around the centerpoint that makes a church community become the church. Following the writings of Rowan Williams, Moynagh has helpfully articulated a way of seeing this core nature of the church. He takes it from the reality of Jesus in life—*upwards, inwards, outwards,*

17. Koyama, *Water Buffalo Theology*, viii.

18. Koyama, *Theology in Contact*, 67–68.

19. Fowler, *Faithful Change*, 220.

and *around*.[20] The church community is inspired through an *upward* relationship, "participating in the life of the Trinity." It is perpetuated with *inward* relationships "through fellowship within the gathering." It is turned *outwardly* through relationships "in love for and service to the world." It is undergirded through relationships "as part of the whole body, *through connections* with the wider Church."[21]

To be an effective countercultural force, a contrast community that encounters, engages, and is prophetic to the context within which it exists, the church community needs to fully acknowledge that it is these relationships that make it what it is.

The church can no longer be defined by its physical image, its wealth accounts, its status, or its professional workforce. It can only be truly defined by its obedience to Christ, by the referent power he instills, by the relationships that hold it together. It can only be defined by its iconic reflection of Jesus, who points them upwards to God in his fullness. It can only be identified by the love each member has for the other brothers and sisters in Christ. It can only be engaged with through the love and service that it offers to the surrounding community. It can grow increasingly in stature through the affirmation and support of the wider, global body of believers.

Further, the nature of such a church community, existing in and through these relationships, is not a static one. It cannot stand still. It can either regress—by fracturing into frigidity, set patterns, rules, structures, and security—or it can move riskily forward into maturity, into "attaining to the whole measure of the fullness of Christ."[22] It can only do this as a whole, with every member participating, and without the imbalance of a dualistic approach to ministry. It can only do this when all these four sets of relationships interlock and grow together "with God, with the wider Church, the world, and within the fellowship."[23] As that growth and maturity improves, the mission of God can become an increasing influence in the life of humanity.

## 11.6 HOLISTIC MINISTRY

The dynamic of relationships within such Christian communities is absolutely crucial. The nature of an emergent Christian community is one that gains its identity from the bottom up, from the ministry of the baptized,

20. Moynagh, *Church for Every Context*, 106–12.

21. Moynagh, *Church for Every Context*, 107.

22. Eph 4:13.

23. Moynagh, *Church for Every Context*, 115.

from the primary presence of the spirit of Christ, with any ordained role being subservient to that principle. If such a dynamic can be established and maintained, then a holistic view of ministry could be achieved from whence the whole of society could benefit.

Hierarchical church structure reflects a traditional ethos of order. However, a relational, emergent community church will require a radical rethink of the role of the ordained.

If the fulcrum of the church springs from the ministry of the baptized, an iconic, servant-episcopal role—following Tom Ray's three points—could enhance the overall ministry of the witnessing community. Such an iconic servant-episcopal role could continuously redirect members to the centrality of Jesus, curate and platform resources to assist the ministry of the baptized, draw to the attention of the membership its place in the wider global body of believers, and, finally, constantly remind the believing community of their countercultural role within the local community to whom Christ came. Such a balance between the ministry of the baptized and the iconic servant-episcopal ministry of the ordained could well reflect a very different image of the church to the third decade.

# Chapter 12

## A Context to Critique

### 12.1 CRITICAL ISSUES

The most exciting element to the world in which we live is that you never know what is going to happen next. It is like porridge bubbling on a stove, or a mud pool in Rotorua, New Zealand, or in Iceland. There are continuous mini explosions of gas and air, escaping from the surface of the boiling liquid. Our innovative society is just like that. Looking at it with a glass half-full attitude, it is primarily exciting. Looking at it with a glass half-empty attitude, it is fundamentally bewildering. There are so many new things, questions, and experiences arising it is not easy to know where to turn to next, or to find peace of mind. It is an inherently unstable situation, constantly being disturbed by disequilibrium as disruption is celebrated as a creative art form.

It is in this third-decade melting pot of mini explosions and old craters that those committed to a mission-of-God countercultural role walk hesitatingly along an unmapped journey, to an edge they can't see but still know to be there. The bubbling surface of the liquid, from whence the gas and air escape, is the context of their lives. What is escaping is not only innovative creations, but also fresh questions, consequent issues, and value judgments. These put strain on practical decision-making and our pluralist ethical and moral framework. Often they force us to question our primary presuppositions, asking whether they still ring true in such a technocratic, ever-changing context. In particular they open up the barriers and boundaries—like the continual repositioning of tectonic plates, irritating each other at the edges—between the three worldviews mentioned earlier: the posthumanist, substance, market and achievement-oriented, mechanistic approach; the creator-inspired, relational Christian stance; and the mystical, holistic approach of Eastern wisdom. Each set of presuppositions is faced with the same primary question that urgently requires an answer: "How do we discern the difference between benevolence and malevolence in society?" It is quickly followed by an even more difficult supplementary: "If we could agree on a global answer, how could we implement it in reality?"

These questions and issues should therefore be the bread and butter of today's contextual, conjunctive, and countercultural church. They become the building blocks of an emergent church, fully engaged with the postmillennial Generation Z. They arise from the reality of life and need to be addressed by the membership of faith within their own local context. This needs to be a bottom-up process that replaces the top-down, cerebral answers of experts—the theolocracy. What then are these questions and issues, and how can the upward pull of unrealized potential be released from the ministry of the baptized to respond to them? And if such a direction was accepted how would the existing ordained ministry fit into the equation? If the groundwork of debate took place on the shop floor, could the representational ministry be reimagined into an iconic, resourcing, curating role, undergirding and sustaining the countercultural body as it platforms a way of life to an uncertain society? If this could happen then the ministry of the baptized, assisted by the representative ministry, could mutually work towards, and achieve, a genuine expansion of the mission of God well into the third decade.

There follows an illustrative list of contemporary questions and issues. Here is not the place to offer definite answers or a definitive list, but simply to highlight the complexity, magnitude, and significance of key unanswered uncertainties facing society today.

## 12.2 GOOD AND EVIL

As human potential is continuously proving to be exponential in growth, as technocratic development leads us to unimaginable futures, the question surrounding each innovation is whether its implementation and long-term effect will be benevolent or malevolent to humanity. Can we be confident of "an unrealistic optimism about the future . . . optimistic utopianism centered around the real though temporal successes of science, medicine and technology"; or whether we are alternatively weighted down by "a massive discontent and despair about society, about violence, about economic forces . . . something inevitable about the passing on of social inadequacy and communal conflict from one generation to another."[1]

And even if we were able to agree on what constitutes benevolent as compared to malevolent development, how do we achieve mutual global determination to implement that agreement in a world that plays down the universal and espouses relative values relating to differing contexts? As has been said, one man's elixir is another man's poison. One part of society might view a particular group as kitchen-sink biotech terrorists, whereas others might describe them as martyrs to the cause.

So can we ever all get to the point of the phrase attributed to Ghandi, that "noncooperation with evil is a moral duty?" Will it ever be possible to define good and evil clearly? Can a reasonable consensus ever be achieved concerning humanity's intrinsic impulse for good? At the moment, a general consensus might be identified over the issues of pedophilia and to an extent, terrorism. But consensus doesn't go much further than that. As innovative potential expands, the significance of the central dilemma is enhanced, with mutual answers more urgently desired.

In the past a Christian view of right and wrong has strongly influenced Western society and established certain norms. Now, in today's pluralist and global society, Enlightenment influence, the rise of Islam, and the emergence of an Eastern/Oceanic worldview have all contributed to a more complex and unresolved debate as to where to draw the line. Now, a countercultural church is being called to rearticulate the standards and the values of the mission of God, including where to draw the line between good and evil. The New Testament talks of principalities and powers, and the church has traditionally seen itself opposing those values and practices. But today the line between benevolence and malevolence is increasingly difficult to draw, or even to predict.

Already we have referred to Bill Joy, Satya Nadella—the CEO of Microsoft—and the House of Lords report, all urging the need for ethical guidelines within AI research, and the threat of biotech viruses—highlighted by the Covid 19 pandemic of 2020. For years now medical ethics has been in the forefront of debate on stem cell research, genetic engineering, and embryo research. Genetically modified crops are welcomed by some and resisted by others. Genetic human enhancement opens up a huge, fresh, far-reaching debate.

Recently the boundaries of this debate have been broken in Shenzhen, China, by He Jiankui's groundbreaking gene-snipping at the single cell stage

---

1. Young, *Face to Face*, 213–14.

of an embryo, which he allowed to develop through to the birth of twins. This first birth, following embryonic experimentation, gave vent to overwhelming international condemnation, for a whole range of scientific and medical reasons. Nevertheless, many see it as opening the gates to other maverick and profit-minded research and experimentation—others would suggest that the race between China and the West, in all forms of technological development, is most probably fueling such research and other possibly unreported developments. As Fowler has put it, "Our ethical sense cannot keep pace with their range of applications."[2]

On the social media front, policing the disinformation ecosystem of Pinterest or Facebook's platform is said to be addressed by the management, but the algorithms behind the whole posting process remains in situ; it is ultimately governed by economic and commercial demands. Contextual approaches to contentious issues in this relativistic society can easily veer toward situational ethics. Countercultural Christian ethics are not so easy to defend in a pluralistic world, where there are so many differing ethical starting points. Nevertheless, it is a crucial area in which the countercultural church should invest, and in which the mission of God has a prophetic bisolational role.

## 12.3 INEQUALITY

The Old Testament is full of illustrations, particularly with the prophets, where God opposes extremes of poverty and wealth. It is accepted that the poor will always be with us. Yet at the same time, the jubilee principle,[3] as we have seen, was set out to stop extreme poverty becoming endemic in Israel's society, even if there is doubt that it was ever implemented. Similarly, Jesus' identification with those who are not, the marginalized, and the outcast, and his condemnation of those in possession of unquestionable power and authority, all go to endorse a Christian rejection of extreme inequality: a hermeneutic of justice.

However, if one issue appears to overwhelm all else in this postmillennial period, it is that of rising inequality. Sir Martin Rees, Astronomer Royal and former President of the Royal Society, reflects vehemently on our present responses to this inequality: "failure to respond to this humanitarian imperative, which nations have power to remedy, surely casts doubt on any claims to institutional moral progress."[4] We have seen that Western society's

2. Fowler, *Faithful Change*, 198.

3. Lev 25:8–17.

4. Appleyard, "Keep Gazing at the Stars," 25.

technological development, empowered by algorithms, data-harvesting and surveillance capitalism, together with the potential, exponential benefits of a quantum computing/AI tie-up, have and will continue to give rise to the irresistible dominance of Western/Chinese giant conglomerates. Capitalism appears to be degenerating into a success-/achievement-oriented, winner-takes-all dynamic whereby those in control of investment, innovation, and production/consumer market transactions, give rise to elite wealth. At the same time, with technological development, algorithmic research, data harvesting, and robotic intelligence expanding into increasing areas of application, the superfluous and peripheral position of ordinary working people results in growing unemployment, and hence poverty and purpose-less living. As it stands at the moment, Western society is building up a recipe for extremes of poverty and wealth, with what many are calling a "superhuman" species being counterbalanced by those who will be forever excluded from the club. As Fei Fei Li, renowned computer scientist and Founder of Stamford University's Human-Centered AI Institute, has put it "If we don't harness AI responsibly and share gains equitably, it will lead to greater concentrations of wealth and power for the elite few, who usher in the new age—and poverty, powerlessness and a lost sense of purpose for the global majority." [5]

The countercultural church, therefore, has a clear task on its hands to challenge that trend unequivocally with its hermeneutic of justice. The inex-orable rise of inequality threatens the very concept of humanity being held together in peace as the embodiment of life. If the church could withdraw its close association with the wielders of power, it could grow into a more effective role of being alongside the powerless, of standing alongside non-achievers, accepting vulnerability as a primary attitude of the Christian faith itself. What the faith says on this issue can be articulated not by academic theologians in ivory towers but by ordinary people, themselves gripped by the experience of poverty. Bottom-up theologizing—Moltmann's "where the Church is"—is the only effective way to radically face up to extremes of poverty and wealth.

The real weapon in the hands of the countercultural church is the mes-sage of the mission of God. It is built not on the supposed equilibrium of market transactions of substance, but rather on the complete disequilibrium created by the offering of a free gift of love, inaugurated by Christ himself. The referent power of the church arises out of its reflection and perpetuation of Christ's free gift towards those who feel they have nothing to give. That offer of a free gift is what provides hope and determination to all who want

5  Danny Fortson. Beijing call Shots in AI. Sunday Times Business. 01/03/2020. p 7.

to claim their right to be fully human, by challenging the inequality that is overwhelming future human dreams.

## 12.4 WHAT IS HUMAN, WHAT IS REAL?

This leads us on to the *Blade Runner* question. Much of this question has already been raised through references to complex computer gaming, internet relationships, video friendships, social media posts, platforming of airbrushed photos of personalities, Instagram/Pinterest memes of people juxtaposed in front of completely different backgrounds, computers becoming more intelligent than humans, and digital harvesting guiding companies as far as what to produce to satisfy consumer needs without the consumer realizing the manipulation.

The stakes are raised even higher when the possibility of genetic engineering, gene reordering enhancement, and computer/brain linkups, appear on the horizon. How would the essential nature of humanity be affected if the financial elite could extend longevity, increase memory/intelligence, and improve disease resistance, thereby creating, in effect, a superhuman category? How would we respond to the concept of developing life beyond human DNA by means of mechanical and electronic processes such as prosthetic limbs and mind-controlled keyboards? At present such ideas may be beyond the horizon, but governments will very soon have to debate the issues/ethics in principle, thereby shutting or opening the gates to further research and development.

On the one hand, if you are immersed in a framework of a material, mechanistic, technological, problem-solving culture, your response to new understandings of humanity might be quite positive. It would be exciting to think that computers might soon be able to think and feel like our ordinary human selves. It might be stimulating to imagine how molecules from one substance are able to be manipulated and make a completely different substance through nanotechnology. It might be challenging if humans were cloned or genetically engineered into becoming a superhuman being. It might be enticing to think that life expectancy could be increased ad infinitum by those who were prepared to risk the treatment, those who could afford to pay for it and for those who freeze their corpses in anticipation of new medical breakthroughs.

On the other hand, if you were a participant in the mission of God, based on the reality of a creator Other acting within his creation, affirming humankind in his image, discernable in past action, experienced in the present, and believable for the future—then one might arrive at a very different view on humanity and reality. In no way should such an approach deny the capability and potentiality of human innovation. But it would reserve the right to define human features as reflecting the nature of a creator God rather than being determined by an amoral, problem-solving, mechanistic/ algorithmic mentality.

## 12.5 FACE TO FACE

Maybe this difference in the understanding of humanity is best expressed in the area of relationships. Today's image of society is typified in the mobile phone. Phones have become computers that are a symbiotic extension of our hands. As we all know, in a bus or tube, no one talks to those around them anymore. Everyone is glued to their phones. The big giants spend their investments enabling the phone/watch to take over more and more of our lives, in the same way that online shopping has taken over from the High Street.

We have become an online generation that deals through the internet, emails, and algorithms, in what has become a virtual world. The experience of face-to-face encounter, a direct person-to-person relationship, is fast becoming a minority experience.

In contrast the Christian faith is one centered around personal relationships. It emanates from God, whom we are encouraged to call *Abba*, "Daddy." This unbelievable situation is where the creator of our cosmic experience and beyond wishes to have a personal relationship with each one of us. Following on from that, his son dedicated his personal being to our lives, engaging face to face with those around him. He left, after Pentecost, a community with a sense of daughter and sonship, and one that encouraged brotherly and sisterly relationships. The central act of worship was for all, regardless of position or status, seated together around a table, sharing a meal, drinking with a communal cup. In a world of CJD, AIDS, Covid 19 and so many other infectious diseases, you can't get more personal than that.

The Christian faith therefore has a great deal to offer to a world that is increasingly becoming virtual, mechanistic, and computer oriented. The more the world moves in that direction, the more the faith becomes countercultural. One of the flip sides of a technocentric society is that it has highlighted achievement-oriented problem solving to a pinnacle, thereby relegating emotions, feelings, caring, and love to the sidelines. These experiences and feelings are not quantifiable or calculable. One thing that a robot will never really be able to do is be an effective carer at an old people's care home—although in Japan certain programmable tasks are already being undertaken by robots. The medical profession is undoubtedly, scientifically, and methodically trained, and assisted by huge amounts of computer research into the causes of illness. But it could never function without care, love, and dedication towards other people's lives—beautifully encapsulated by the warm words of appreciation uttered by so many patients, including the Prime Minister, leaving hospital after recovery from Covid 19. It is that kind of positive contribution that the Christian faith can make as it stands alongside the nonachiever, shares the soul of the marginalized, and engages with situations that can benefit from a palliative approach.

Streeck and the writers of *Econocracy* both make reference to the centrality of the Treasury Economic Model for the calculation of the British economy. They point out that the Treasury model is deeply flawed in one aspect, which, they infer, was partially responsible for the 2008 economic crash. The model has an entirely mechanistic, transactional, materialistic method. It takes no account of the fact that economics is embedded in the lives of people, and that people are not just automated robots. People have feelings, intuitions, preferences, and a unique biological makeup. In essence, people are not predictable, leading to reactions that can't be quantified by calculations/algorithms or processed by computers—a fact which is further endorsed by Harari's point about intelligence and consciousness. Because of the wholeness of the human being, the Treasury model—and so much of our technocratic, consumer-oriented world—offers inadequate conclusions. What they depend on/center around, does not reflect the width of either humanity or truth. Personal, face-to-face relationships and trust add a wider perspective on humanity; that is central to humanity and truth itself.

This deep-seated point was summed up to me in a kind of satirical way by one sentence in a novel. The story describes a particular person who was reflecting on another person who was in love. The central person reflects, "this type of relationship is the unmistakable sign of the psychiatric disorder commonly called love."[6] The gift of love is unquantifiable, unpredictable, and often transforming, but in all its forms, it is hugely influential in person-to-person relationships. Once again, the faith and its belief in Christ's gift of love offers great countercultural perspectives in the growing gap between the automated, virtual world, and the face-to-face world.

Nowhere can this be better illustrated that in the sexual learning experience of teenagers. As has been pointed out, many young people find out about sexual relationships and sexual intercourse through watching it on pornographic videos. They build up a virtual understanding of sex before they actually experience it for themselves with another person. In doing so in this way they are ill equipped to handle real emotional, sexual relations

6. Goddard, *Closed Circle*, 28.

with other teenager, in a real-life situation. What they saw being simulated and depicted on a computer or phone screen bears little resemblance to the emotional and relational nature of face-to-face relationships. Life turns out to be very much more than a screenshot. In all their uncertainty and inadequacy, such young people need the support of those with interpersonal understanding and skills. In this whole area of personal relationships, as compared to screen world dynamics, the Christian faith has a great deal to contribute. The more Western society norms follow a mechanistic, algorithmic, transactional model, the more the Christian relational alternative will prove relevant. It is not an either/or situation, but more a both/and one. As well as affirming the innovation and celebration of technocratic development, it would be wise to pay attention to face-to-face encounter, which is neither predictable nor quantifiable, but can often be most enjoyable.

## 12.6 GLOBALISM—MUTUAL GLOBAL DECISION-MAKING

It is quite clear that postmillennial Western society faces an increasing transition from a national to a global scenario. Although nationalism, populism, and localism are still significant factors, sprouting up strongly from time to time, globalization is increasingly becoming the overarching context. With the corporate giants dominating innovation, production, and the marketplace, national governments and their legislation are increasingly being overwhelmed. On the other hand, questions and issues, such as ethical guidelines for AI research, arise that cannot be reduced to national responses, and require globalist consensus. Stuart Russell, in an interview with Danny Fortson, calls for a fundamental overhaul of how we, as a corpus of nearly eight billion people, organize, value, and educate ourselves, describing our predicament as "we're sort of in a bus and the bus is going fast, and no one has any plans to stop. Where's the bus going? Off the cliff."[7]

David Goodhart's analysis of our nation being divided into somewheres and anywhere, and the "orthodox/progressive" divide, have indicated that finding mutual agreement and consensus decisions is often extremely difficult: the gap between developed and under-developed countries is similarly diverse, as needs and expectations/dreams can be spectacularly different. Yet there is not even a comprehensive forum where these matters can be discussed, let alone decided upon. The Paris Accord on Climate Change pointed in that direction, and even that achieved far less than what was required and was broken soon after by one of the lead players. Even when

7. Russell, in Fortson, "End of Humanity," 21.

the Covid 19 Pandemic dramatically highlighted the need for such a global response, there was only limited cohesion between the responses of different countries and continents.

This need for a globalist approach within the context of national aspirations is one that those born from the millennium onwards need to grasp, regardless of how universalism runs against the flow of postmodernism. Once again, the Christian faith has a considerable track record in this field. Far from perfect, yet, even so, the church does exhibit a global perspective. Arising in one fraught Middle Eastern context it spread to encompass the world. Undoubtedly it has intransigent difficulties to face, as is seen in the divergence of opinion arising from different continents on the subject of gay marriage. But at the same time, it maintains a universality of membership, offering a hope for the future. However, central to its model is its emphasis on love, reconciliation and an ability to live with suffering. The road to mutual decision-making will be costly. But once again, a Christian, countercultural contribution could be of real benefit to a world torn between national/local aspirations and globalist decision-making, for a healthy and benevolent humankind.

## 12.7 ENDNOTE

Earlier the case was made for the church to face the contextual challenge of the postmillennial third decade. Now the faith/church is challenged to offer a countercultural alternative to postmodern assumptions and values, to technological development centered around material wealth, power, and possessions. How to keep the contextual and the countercultural in conjunctive balance, as an expression of the mission of God, by the whole body of Christ, is surely a contemporary outworking of being, both in and not of the world, of being the mission and the kingdom of God.

# Conclusion/Postscript

The introduction of this book draws attention to a line from a poem by W. B. Yeats, "Things fall apart: the centre cannot hold," and asks whether there is relevance in it for the situation facing the church today.

For Yeats, his prophecy was not fulfilled. The Irish Free State did and does survive, despite the turmoil it underwent during that birthing experience. Yeats himself went on to become a pillar of that establishment, and a famous son of the nation.

The questions remain, however, with regard to his poem's relevance to established churches today: Can the center hold? Will the center hold? Should the center hold? The journey of this book suggests that some form of modal rump, within the large city/towns, its suburbs and environments, could well survive. Alternatively, instead of fighting for institutional order/ identity, the churches could accept that the center will not and should not hold, that a new form—new wineskins—of church could now become more appropriate.

One of the most striking TV images that has stuck in my mind over recent years has been that of erecting the final structure, the pinnacle, of the Shard in South London. At those dizzying heights, construction workers received the steel frame airlifted in by helicopter, and bolted it onto the girders on which they walked—held only by a safety harness—with such confidence and composure. Similarly, on the top platforms of the Twin Towers of Kuala Lumpur, freefall base jumpers throw themselves off into the void with only a parachute between them and death.

These images, sharp as they may appear, come to mind as I ponder the choices before established denominations, as they face an adaptation of Yeats's perennial conundrum. Can and should the center hold? As the third decade approaches, is there an expectation of hope, a wave of momentum, a preparedness to take risks that could inspire the church to bungy-jump into the future, relying steadfastly on the umbilical cord of faith? Such a faith would be a witness to the gift of Christ, relying on a relationship with every part of the Trinity.

Encouragement towards such an attitude comes from Rutger Bregman. Bregman, a young Dutch historian—a son of a Dutch Protestant preacher, but not a practicing Christian now—has just published "Utopia for Realists—And How We Can Get There." In it he draws some thought-provoking conclusions. To someone from the Middle Ages, he suggests, we already have Utopia. For such a person, the thought of a National Health Service and of free education for all would appear totally impossible. Yet for us today, both are a reality. "Present utopianisms can become future realities." He goes on to reflect "I am really interested in how the impossible can become inevitable, how things that seem unrealistic now, come to be seen as realistic in the future."[1]

If an historian, without benefit of faith, can have such imaginative thoughts, then surely those who look back to the New Testament church, and forward to the consummation of the kingdom, can imagine, and even expect to see, such an emergent church arising out of the third decade.

The purpose of this book is to consider whether a contextual and countercultural jump of faith/risk is an appropriate step for the church to take. The book has sought to undergird that proposal to jump by addressing four disjunctions within the existing church: between the security of power and the faithfulness of vulnerability, between hierarchy, authority, order, and the networking potential of the ministry of the baptized; between the cerebral "somewheres" approach of existing church institutions, and the innovative, intuitive, "anywheres," experiential, personal faith, found in networked Christian communities, freshly inspired by the Holy Spirit; and between contextual safety and countercultural risk.

The book has concluded, following the ministry of Jesus, that vulnerability is of greater influence than the power of structure, substance, and status, that a bottom-up, empathetic, emergent network is more appropriate than a top-down, constricting authority; that a rebalancing of a more experiential, intuitional, community-oriented approach, with the existing cerebral, narrative, institutional structure, could be beneficial; that bottom-up, lay-vocational, countercultural, prophetic witness should blossom alongside contextual adjustment. To work through these questions would require a paradigm shift in institutional thinking, a step of faith/risk from security to uncertainty, a mutuality and conjunction arising from the merging of the theocracy of experts with grassroots faith/witness, and an engagement between the context of the third decade and the unique message of the gospel.

---

1. Bregman, in Smith, Review of *Utopia for Realists*, 32.

Such a journey, it is believed, would lead to a sharper alignment between medium and message, between the outer and inner identities of the church.

Such a journey is that which faces Generation Z/postmillennials, encompassed by a post-Christendom context, and with the pre-Enlightenment understanding of truth slipping away from Western society. These members of the third decade—challenged by the post-enlightenment, post-human, technocratic age of artificial intelligence—have fresh and daunting choices to make. Maybe what is most important for them to remember is that in the similar, agnostic ethos of the first century, people who heard about the Jesus story and the ensuing Pentecost event responded to those events, with the result that their lives were forever transformed.

---

**MAXINE**

Such a call to transformation is the true challenge facing young people, such as Maxine—mentioned at the start of the book—her siblings, cousins, and friends. As they face the consumer bubble reality offered by mega corporations, they would surely benefit from a community of Pentecostal faith: personal to them, reflecting Christ with interlinking biblical unity and authority, relevant to their contemporary culture, and challenging to the technocentric ethos of the third decade.

---

Such a challenge could benefit from being reminded of the first and last stanzas of Yeats's poem. The poem begins "Turning and turning in the widening gyre the falcon cannot hear the falconer. Things fall apart: the centre cannot hold," a stanza that suggests that Western society—the falcon—has failed to keep touch with its Creator—the falconer. It ends by poetically imagining an unlikely but possible scenario: "what rough beast, its hour come round at last, slouches toward Bethlehem to be born." In other words, this coming decade could well become the time when the Authority behind that Bethlehem event challenges afresh Western Society, as we know it.

This book calls on the generations of tomorrow to believe, reflect and act, within their local communities, as inspired and empowered daughters and sons of God, in the knowledge that Jesus Christ provides a radical new paradigm for living through these times of epochal change.

# Glossary

acrasin—Cyclic AMP—adenosine monophosphate. A chemical which aids communication in slimemould.

algorithm—Definitions in Ch 1 Introduction: H of Lords (3), and Harari (4).

Anabaptists—Protestant Christian movement originating from sixteenth-century Germany. Emphasized the "Great Commission" but separated themselves from the state and from other Reformation groupings.

Anthropocene—Proposed epoch dating from the start of human impact on earth's geology and ecosystems, including anthropogenic climate change.

anthropocentric—Centered around human beings/humanity.

anywheres—A term used by Goodhart where he describes British society as divided into Somewheres and Anywheres—2.7.

artificial intelligence—Advanced computer intelligence/robots. Divided into general (AGI)—singularity/sentient computers, and narrow (AI)—the normal use of the term.

avatar—An imaginary manifestation of a human robotic/cartoon form.

big data—Vast libraries—troves—of data stored and available for analysis, extraction, and interpretation. Cross-referenced and available for both structured and unstructured searches—1.6.

bisociation—Being able to see "what is," the here and now, but also being able to declare "what might be," God's eternal purposes—5.2: the role of the prophets in the OT.

bootstrapping—Self-starting process in creation/evolution, that is believed to proceed without external input.

Byzantine—From Byzantium, an ancient Greek city on the Bosporus: the continuum of the Roman Empire to the East.

capitalism—Economic system based on the private ownership of the means of production and their operation for profit. Subdivided into laissez-faire—free market—welfare, state, and surveillance: all with varying degrees of state welfare intervention—2.1.

carapace—An external body structure: the shell of a turtle.

chaordic—Where both chaos and order are simultaneously combined and held together by individuals and organizations—1.6.

complexity—A system or model with many parts which react together in ways that lead to a higher order than the sum of the parts—1.4.

conjunction—Being able to hold opposites together in a single frame—7.2.2.

CRISPR (Clustered Regularly Interspaced Short Palindromic Repeats)—A family of DNA sequences found within the genomes of certain bacteria, having a key role in anti-viral defense systems; used extensively in gene editing and disease treatment.

curation—The collation, processing, annotation, and integration of data—10.3.2.

data barons—Giant, high-tech, Silicon Valley conglomerates.

database—Digital storage of information, observation, measurements, or facts; drawn, stored, and analyzed by computer.

dataism—The universe consists of data flows, and the value of any phenomenon or entity is determined by its contribution to data processing—*Homo Deus*, p. 428.

deep learning systems—See neural networks.

demography—The study of human populations.

digital—Referring to something using digits, often binary digits, 0 and 1. Used extensively in the fields of technology, electronics, data, communication, and commerce/economy/society.

disruption—Disturbance or problems that interrupt an event, activity, or process; often used in Business with reference to "disruptive innovation," the introduction of new ideas or products to an existing activity or market.

dystopia—"Not a good place." A society, often described in the future, such as in *Brave New World*, *Animal Farm*, *Blade Runner*, or *The Hunger*

*Games*: characterized by dehumanizing, tyrannical, and cataclysmic decline.

econocracy—Prioritizes management of the economy, subordinating other policy areas of government to economic policy. It is often led by self-proclaimed "experts" in the field, thereby discouraging wider contributions and undermining democratic and deliberative debate—2.1.

embryonic experimentation—Genetic experimentation/manipulation of the human genome at a very early embryonic stage of development—1.9.

emergence—A movement from lower levels to higher levels of sophistication, whereby disparate agents can unwittingly create a higher-level order without recourse to a higher level of leadership—1.5, 9.5.5.

established church—A church with specific links to a national state or government—as compared to churches which have no direct association with the state.

existential—A philosophy that begins with the human, living, feeling individual, centering around present experience and human existence.

exponential—Something moving very fast, and getting faster and faster, as in the case of computing power. Graphically it is a curve that gets steeper and steeper going up towards the point of infinity. Exponential decreases get slower and slower, as in the case of radioactive waste.

fiduciary—An accepted framework around which more is added; something bound to act in trust for another; a relationship between trustee and beneficiary.

functional—Practical, active working role, carrying out and fulfilling specific, often professional, responsibilities.

genetic engineering/enhancement—Improvement of human DNA to reduce illness or to enhance human capability and/or longevity—1.9.

genome—Complete set of nucleic acid sequences for humans, encoded as DNA within twenty-three pairs of chromosomes.

globalism—Planning economic and foreign policy on a global basis—12.6.

globalization—Process of the world becoming increasingly interconnected through massively increased trade and cultural exchange—2.6.

grey goo—Hypothetical scenario involving molecular nanotechnology where out-of-control self-replicating robots consume all biomass on earth while building more of themselves—1.7.

haiku—A short form of Japanese poetry; composed of three phrases, typically characterized by three qualities.

haptic technology—Uses touch to control and interact with computers; sensory feedback system between machine and user, so that one could "play things into existence"—Chapter 3 Introduction.

Hellenist—Mediterranean civilization between 323 BC and 31 BC.

heterodox economics—Alternative economic policies and schools of thought, as compared to neo-classical economics—2.1.

hierarchy—Systems, persons, or things arranged in a graded order; pyramidical organizational structure—1.1.

humanism—A philosophical and ethical stance emphasizing human beings, both individually and collectively; preferring critical thinking over dogma and belief.

iconic—A reflection or representation of particular opinions or times; sometimes famous, popular, or distinctively excellent.

Ignatius—Bishop of Antioch at the turn of the first century.

individuative-reflective—Individual/collective faith expressed through rigorous questioning of religious tradition and societal culture; used by Fowler—7.2.2.

infostructure—A structure of information as compared to an infrastructure of communications/transport.

inherited church—Church life/practice based on past traditions of the church, or of traditional interpretations of faith.

intellectual property—Rights of ownership of an idea, design, or discovery.

*kenosis*—Refers back to the "self-emptying" of Christ on the cross; renunciation, at least in part, of Christ's divine nature.

laager—An encampment formed by a circle of wagons.

*laos*—Greek word for "people"; usually referring to the total membership of the church who are not ordained.

latitudinarianism—Liberal religious views arising after the time of the Enlightenment.

learning networks—See neural networks.

Maccabean uprising- Jewish uprising against Rome in 300BC.

machine-centered/mechanistic—A process/technique concerning the equilibrium or motion of bodies; designing, constructing, operating machines.

macromolecular—Very large molecules, often comprised of thousands of atoms, commonly created by the polymerization of small subunits.

market equilibrium/market forces—Transaction between those who wish to sell and those who wish to buy goods; an equilibrium of "reasonable satisfaction" for both parties.

meritocracy—Social system based on rule by people of superior talent or intellect.

*metanoia*—Change resulting from repentance.

"Ministry of the baptized"—Ministry of all those who have discovered and entered the Christian faith.

modal—The norm; the established structure, as compared to the "sodal," the offshoot—4.5.

molecular construction/assembly/manufacture—See nanotechnology.

nanotechnology—Anything being manufactured at tiny molecular levels; the ability to work at the molecular level, atom by atom, to create large structures with fundamentally new molecular organization—1.7.

Neo-classical economics—An economic policy midway between a totally free market and considerable state planning/intervention; tendency toward self-regulation of the private sector, privatization of state operations, deregulation of trade restrictions—2.1.

Neo-feudalism—A contemporary return to the medieval social system, whereby lords ruled over and protected their subjects—serfs—expecting them to fight their battles, if so required.

neural networks/deep learning systems—A system/structure of interconnected points, often seen as horizontally, rather than vertically structured. Artificial neural networks in computers are inspired by biological neural networks in the human brain.

neurons—Cells within the nervous system that transmit information to other nerve cells or muscles.

neuroscience—Multidisciplinary study of the structure and function of the nervous system.

New Shanzhai—Open-sourced innovation on hyper-speed, where creators build on each other's work, coopt, repurpose, and remix in a decentralized way.

node—A point from which growth emanates; the point in a plant stem from which leaves emerge.

objectivism/objective critical realism—A philosophy encompassing the existence of an entity independent of the mind—real—: something undistorted by personal feelings/bias—objective opinion/evidence relating to facts rather than feelings.

*oikophiles*—Those orientated and rooted to a physical place/local community—2.6.

*oikophobes*—Those for whom place or nationhood mean very little—2.6.

oligarchs—A small body of people ruling/controlling a social system/organization.

oligopoly—A state/organization completely dominated by a small, all-powerful elite.

ontology—The study of the nature of being.

paradigm shift—A complete change of model/pattern; a distinct jump from one model/pattern to another—Introduction.

pheromones—A chemical substance secreted or excreted by animals that trigger social responses in members of the same species—1.5, 9.5.6.

pietists—A seventeenth-century reform movement of German Lutherans; emphasizing personal faith over doctrine and theology.

Pinterest—A social media chat-site—12.4.

platforms—A computer platform is a set of hardware or software that is the base from which programs run; a place where information is collated—10.3.2.

postmillennials—Those born after 1997—a date of key political, economic, and social change; those who are then followed by Generation Z.

postmodernism—Following modernism; a movement of philosophy, arts, architecture, and criticism developed from the mid-twentieth century onwards—6.4.

prelate—A church dignitary, such as a bishop.

publishing—An expression of opinion on collated material; as distinct from platforming that material—10.3.2.

quantum computing—The use of quantum-mechanical phenomena, such as superposition and entanglement to perform computation. Information is stored in qubits, where data can be stored in two different states simultaneously, making it up to a million times faster than some classical computers. The expectation is to double the number of qubits every year, and hence double the quantum computer's processing power annually.

quantum theory—Concerns the behavior of physical systems, based on the idea that they can only possess certain properties, such as energy and angular momentum, in discreet amounts; the smallest quantity of some physical property that a system can possess.

quisling—A collaborator/traitor who aids an occupying enemy force—8.2.

radical constructivism—All learning has to be deduced or constructed.

referent power—It flows from an inspirational person in the light of their perceived attractiveness, worthiness, or their right to the respect of others—8.1.

relationship, relational—Social, personal, political, mutual dealings/connections between people/groups—9.5.4.

relativism—Views are relative to differences in perception/consideration/context; there is consequently no concept of universal objective truth.

Renaissance—Period of European cultural, artistic, political, and economic growth from the fourteenth to the seventeenth centuries; having an anthropocentric rather than a theocentric orientation.

replicant—A fictional bioengineered android; a mechanistically constructed/programmed, human-like robot—*Blade Runner* films.

representational ministry—Ministry performed by an officially authorized, professional, ordained body of ministers—7.3.1.

reverse engineering—Deconstructing the design and complexity of the brain in order to apply to and enhance computer capability; linked with connecting the brain and computer together through transcranial helmets—1.8.

robotics—Machines programmed to perform specific tasks in a human manner—6.5.

S-curves—A growth pattern of technology, beginning with exponential growth followed by plateauing, followed by a staircase of "growth/plateau" ascending curves—1.6.

secularization—The process by which religious thinking, practices, and institutions lose their significance influence in relation to the operating of a social system; where faith lacks cultural authority and religious organizations have little social power—10.4.3.

sentient—Thinking, conscious, human-like—when describing a computer.

serf—An underclass of people in the control of a lord in medieval times; subservient.

Sigmoid Curve—A graphic description of organizational life; through inception, growth, plateau, decline, death—1.2.

Silicon Valley—A valley in California centered around San José; a synonym for companies built on the rise of digital, electronic, computer, technological development.

singularity—A word taken from physics; used in the technological sphere to denote a discontinuity in human progress that would be fundamentally opaque until it occurs; used to relate to thinking—sentient—computers, that match and exceed all human capability—1.7.

slimemould—An algae found in rotting vegetation—1.5, 9.5.6.

sodal—Brotherly; an offshoot alternative to the modal norm; a side line that diverts from the main line—4.5

somewheres—A term used by Goodhart, where he describes a section of British society—2.7.

Stoic. Greek school of philosophy; virtue/happiness can be achieved only by submission to destiny; accepting your present condition.

substance—One of Aristotle's ten key attributes of life; center point of a materialistic society based on an individualistic world view—9.5.4.

superhuman—Combining the human brain with computer capability; improvement of human DNA to eliminate faulty genes—responsible for certain illnesses— or for "enhancement" of human capability; creating digital surrogates/clones—1.9.

surveillance capitalism—Domination by market leaders to control the economy through collation, extraction, analysis, interpretation, and application of "big data"—2.1.

synapses—Electrical switches in the human nervous system.

synthetic conventional—Traditional approach to faith, centered around preenlightenment attributes; term used by Fowler—7.2.2.

system malfunctions—A malevolent side-effect resulting from technological development.

technocentric—A world view centered around technological development.

technohumanism—Term used by Harari; the use of technology to create a superior human model; retaining essential human features but upgrading physical and mental abilities.

theistic emergentism—God's self-revelation through the human capacity to know God—9.5.1.

theocentric—Worldview centered around the existence of a creator God—5.1.

theolocracy—Theology expressed through the work of a small group of theological experts—7.6.

3-D printers—Builds three-dimensional objects from a computer-aided design by adding material layer upon layer.

transcranial simulator helmets—Produce weak magnetic fields that are directed toward the brain to stimulate or inhibit select brain activities; interaction between computer and brain; used by American military—1.8.

tsunami—A tidal wave; often used as a metaphor for other extreme/influential events.

universal basic wage/income—Regular payment made to every citizen of a country, without reference to work—2.4.

UVF—Ulster Volunteer Force; Protestant paramilitary force in Northern Ireland—9.5.2.

# Bibliography

Alberts, David S., and Richard E. Hayes. *Campaigns of Experimentation: Pathways to Innovation and Transformation*. s.l.: CCRP, 2005.

———. *Power to the Edge: Command . . . Control . . . In the Information Age*. s.l.: CCRP, 2003.

Allen, Roland. *Missionary Methods—St Paul's or Ours?* London: Lutterworth, 1968.

Appleyard, Brian. "Facebook, Amazon, Google, Twitter: The Dudes of the Valley Become Robber Barons in Trainers." *Sunday Times*, 27/10/2018. www.thetimes. co.uk/article/facebook-amazon-google-twitter-the-dudes-of-the-valley-have become-robber-barons-in-trainers-mtkhvoqk7.

———. "Keep Gazing at the Stars." *Sunday Times*, 26/08/2018. www.thetimes.co.uk/ article/martin-rees-keep-gazing-at-the-stars-and-avoid-terror-bugs-m7196hhmw.

———. "Not OK Computer." *Sunday Times*, 08/01/2017. www.thetimes.co.uk/article/ not-ok-computer-pr7s6738t.

———. Review of *The Age of Surveillance Capitalism*, by Shoshana Zuboff. *Sunday Times Culture*, 20/01/2019. www.thetimes.co.uk/article/review-the-age-of-surveillance-capitalism-the-fight- for-the-future- of-the-new-frontier-of-power-by-shoshana-zuboff-big-tech-is-stealing-our-lives-b6sovhqrd.

Arlidge, John. "Held to Account: Review of *Bean Counters*, by Richard Brooks." *Sunday Times*, 17/06/2018. www.thetimes.co.uk/article/review-bean-counters-the-triumph-of-the-accountants-and-how-they-broke-capitalism-by-richard-brooks-an-angry-indictment-of-the-big-four-firms.

———. "Humans Aren't Working." *Sunday Times*, 27/08/2017. www.thetimes.co.uk/ article/what-will-happen-when robots-take-our-jobs-ai-pglfwmxmw.

Baddiel, David. "How We are All Becoming Cyborgs." *Sunday Times*, 22/10/2017. www.thetimes.co.uk/article/tech-david-baddiel-on-how-we-are-all-becoming-cyborgs-lxo9w6bvr.

Bailey, Ken. *Finding the Lost: Cultural Keys to Luke 15*. St. Louis: Concordia, 1992.

Baines, Nick. "Notre Dame, Like Easter, Tells Us Death Can't Have the Last Word." *Sunday Times*, 21/04/2019. www.thetimes.co.uk/article/notre-dame-like-easter-tells-us-death-can't-have-the-last-word-8oj3rb59k.

Baldwin, Richard. *Great Convergence: Information Technology and the new Globalization*. Cambridge, MA: Belknap, 2016.

Banks, Robert. *Home Church: Going to Church in the 1ˢᵗ Century*. Jacksonville, FL: Seedsowers, 2008.

Bartlett, Jamie.. "Secrets of Silicon Valley—The Disruptors." Episode 1. BBC2 6/8/17. www.bbc.co.uk/programmes/b0916ghq.

Benington, John, and Mark H. Moore. *Public Value: Theory and Practice*. Basingstoke, UK: Palgrave Macmillan, 2011.

Benington, John, and Jean Hartley. *Whole Systems Go!: Improving Leadership across the Whole Public Service System*. London: National School of Government, 2009.

Berger, Peter, ed. *Desecularization of the World*. Grand Rapids: Eerdmans, 1999.

Berry, Thomas. *The Great Work: Our Way into the Future*. New York: Crown, 2000.

Bevans, Steven. *Models of Contextual Theology*. New York: Orbis, 1992.

Bible Society Journal. "Salt and Light." 7 (2018) 3–5.

Bosch, David. *Transforming Mission*. New York: Orbis, 1991.

Bradley, Tony. *Guidelines for the Ministry, Diocese of Coventry*. Coventry: Diocesan Office 1991.

Brafman, Ori, and Rod A. Beckstrom. *Starfish and the Spider: The Unstoppable Power of Leaderless Organizations*. New York: Penguin, 2006.

Breen, Mike, and Bob Hoskins. *Clusters: Creative Mid-sized Missional Communities*. Reading, UK: ACPI, 2008.

Bregman, Rutger. *Utopia for Realists—And How We Can Get There*. London: Bloomsbury, 2017.

Brewin, Kester. *Signs of Emergence: A Vision of Church that is Organic/Networked/ Decentralized/Bottom-Up/Communal/Flexible/Always Evolving*. Grand Rapids: Baker, 2007.

Bringhurst, Robert, and Jan Zwicky. *Learning How to Die: Wisdom in the Age of Climate Crisis*. Regina, SK: University of Regina Press, 2018.

Brink, André. *A Fork in the Road*. London: Vintage, 2010.

British Anglican Cursillo Council. "What is Cursillo? A Brief History." www. anglicancursillo.co.uk/what-is-cursillo.php.

Brooks, Richard. *Bean Counters: The Triumphs of the Accountants and How they Broke Capitalism*. London: Atlantic, 2018.

Brown, Brené. "Power of Vulnerability." Filmed June 2010 in Houston, TX. TED video, 20:04. www.ted.com/talks/brene_brown_the_power_of_vulnerability?language-en.

Brown, Gordon. *Beyond the Crash: Overcoming the First Crisis in Globalization*. New York: Simon and Schuster, 2010

———. *My Life, Our Times*. London: Bodley Head, 2017.

Brueggemann, Walter. *Texts Under Negotiation: The Bible and Postmodern Imagination*. Minneapolis: Fortress, 1993.

*Canons of the Church of England*. 7th ed. London: Church House, 2017.

Capper, Brian J. "Order and Ministry in the Social Pattern of the New Testament Church." In *Order and Ministry*, edited by Christine Hall and Robert Hannaford, 61–104. Leominster, UK: Gracewing, 1996.

Castells, Manuel. *Information Age: Economy, Society and Culture: Vol. 1, The Rise of the Network Society*. 3 vols. Hoboken, NJ: Wiley-Blackwell, 2000.

———. *Information Age: Economy, Society and Culture: Vol. 2, Power of Identity*. 3 vols. Hoboken, NJ: Wiley-Blackwell, 2009.

Cavendish, Camilla. Review of *People vs. Tech*, by Jamie Bartlett. *Sunday Times*, 15/04/2018. www.thetimes.co.uk/article/the-people-vs-tech-how-the-internet-is-killing -democracy-and-how-we-can-save-it-bartlett-review-ptknlnkgw.

Chakrobortty, Aditya. "The *Econocracy* Review: How Three Students Caused a Global Crisis in Economics" by Joe Earle, Cahal Moran, and Zach Ward-Perkins.

*The Guardian*, 09/02/2019. www.theguardian.com/books/2017/feb/09/the-econocracy-review-joe-earle-cahal-moran-zach-ward-perkins.

Chambers, Robert. "Normal Professionalism, New Paradigms and Development." In *Poverty, Development and Food*, edited by Edward Clay and John Shaw, 229–55. Basingstoke, UK: Macmillan, 1987.

———. *Rural Development: Putting the Last First*. Abingdon, UK: Routledge, 2014.

Childs, Peter. *Modernism: The New Critical Idiom*. 2nd ed. Abingdon, UK: Routledge. 2007.

Christian, David. *Origin Story: Big History of Everything*. London: Allen Lane, 2018.

Church Buildings Review Group. *Church Buildings Report Summary*. London: CIO, 2016.

Church Urban Fund. *Tackling Poverty in England: An Asset-Based Approach*. London: CIO, 2013.

Commission on Evangelism. *Towards the Conversion of England: A Plan Dedicated to the Memory of Archbishop William Temple*. London: Press and Publications Board of the Church Assembly, 1945.

Cocksworth, Christopher, and Rosalind Brown. *Being a Priest Today*. Norwich, UK: Canterbury, 2002.

Collins, John. *Diakonia: Re-Interpreting the Ancient Sources*. Oxford: Oxford University Press, 1990.

Connor, Marcia. *Chaordic Alliance in Birth of the Chaordic Age: Dee Hock*. San Francisco: Berrett-Koehler, 1999.

Cooke, Bill, and Uma Kothari, eds. *Participation: The New Tyranny?* New York: Zed, 2001.

Costas, Orlando. *Church and its Mission*. Carol Stream, IL: Tyndale House, 1974.

Croft, Steven. *Ministry in Three Dimensions: Ordination and Leadership in the Local Church*. London: Darton, Longman and Todd, 1999.

Cundy Ian, ed. *Tomorrow is Another Country: GS Misc 467*. London: Church House, 1996.

Cundy, Ian, and Justin Welby. "Taking the Cat for a Walk: Can a Bishop Order a Diocese?" In *Managing the Church*, edited by G. R. Evans and Martyn Percy, 25–48. Sheffield: Sheffield Academic, 2000.

Dalio, Ray. "Why and How Capitalism Needs to Be Reformed." https://linkedin.com/pulse/why-how-capitalism-needs-reformed-parts-1-2-ray-dalio.

Davie, Grace. "Europe: The Exception that Proves the Rule." In *Desecularization of the World*, edited by Peter Berger, 65–83. Grand Rapids: Eerdmans, 1999.

———. *Religion in Britain*. Hoboken, NJ: Wiley-Blackwell 2015.

Davis, Nicola. "Soviet Submarine Officer Who Averted Nuclear War Honoured with Prize." *The Guardian*, 27/10/2017. www.theguardian.com/science/2017/oct/27/vasili-arkhipov-soviet-submarine-captain-who-averted-nuclear-war-awarded-future-of-life-prize.

Dewar, Francis. *Called or Collared*. London: SPCK, 1991.

Donovan, Vincent. *Christianity Rediscovered*. New York: Orbis, 1982.

Driscoll, Mark. "Relevants, Reconstructionists and Revisionists: A Pastoral Perspective on the Emergent Church." *Criswell Theological Review* 3.2 (Spring 2006), 87–93.

Dulles, Avery. *Models of the Church*. New York: Doubleday, 1974.

Earle, Joe, et al. *Econocracy: The Perils of Leaving Economics to the Experts*. Manchester, UK: Manchester University Press, 2017.

Enlow, John. *Seven Mountain Prophecy*. Lake Mary, FL: Creation House, 2009.

Ferguson, Niall. *Square and the Tower: Networks, Hierarchies and the Struggle for Global Power*. London: Allen Lane, 2017.

Fletcher, Joseph. *Situation Ethics*. London: SCM, 1966.

Ford, Martin. *Rise of the Robots: Technology and the Threat of Mass Unemployment*. London: Oneworld, 2015.

Forrester, Kevin T. *Theology of Mutual Ministry*. Marquette: Diocese of Northern Michigan, 2001.

Fortson, Danny. "Beijing Will Call All the Shots." *Sunday Times Business*, 01/03/2020. www.thetimes.co.uk/article/beijing-will-call-all-the-shots-in-the-AI-age-warns-silicon-valley-7t9kss8nr.

———. "End of Humanity." *Sunday Times*, 27/10/2019. www.thetimes.co.uk/article/the-end-of-humanity-will-artificial-intelligence-free-us-enslave-us-or-exterminate-us-bb9903klr.

Fowler, James. *Faithful Change: Personal and Public Challenges of Post-modern Life*. Nashville: Abingdon, 1996.

———. *Stages of Faith*. Harper Collins: New York, 1981.

French, John, and Bertram Raven. "Bases of Social Power." In *Group Dynamics*, edited by Dorwin Cartwright and Alvin F. Zander, 259–69. New York: Harper and Row, 1959.

Frensdorff, Wesley. "The Dream." www.thefunstons.com/rectors-address-the-dream-by-wesley-frensdorff-conversion-of-st-paul-tr-january-27-2013/.

Friedman, Thomas. *Thank You for Being Late: An Optimist's Guide to Thriving in the Age of Accelerations*. New York: Penguin, 2017.

Friere, Paulo. *Pedagogy of the Oppressed*. London: Sheed and Ward, 1972.

Frost, Matthew. *Setting God's People Free*. GS2056. London: Church House, 2017.

Frost, Michael, and Alan Hirsch. *The Shaping of Things to Come: Innovation and Mission for the 21st Century*. Peabody, MA: Hendrickson, 2003.

Fukuyama, Francis. *Contemporary Identity Politics and the Struggle for Recognition*. London: Profile, 2018.

General Synod, Anglican. *Report on Children and Youth Ministry*. GS 2161. London: Church House, 2020.

———. *Report on Partnership in Mission: To a Rebellious House?* London: CIO, 1981.

Gibbs, Eddie, and Ryan Bolger. *Emerging Churches: Creating Christian Communities in Post-modern Cultures*. London: SPCK, 2006.

Goddard, Robert. *Closed Circle*. London: Corgi, 2011.

Goodhart, David. *Road to Somewhere: The Populist Revolt and the Future of Politics*. London: Hurst, 2017.

Green, Stephen. *Green Report*. London: Church House, 2014.

Greenwood, Robin, and Caroline Pascoe, eds. *Local Ministry: Story, Process and Meaning*. London: SPCK, 2006.

Handy, Charles. *Empty Raincoat*. London: Hutchinson, 1994.

Hanson, Anthony. *Pioneer Ministry*. London: SPCK, 1961.

Harari, Yuval Noah. *Homo Deus: A Brief History of Tomorrow*. London: Harvill Secker, 2016.

———. *Twenty-one Lessons for the Twenty-First Century*. New York: Vintage, 2019.

Hastings, Max. Review of *The Road to Somewhere*, by David Goodheart. *Sunday Times Culture*, 26/03/2017. www.thetimes.co.uk/article/books-the-road-to-somewhere-the-populist-revolt-and-the-future-of-politics-by-david-goodheart-n3zwvcbdx.

Hawking, Stephen. *Brief Answers to the Big Questions*. London: Murray, 2018.

———. "Will Robots Outsmart Us?" *Sunday Times*, 14/10/2018. www.thetimes.co.uk/article/stephen-hawking-ai-will-robots-outsmart-us-big-questions-facing-humanity-q95gdtq6w.

Herbert, George. *The Country Parson and the Temple*. Mahwah, NJ: Paulist, 1981.

Herrero, Leandro. *Viral Change: The Alternative to Slow, Painful and Unsuccessful Management of Change in Organizations*. Heemstede, Holland: Meetingminds, 2008.

Heywood, David. *Reimagining Ministry*. London: SCM, 2011.

Hickey, Samuel, and Giles Mohan, eds. *Participation—From Tyranny to Transformation?: Exploring New Approaches to Participation in Development*. London: Zed, 2004.

Himanen, Pekka. "Challenges of the Global Network Society." In *The Network Society: From Knowledge to Policy*, edited by Manuel Castells and Gustavo Cardose, 337–71. Washington DC: John Hopkins Centre of Transatlantic Relations, 2005.

Hirsch, Sandra K., and Jane A. G. Kise. *Introduction to Type and Coaching*. Mountain View, CA: CPP, 2011.

Hock, Dee. *Birth of the Chaordic Age*. San Francisco: Berrett-Koehler, 1999.

Hoffman, Donald D. *Case Against Reality: How Evolution Hid the Truth from Our Eyes*. London: Allen Lane, 2019.

Holland, Tom. *Dominion: The Making of the Western Mind*. Boston: Little, Brown, 2019.

Horle, T. *Article in Transmission*. London: Bible Society, 2015.

House of Lords Report. *AI in the UK: Ready, Willing and Able?* London: Authority of the House of Lords, 2018.

Inter Anglican Theological and Doctrinal Commission. *Communion, Conflict and Hope: The Kuala Lumpur Report*. London: Church House, 2008.

"Intergovernmental Panel on Climate Change." Presented at the United Nations, Geneva, in March 2018.

Jackson, Bob. *Road to Growth: Towards a Thriving Church*. London: Church House, 2005.

Johnson, Steven. *Emergence*. London: Penguin, 2001.

Joy, Bill. "Why the Future Doesn't Need Us." *Wired*, 04/08/2000. www.wired.com/2000/04/joy-2/.

Kaye, Bruce. "Vocation of the Laity." In *Called to Minister*, edited by Thomas R. Frame, 37–52. Canberra: Barton, 2009.

Kemp, Peter. "Machines Like Me by Ian McEwan Review." *Sunday Times*, 14/04/2019. www.thetimes.co.uk/article/machines-like-me-by-ian-mcewan-review-when-the-robots-came-of8kxn8fs.

Kinnaman, David. *Faith for Exiles: 5 Ways for a New Generation to Follow Jesus in Digital Babylon*. Grand Rapids: Baker, 2019.

Kotter, John. "Accelerate." *Harvard Business Review* 90.11 (Nov 2012) 44–52, 54–58, 149.

———. *Accelerate (XLR8)*. Brighton, MA: Harvard Business Review Press, 2014.

———. *Our Iceburg is Melting: Changing and Succeeding Under Any Conditions*. New York: Macmillan, 2017.

Koyama, Kosuke. *Theology in Contact*. Madras: Christian Literature Society, 1975.

————. *Water Buffalo Theology*. London: SCM, 1974.

Kreider, Alan. "Beyond Bosch: The Early Church and the Christendom Shift." *International Missionary Research* 29.2 (2005) 59–68.

Lambeth Conference. *Official Report on the Conference*. London: Church House, 1998.

Lanier, Jaron. *Dawn of the New Everything: A Journey through Virtual Reality*. Basingstoke, UK: Macmillan, 2017.

————. *10 Arguments for Deleting Your Social Media Right Now*. London: Bodley Head, 2018.

————. Review of *Ten Arguments*, by Ian Critchley. *Sunday Times*, 27/05/2018. www.thetimes.co.uk/article/review-ten-arguments-for-deleting-your-social-media-accounts-right-now-by-jaron-lanier-how-to-take-back-control-rhsgvb717.

Lessem, Ronnie, and Alexander Schieffer. *Integral Development: Realising the Transformational Potential of Individuals, Organizations and Society*. Farnham, UK: Gower, 2010.

Lessing, G. E. On the Proof of the Spirit and of Power. S.l.: n.p., 1777.

Lind, Michael. *New Class War: Saving Democracy from the Metropolitan Elite*. London: Atlantic, 2020.

Lings, George. *Day of Small Things*. Sheffield: Church Army Research Unit, 2016.

————. "Modality and Sodality." Paper presented in Seoul, 1973. www.churcharmy.org.uk/Publisher/File.aspx?ID-236486.

Longo, Matthew. "Book Review: For a Left Populism, by Chantal Mouffe." https://blogs.lse.ac.uk/lsereviewofbooks/2018/08/29/book-review-for-a-left-populism-by-chantal-mouffe/

Lovelock, James. *Novacene*. London: Penguin, 2019.

McEwan, Ian. *Machines Like Me*. London: Cape, 2019.

MacIntyre, Alasdair. *After Virtue*. Notre Dame: University of Notre Dame Press, 1981.

Male, Dave. "Pioneer Ministry/Fresh Expressions." https://freshexpressions.org.uk/get-started/pioneer-ministry/.

Manning, Russell. "Mere Summing Up?" *Science and Christian Belief* 19.1 (2007) 37–58.

Marti, Gerado, and Gladys Ganiel. *Deconstructed Church: Understanding Emerging Christianity*. New York, Oxford University Press, 2014.

Maslow, Abraham. "Hierarchy of Needs: Self Actualization." *American Psychological Review* 50.4 (1943) 370–96.

Mason, Kenneth. *Priesthood and Society*. Norwich, UK: Canterbury, 1992.

McConnachie, James. "What's in Store for Us? Review of Brief Answers to Big Questions, by Stephen Hawking and *On the Future: Prospects for Humanity*, by Martin Rees." *Sunday Times Culture*, 21/10/2018. www.thetimes.co.uk/article/reviews-brief-answers-to-big-questions-stephen-hawking-on-the-future-prospects-for-humanity-martin-rees-xr7kzjbw6.

————. "The Wired Generation: How Technology has Changed Childhood." *Sunday Times*, 03/12/2017. www.thetimes.co.uk/article/the-wild-generation-how-technology-has-changed-childhood-srxov3dzs.

McLaren, Brian. *Finding Our Way Again: The Return of Ancient Practices*. Nashville: Thomas Nelson, 2008.

————. *A Generous Orthodoxy*. Grand Rapids: Zondervan, 2004.

McLuhan, Marshall. *Understanding Media: The Extensions of Man*. New York: Mentor, 1964.

Middleton, J. Richard, and Brian J. Walsh. *Truth is Stranger than it Used to Be: Biblical Faith in a Post-modern Age.* London: SPCK, 1995.

Miller, David W. *God at Work: The History and Promise of the Faith at Work Movement.* Oxford: Oxford University Press, 2007.

Miranda, Jose. *Marx and the Bible: A Critique of the Philosophy of Oppression.* New York: Orbis, 1974.

Moberley, Robert. C. *Ministerial Priesthood.* London: SPCK, 1969.

Mobsby, Ian. *Emerging and Fresh Expressions of Church.* London: Moot Community, 2007.

Moltmann, Jurgen. *Experiment of Hope: Theology for a World in Peril.* London: SCM, 1975.

———. *Open Church.* London: SCM, 1978.

Moltmann, Jurgen, and James W. Leitch. *Theology of Hope.* Minneapolis: Augsburg Fortress. 1993.

Moody, Katherine S. *Radical Theology and Emerging Christianity: Deconstruction, Materialism and Religious Practices.* New York: Routledge, 2016.

Morisy, Ann. *Beyond the Good Samaritan: Community, Ministry and Mission.* London: Mowbray, 1997.

———. *Journeying Out: New Approach to Christian Mission.* London: Continuum, 2004.

Morrell, Margot, and Stephanie Capparell. *Shackleton's Way.* London: Penguin, 2002.

Mouffe, Chantal. *For a Left Populism.* New York: Verso, 2018.

Moule, C. D. F. "The Manhood of Jesus." In *Christ, Faith and History,* edited by S. W. Sykes and J. P. Clayton, 95–110. Cambridge Studies in Christology. Cambridge: Cambridge University Press, 1972.

Moynagh, Michael. *Church for Every Context: An Introduction to Theology and Practice.* London: SCM, 2012.

———. *Mission-Shaped Church: Church Planting and Fresh Expressions of Church in a Changing Context.* London: Church House, 2004.

Murray, Stuart. *Biblical Interpretation in the Anabaptist Tradition.* Kitchener, ON: Pandora, 2000.

———. *Post-Christendom: Church and Mission in a Strange New World.* 2nd ed. London: SCM, 2018.

Nadella, Satya. "I Believe Right Now Microsoft is Probably on the Right Side of History." *Sunday Telegraph,* 27/05/2018. www.telegraph.co.uk/technology/2018/05/27/microsoft-chief-satya-nadella-right-side-history/.

Nazir-Ali, Michael. *Shapes of the Church to Come.* GS 1455. London: CIO, 2000.

Nelson, Nici, and Susan Wright. *Power and Participatory Development.* Bradford, UK: Intermediate Technology Development Group, 1995.

Newbigin, Lesslie. *Foolishness to the Greeks: Gospel and Western Culture.* London: SPCK, 1986.

———. *Gospel in a Pluralist Society.* London: SPCK, 1989.

Niebuhr, Richard H. *Christ and Culture.* New York: Harper, 1975.

———. *The Kingdom of God in America.* New York: Harper, 1937.

Njoroge, Francis, et al. *Umoja Co-ordinator's Guide.* London: TearFund, 2009.

———. *Umoja Facilitator's Guide.* London: TearFund, 2009.

O'Donovan, Oliver. "What Kind of Community is the Church?" *Ecclesiology* 3.2 (2007) 171–93.

Paget-Wilkes, Michael. *Church and the Land: Rapid Social Change Study.* Dodoma, Tanzania: Central Tanganika Press, 1968.

———. *Poverty, Revolution and the Church.* London: Paternoster, 1981.

Paton, David ed. *Reform of the Ministry.* Cambridge, UK: Lutterworth, 2002.

Peachey, Paul. "New Ethical Possibility: Task of Post Christendom Ethics." *Union Seminary Magazine* 19.1 (1965) 26–38.

Peterson, Eugene. *Gift: Reflections on Christian Ministry.* London: Pickering, 1995.

Phillips, Trevor. "Help, My Laptop's a Sexist, Racist Pig." *Sunday Times,* 27/08/2017. www.thetimes.co.uk/article/how-silicon-valley-has-made-your-computer-sexist-and-racist-h78jp2wzm/arti.

Pickard, Stephen. *Theological Foundations for Collaborative Leadership.* London: Ashgate, 2009.

Piketty, Thomas. *Capital in the Twenty-First Century.* London: Harper Collins, 2013.

Pogrund, Gabriel. "Clear Browsing History?" *Sunday Times,* 27/08/2017. www.thetimes.co.uk/profile/gabriel-pogrund?page-13.

Priest, Doug. *Doing Theology with the Maasai.* Pasadena, CA: William Carey Library, 1990.

Rather, David Mark. *Baptists and the Emerging Church Movement: A Baptistic Assessment of Four Themes of Emerging Church Ecclesiology.* Eugene, OR: Wipf and Stock, 2014.

Reason, Peter, and John Heron. "Co-operative Inquiry." In *Rethinking Methods of Psychology,* edited by Jonathan A. Smith et al., 122–42. London: Sage, 1995.

Rees, Martin. *On the Future: Prospects for Humanity.* Princeton: Princeton University Press, 2018.

Rhymer, David W. "Jeremiah 31:31–34." *Interpretation* 59.3 (July 2005) 294–96.

Roberts, Richard. *Religion, Theology and the Human Sciences.* Cambridge: Cambridge University Press, 2002.

Rohr, Richard. *Divine Dance.* London: SPCK, 2016.

Russell, Anthony. *Country Parson.* London: SPCK, 1993.

Russell, Stuart. *Human Compatible: AI and the Problem of Control.* London: Penguin, 2020.

Rutger, Bregman. *Utopia for Realists: How Can We Get There?* London: Bloomsbury, 2017.

Schluter, Michael, and John Ashcroft. *Jubilee Manifesto: A Framework, Agenda and Strategy for Christian Social Reform.* Leicester, UK: IVP, 2005.

Schnabel, Eckhard J. *Paul, the Missionary: Realities, Strategies and Methods.* Downers Grove, IL: IVP Academic, 2008.

Schnarch, David. *Passionate Marriage: Keeping Love and Intimacy Alive in Committed Relationships.* New York: Norton, 2009.

Scott, Des, et al. *Report of the Lay Ministries Working Group: Serving Together.* London: CIO, 2016.

Scott, W. Richard. *Institutions and Organizations: Ideas, Interests and Identities.* 4th ed. Cambridge, UK: Sage, 2014.

Scruton, Roger. "The Tories Will Stay Lost Until They Relearn How to Be Conservative." *Sunday Times,* 13/08/2017. www.thetimes.co.uk/article/the-tories-will-stay-lost-until-they-relearn-how-to be-conservative-xn81g36jw.

———. *Where We are: The State of Britain Now.* London: Bloomsbury, 2017.

Shenk, Wilbert. "New Wineskins for New Wine: Towards a Post Christendom Ecclesiology." *International Bulletin of Missionary Research* 29.2 (2005) 73–79.

Shults, F. LeRon, and Steven J. Sandage. *Transforming Spirituality: Integrating Theology and Psychology*. Grand Rapids: Baker, 2006.

Siedentop, Larry. *Inventing the Individual: The Origins of Western Liberalism*. London: Allen Lane, 2014.

Smith, David. Review of *Utopia for Realists*, by Rutget Bregman. *Sunday Times*, 26/03/2017. www.thetimes.co.uk/article/books-utopia-for-realists-and-how-we-can-get-there-by-rutger-bregman-basic-income-a-radical-proposal-for-a-free-society-and-a-sane-economy-by- philippe-van-parijs-and-yannick-vanderborght-ogtkqs23x.

Stephenson, Neal. *Snow Crash*. New York: Bantam, 1992.

Streeck, Wolfgang. *How Will Capitalism End? Essays on a Failing System*. New York: Verso, 2016.

Susskind, Jamie. *Future Politics. Living Together in a World Transformed by Technology*. Oxford: Oxford University Press, 2018.

Tacey, David. *Spirituality Revolution: The Emergence of Contemporary Spirituality*. Sydney: Harper Collins, 2003.

Taylor, John. *Go-between God*. London: SCM, 1972.

Taylor Review. *Sustainability of English Churches and Cathedrals*. London: Government Publishing Service, Dept for Digital, Culture, Media and Sport, 2017.

Thompson, Grahame, et al. *Markets, Hierarchies, and Networks: Coordination of Social Life*. Cambridge, UK: Sage, 1991.

Tiller, John. *Strategy for the Church's Ministry*. London: CIO, 1983.

Tooze, Adam. *Crashed: How a Decade of Financial Crises Changed the World*. London: Allen Lane, 2018.

Tzu, Sun. *The Art of War*. Boston: Shambhala, 2002.

Villeneuve, Jean, dir. *Blade Runner 2049*. 2017. Alcon Entertainment, 2017.

Walls, Andrew. *Missionary Movement in Christian History*. New York: Orbis, 1996.

Watson, Richard, and Oliver Freeman. *Futurevision: Scenarios for the World in 2040*. Brunswick, VIC: Scribe, 2012.

Welby, Justin. "Capitalism Must 'Draw Alongside the Suffering,' Says Archbishop." www.archbishopofcanterbury.org/news/latest-news/news-archive-2015/capitalism-must-draw-alongside-suffering-says-archbishop.

———. *Dethroning Mammon: Making Money to Serve Grace*. London: Bloomsbury, 2017.

———. "Inclusive Capitalism." *Daily Telegraph*, 25/06/2015. www.telegraph.co.uk/news/religion/11696974/Capitalism-should-stop-being-so-self-serving.html.

Wells, Samuel. *Community-led Regeneration and the Local Church*. Cambridge, UK: Grove, 2003.

Wheatcroft, Patience. "A Capitalism that Makes Everyone Richer." *Sunday Times*, 19/05/2019. www.thetimes.co.uk/article/a-capitalism-that-makes-everyone-richer-by-giving-it-all-away-tf5cwsdsp.

Wignall, Paul. *Collaborative Ministry Review*. Coventry, UK: Coventry Anglican Diocese, 2008.

———. "Praying for the City." Unpublished Paper. Coventry Anglican Diocese. 2009 www.dioceseofcoventry.org/contact/contact_office.

———. "Kenosis and Total Ministry." Coventry Anglican Diocese. 2009 www. dioceseofcoventry.org/contact/contact_office.

Wink, Walter. *Engaging the Powers*. Minneapolis: Fortress, 1992.

Wright, Christopher J. H. *Mission of God: Unlocking the Bible's Grand Narrative*. Nottingham: IVP, 2006.

Wright, Tom. *Spiritual and Religious: The Gospel in an Age of Paganism*. London: SPCK, 2017.

Young, Frances. *Face to Face*. Edinburgh: T. and T. Clark, 1990.

Zorgdrager, Rebekah. "Ecclesiology of the Emerging Church." *The Gospel and Our Culture Network*, 24/7/19. https://gocn.org/library/ecclesiology-of-the-emerging-church/.

Zuboff, Shoshana. *Age of Surveillance Capitalism*. London: Profile, 2019.

———. "'Big Other': Surveillance Capitalism and the Prospects of an Information Civilization." *Journal of Information Technology* 30.1 (2015) 75–89.

———. "Big Other: A Theory of Surveillance Capitalism." *New Labour Forum* 22/01/2019. https://newlabourforum.cuny.edu/2019/01/22/big-other-surveillance-capitalism/.

# Index